Ocean

a participant° guide
MEDIA

oceans

THE THREATS TO OUR SEAS AND
WHAT YOU CAN DO TO TURN THE TIDE

Edited by Jon Bowermaster

PUBLICAFFAIRS
New York

Published in the United States by PublicAffairs™, a member of the Perseus Books Group.

PublicAffairs books are available at special discounts for bulk purchases in the U.S. by corporations, institutions, and other organizations. For more information, please contact the Special Markets Department at the Perseus Books Group, 2300 Chestnut Street, Suite 200, Philadelphia, PA 19103, call (800) 810-4145, ext. 5000, or e-mail special.markets@perseusbooks.com.

Book design and production by Eclipse Publishing Services
Map by Chris Erichsen

Library of Congress Cataloging-in-Publication Data

Oceans : the threats to our seas and what you can do to turn the tide : a participant media guide / edited by Jon Bowermaster.
     p. cm.
  Includes bibliographical references and index.
  ISBN 978-1-58648-830-7 (pbk.)
  1. Marine resources conservation. 2. Ocean—Environmental aspects. 3. Oceanography. 4. Marine biology. I. Bowermaster, Jon, 1954-
  GC1018.O26 2010
  333.91'64--dc22
                              2010002192

First Edition
10 9 8 7 6 5 4 3 2 1

CONTENTS

PART II: LOSING IT

There are officially five oceans—Atlantic, Pacific, Indian, Arctic, and Southern—though it is easy to see by looking at the map that a strong argument could be made that there is just one big and connected ocean, covering 70 percent of the planet. Labeled are many of the locations visited by our authors in the course of various explorations and in their writings.

ARCTIC OCEAN

North America

Euro

British Columbia

Columbia River

Monaco

Hudson River, New York

Lazy Point, Long Island

Monterey Bay Aquarium

North Pacific Garbage Patch

San Ignacio Lagoon

Dead Zone

Tropic of Cancer

Baja, Mexico

ATLANTIC

Meso-Amerian Reef, Belize

Dominican Republic

A f

PACIFIC

Venezuela

Gabo

Paita, Peru

South America

Marquesas Islands

OCEAN

Nan

Tuamotu Archipelago

Tropic of Capricorn

OCEAN

Chilean Sea Bass - Patagonia Toothfish

King George Island, Antar

Antarctic Peninsula

SOUTHERN OCEAN

OCEANS MAP

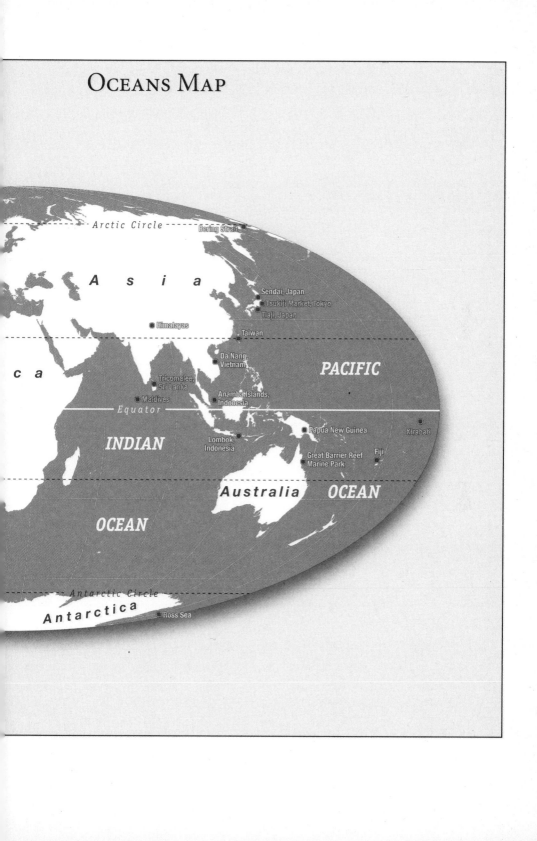

Arctic Circle --- Bering Strait

A s i a

Sendai, Japan
Tsukiji Market, Tokyo
Taiji, Japan

Himalayas

Taiwan

c a

Da Nang,
Vietnam

PACIFIC

Tricomalee,
Sri Lanka
Maldives

Anamba Islands,
Indonesia

Equator

INDIAN

Lombok,
Indonesia

Papua New Guinea

Kiribati

Great Barrier Reef
Marine Park

Fiji

Australia

OCEAN

OCEAN

Antarctic Circle

Antarctica

Ross Sea

Where Blue Meets Blue: Trouble on the Horizon

Jon Bowermaster

Who isn't made blissful sitting at water's edge, staring at the horizon, hypnotized by that delicate, nearly imperceptible yet somehow distinct line where blue meets blue? Who among us doesn't count those solitary, sun-washed moments—whether afloat on a boat or feet dug deep into the sand—as among the favorites of a lifetime?

Cliché? Perhaps. But if the views off land's edges are not the most soothing, the most renewing on the planet, why do so many of us flock there to live, to work, to rejuvenate? Which raises the issue of why we call this Planet Earth when 71 percent of it is ocean. That this is not known as Planet Ocean speaks only to the ego of man because it has nothing to do with reality. It also raises the question of exactly how many oceans there are. Go get your atlas. Inside, you'll find five mildly distinct bodies with labels (Pacific, Atlantic, Indian, Arctic, and Southern). I, like most whose writing graces these pages, believe there are no real distinctions, that this big body of water encircling the planet is just one ocean.

For the past twenty years a variety of explorations have given me a unique perspective on both the health of the ocean and the lives of people who depend on it. I've followed a meandering route leading me from remote Bering Sea and Pacific islands; down the coasts of Vietnam and all of South America; around the various seas that surround Europe; parallel along sandy beaches in Peru and India; and along rocky ones in Croatia, Tasmania, and Kamchatka. At each stop, I have spent time with the people whose days are most defined and shaped by the ocean.

For all the differences each place offers—from browsing forest elephants and surfing hippos along the beaches of Gabon to eighty-mile-an-hour winds raking the Aleutian Islands, from horrifically polluted bays off the South China Sea to centuries-old ritual celebrations still practiced on remote South Pacific atolls—similarities link them all. The same is true for ocean people. Although their cultures may differ in dress, food, religion, and more, the people who live along coastlines have far more in common than they have differences. Instinctively, the very first thing each does in the morning is scan the horizon line, the seascape, checking the morning sky and what it might portend. Increasingly, too, each is affected by a similar handful of environmental risks now exerting impacts on the ocean, its coastlines, and both its marine and human populations.

As the human population grows, headed fast toward 9 billion, the planet's coastlines grow ever more crowded. Fourteen of the seventeen largest cities are built on the edge of the ocean. Nearly half the world's population, more than 3 billion, lives within an hour's drive of a coast. The rich go for the views and refreshing salt air, the poor for jobs and big dreams, holiday-goers for a brief respite. But we humans are a rapacious species, seemingly incapable of taking good care of any place; over the past five centuries or so, we've done a very good job of taking from the ocean without pause to consider its fragility and the damage we've done to it by our indifference.

How many of those billions who glimpse a sea with frequency wonder about how this big, beautiful ocean of ours is doing? Although it has long seemed limitless, its resources infinite, there are myriad signs that we've now abused the ocean to the point of almost no return. The list of harms is long. Acidification, global warming's evil twin, threatens to make all life in the ocean impossible for many species. Plastic waste is now so pervasive that on many beaches around the world, washed-up flip-flops and bottles are more prevalent than seashells; remote parts of the ocean are choking on it, and it is so dense that it has invaded the very pores and guts of many fishes and seabirds. Warming air and sea temperatures have put the planet's ice at great risk, threatening an unprecedented sea level rise, with severe implications for the 145 million of us who live just a few feet above sea level. Various pollutions, especially fertilizers and runoff from industry and development, threaten our estuaries and gulfs, creating dead zones that kill everything. The reefs that circle the globe, the ocean's warning canaries, are dying from a variety of ills. Eat fish? If so, you *have* to be concerned; experts predict that by 2050, all the fish species we currently survive on will be gone. Do you like tuna sashimi? Get it now because all of the world's bluefin is anticipated to be gone by 2012. Forever. Freshwater supplies are endangered globally; new reports suggest that even in the wealthiest nation (the United States), 20 million people drink polluted water every day.

The bottom line is that what happens to the ocean affects each of us, whether we know it or not. As so many of the writers in the pages that follow suggest, as goes the ocean, so goes the human race. There is some hope for optimism, with marine reserves and both national and international laws in the works that may help make a difference. Let's hope they are enacted and enforced quickly enough to have an effect rather than just preceding an inevitable demise. Around the globe, for example, far too often marine reserves have been set up only *after* the last fish was taken.

Our book, with writings from some of the most thoughtful and committed protectors, explorers, and interpreters of the ocean, is not intended to scare but *to inspire*. Now is not a time for complacency regarding any environmental concern; it is not a time for modest steps. Rather, now is the time for action. We hope you will find some clues in these pages for how you might change your individual life to help keep the ocean both viable and welcoming for centuries to come.

PART I

LOVING IT

On Making *Oceans*
An Interview with Filmmaker Jacques Perrin

Veteran filmmaker Jacques Perrin is best known outside of his native France for his bold, technology-pushing wildlife films, Microcosmos and Winged Migration. His latest film, Oceans— eight years in the making—breaks new ground in terms of both the story it tells and the incredible beauty of its subject matter. I spoke with Perrin on a sunny, early winter day in Paris, two months before the film's release in the U.S.

It started with a simple dream: to swim with the fish and the dolphins, to accompany them underwater and as they crossed the oceans. The desire to forget the little we do know in order to rediscover it and see and hear it anew. To invent a camera as fast and nimble as the sea lion, a camera made for the big screen but using short focal lengths so we can get up close and personal with the animals, sparking new relationships and emotions. To stop watching the spectacle and be a part of it. To never slow down—the sensation of speed and vitality is far too precious. That's what we wanted: a living camera dancing with the whales, leaping with the dolphins, bursting forth with the tuna, and gliding with the manta rays."

That was Jacques Perrin's goal for his new film, *Oceans*. Aided by a cast of many hundreds—including the top echelon of his team: the film's co-producer Jacques Cluzaud, executive producer Jake Eberts, and biologist and writer Francoise Sarano—he managed to pull it off, creating a jaw-droppingly beautiful and powerful film.

Conceived in Perrin's head a decade ago, the filmmaking required to match his vision had been a monumental project, taking the mostly underwater camera crews to fifty-four locations around the globe. (At one point, twenty-six location managers and nineteen cameras were in the field on a single day.) Perrin's films have always been major events. *Oceans,* funded by a long and varied list including the expected (film companies and television channels) and the unexpected (NGOs and philanthropic foundations, banks, businesses, and regional councils) is no different.

His team built thirteen specially modified digital camera systems and sophisticated waterproof housings for each. The camera operators had to be able to use rebreathers to allow them to stay down for long periods and dive without bubbles; each cameraperson was assigned a security diver–rebreather instructor who shadowed his every flipper-stroke and was responsible for managing and maintaining the dive equipment so the cameraperson could focus solely on the pictures. When the diving site was more than two hours from the closest first aid center specializing in diving accidents, the expedition traveled with a pressurized stretcher and an emergency doctor trained in hyperbaric medicine. They built a high-tech crane dubbed *Thetys,* using military secrets; a remotely controlled helicopter camera they called *Birdy Fly;* a torpedo-cam that could be dragged 300 feet behind the boat; and a pole-cam for getting up close to the fishes from above sea level. All that time, energy, and money is apparent on the screen.

They were after something bigger than a nature film or documentary. In the words of the film's co-producer, Jacques Cluzaud, "To tell the story of the oceans, we had to go beyond statistics, following avenues that opened on a magical and fantastic world, revealing the wonders of the microcosm of the coral reef, the heroism of charging dolphins, the graceful dances of the humpback whales and giant cuttlefish, the horrors of the assault on the ocean and its inhabitants, the incredible spectacle of the raging sea in a storm, the silence of a museum of extinct species, and the questioning gaze of a grouper or a sea elephant.

Oceans was not intended to explain behavior patterns and provide information about species. It was not designed to teach, but to make the audience feel."

∼∼∼

Jon Bowermaster: What was the inspiration for this new film?
Jacques Perrin: The idea for *Oceans* came to me about ten years ago when we were finishing *Winged Migration*. Still vague, it was an idea for a fiction film about a defender of whales and oceans based on the story of Captain Paul Watson. Then the sea animals grew increasingly important. Of course, the story continued to fill out, getting richer with more and more characters and points of view—that of the sailor, the diver, the oceanographer, the fisherman, the judge, the polluter, and the ocean traveler—to represent every aspect of the ocean. But it was never enough; the ocean has too many faces. And, more and more, the sea creatures were taking over our script, ever more disconcerting. Clearly, there wasn't just one ocean but thousands of them, making up the great global ocean we couldn't ignore. It filled us with enthusiasm over the days and nights and years that we worked on the script. Jacques Cluzaud and I surrounded ourselves with an indispensable, unbeatable team who helped us develop an intimate understanding of the oceans.

JB: How did the project evolve from there?
JP: After three years of collaborative work, we realized the script we had finally finished was a dead end; at three and a half hours, the film wove the stories of human characters and sea creatures into the greatest impressionistic vision of the ocean—and was way too long. We came to an abrupt, painful stop.

We had to start over, build it from the ground up, using only what was essential: the marine creatures, the best advocates there are for the ocean. As long as you're not just in it to film pretty pictures or vent your pessimism, this kind of filmmaking is the best weapon you have to testify, take a stand, denounce, and convey your indignation, no matter how complex the subject. The evocative power of cinema could truly resonate with that of the ocean.

JB: What were your biggest challenges?
JP: Of course, we're not the first to make a movie about the sea. But we wanted something else. Wasn't it possible to make something different and innovative using images we might have seen before? Naturally, it wasn't easy. The breadth of the ocean cannot be defined from a single point of view. It took a long time: three years of writing and pre-production, nearly four years in production, endless trial and error that allowed us to pinpoint our desires and better define our intentions as we went along.

JB: How did the making of Oceans *compare to that of* Winged Migration?
JP: Though *Winged Migration* was a challenge, *Oceans* was incredibly more complicated. Underwater, our cameramen were physically and visually handicapped, too slow to swim as fast as fish and in an environment where visibility is rarely greater than fifty feet. Yet we wanted to express the life and movements of sea animals as different as the cuttlefish and the sailfish. *Oceans* isn't a documentary; it's a wildlife opera, and each animal played its part, contributing a few notes to the score.

The essence of a documentary is that you start off with a theory that you wish to explain using pictures or images. In a way, it becomes an illustrated text. Our case was a bit different because we spent a long time listening to scientists, learning from them, digesting that information, and re-expressing it by giving full throttle to nature itself, allowing nature to express itself fully, getting really into the heart of what nature could show us, which is a very emotional way of expressing it, and the viewer should feel that emotion.

It's a bit like the end-of-the-nineteenth-century painters doing seascapes, for example. They would show you colors of the sea and colors of the sky and would perhaps describe scientifically what was happening at a particular point of time. What I hoped to do was convey that expression and that emotion in a similar way.

JB: Filming birds in the air versus fish in the sea requires very different techniques. What were your biggest challenges?
JP: With *Winged Migration*, we were trying to see things that we know, animals that we know, but see them differently and therefore discover new

things about them. We've done that in this film in different ways, first in the way in which we filmed and then in the way it's been edited. It's presented to give you that very close feel to the animals, especially by filming them extremely fast, in the speed of their movement. For example, if you are following a dolphin at 10 knots in the water, or 22 knots outside water, you see things differently, in a new light, and that's exactly what we're trying to do. So we're very close to them.

We had all sorts of advisors, but scientists were not dictating to us to do certain things. We just followed the animals; they guided us, kind of telling us what to film, what not to film, and how we should feel. We might be right in the middle of them, but their behavior didn't change with our presence, which is what makes it so special, the fact that we are there, we observe them, but they continue to behave in a completely natural way without being modified in any way.

JB: What do you hope viewers will take away from Oceans? *What has been your experience so far?*

JP: We have heard several times, after private viewings of *Oceans,* people coming out of the theater saying, "We didn't realize the diversity that we talk about so much is an expression of life and movement." To us, that is what is important to show. We are not just talking about ordinary fishes; we are talking about predators and prey, about innate and acquired behavior. We're not just talking about fish that are going to be eaten or displayed in a store or a market but about beautiful, graceful animals moving in a natural, balletic way. What we are trying to do is show that this diversity is something that we belong to as well, that we are not more than these animals, that we are not in any way better or greater but just another species, part of the huge diversity that exists on the planet. We are not just showing them a gallery of pretty animal pictures but all of life's theater, which we hope is going to move them, blow them away.

JB: After all these years of such intense filming, do you find you are more concerned about the ocean and its creatures?

JP: Absolutely. During these eight years, several species of fish have disappeared forever.

JB: What can be done to save the rest?

JP: I truly think individuals can change things. Otherwise, it's just like going to church and lighting a candle and hoping that something is going to happen. We need to do more than that. We need to have tighter regulations, a United Nations of the Sea so to speak, and it should no longer be mere rhetoric for conferences and discussions. We've got to go much further and really have an armed sense of protection of the sea and its nature. I think, however, that more people are becoming aware of these issues and that they are going to put real pressure on governments to take action along these lines.

The ocean is really quite strong and capable of regenerating itself if it is allowed to do so. I think our film is an ode to the ocean, and I think if we sing from the same hymn sheet, so to speak, and we sing in tune, we can make a difference.

The World Is Blue
Sylvia Earle

*Known around the world as "Her Deepness," Sylvia has ocean
experiences that span seven decades and that have taken her to every
corner of the ocean planet. She is the first to remind us that we know
very little about 95 percent of the ocean, its undersea world.
When she talks, all of the world's ocean lovers listen.*

*Standing on the shore and looking out to sea, the boy said,
"There's a lot of water out there." And the wise old ocean-
ographer responded, "And that's only the top of it."*
Richard Ellis, Singing Whales and Flying Squid

One hundred miles south of the mouth of the Mississippi River,
where green inshore water gives way to the ethereal indigo of the open
sea, I was lowered over the side of the NOAA research vessel, *Gordon
Gunter,* in a one-person submersible. According to old records, deep coral
reefs should be somewhere nearby on the seafloor 1,800 feet below, and
I hoped to document them with the camera mounted on the outside of
the little sub.

Water swirled over the clear dome covering my head, and free of the
deployment hook and cable, I touched the sub's foot pedals and began to
descend. Shafts of bright sunlight illuminated the surface waters, a vast
arena of pale blue shading downward to deepening shades of sapphire.
I powered down slowly, passing through a mass of plum-sized comb
jellies, translucent animals with eight bands of iridescent cilia rippling

with rainbows as light struck them at certain angles. Minute flecks of life and small clumps of organic "snow" were barely visible as I passed one hundred feet, about as deep as scuba divers usually go. I was aware at two hundred feet of how nitrogen muddles a diver's mind and how increasing pressure decreases the time allowed without incurring long decompression penalties. Inside the sub, I was protected from the pressure imposed by the weight of the water and had hours, not minutes, of time to explore and no need for decompression.

At four hundred feet, I was at the edge of the almost-light, almost-dark "twilight zone," where the deepening blue fades into a continuous velvety darkness. Sparks of light appeared, the living fire of deep-sea animals whose bodies contain bioluminescent bacteria or the basic chemicals needed to create the flash, sparkle, and glow deep-sea creatures use to signal one another, attract prey, or confuse would-be predators.

At one thousand feet, more than halfway to the bottom, I was keenly aware of how few humans had been privileged to be immersed deep in the heart of the ocean and how much of the planet's liquid space remains unknown, unexplored. The average depth is two-and-a-half miles, the maximum, seven miles, and less than 5 percent has been seen, let alone mapped with the accuracy of what has been charted of the surface of the moon or Mars. I thought how easy it is to go to a place on Earth no one had ever been to before. All you need is a little submarine!

As I approached the seafloor, a scattering of shrimp-like creatures and small fish appeared, then shadowy mounds of what looked like waist-high shrubs. Not coral but, rather, the closely intertwined branches of a very different kind of animal, bearded tube worms, each pale, slim body crowned with a tuft of bright red plumes. Discovered late in the twentieth century, these creatures helped transform concepts about how energy is fixed and passed along by pathways other than those originating with photosynthesis. Here, beyond the reach of sunlight, chemosynthetic bacteria within the worm's tissues and in the surrounding water generate food for themselves, the worms, and a rich assemblage of fish, crabs, starfish, shrimp, anemones, and many others whose history precedes that of humankind by hundreds of millions of years. I felt like a time traveler with a passport to glimpse life on Earth as it existed long before dinosaurs, birds, trees, and flowers appeared.

Diving into the ocean *is* rather like diving into the history of life on Earth. Nearly all of the major divisions of plants, animals, protists, and other forms that have ever existed have at least some representation there, whereas only about half occur on the land. In a single gulp of plankton-filled water, a whale shark may swallow fifteen or so of the great wedges of animal life, fish, copepods, arrow worms, flatworms, jellyfish, comb jellies, salps, the larval stages of starfish, sponges, polychaete worms, peanut worms, ribbon worms, mollusks, brachiopods, and more. Some think of the ocean as a great basin of sand, rocks, and water, but it is really more like an enormous bowl of blue minestrone where all of the bits and pieces are alive. During thousands of hours suspended in the ocean's embrace, I have glided side by side with dozens of dolphins; been nose to nose with humpback whales, wreathed with jewel-like chains of luminous jellies and followed around coral reefs by large inquisitive groupers; and had close encounters with curious squids.

I have come to understand that every drop of ocean has carbon-based life in abundance, although most is too small to be seen without powerful magnification. Thousands of new kinds of microbes recently have been discovered thriving in each spoonful sampled of what appears to be clear, lifeless seawater. Some miniscule blue-green bacteria are so abundant and productive that they generate the oxygen in one of every five breaths we take, but their existence was not detected until the 1990s.

More has been learned about the nature of the ocean—and its importance to all that we care about—in the past half century than during all preceding human history. A turning point came with the view, first seen by astronauts, of Earth as a blue sphere gleaming against the vastness of space. With increasing urgency, people wondered, "Are we alone? Is there life elsewhere in the universe?"

The quest begins by asking, "Where is the water?"

That's the first question astrobiologist Chris McKay poses in his ongoing search for life on Mars, the moons of Jupiter, and beyond. "Water," he says, "is the single nonnegotiable thing life requires. There is plenty of water without life . . . but nowhere is there life without water."

No water, no life; *no blue, no green*; or, as poet W. H. Auden points out, "Thousands have lived without love, not one without water."

Earth is blessed with abundant water, and most of it, 97 percent, is ocean. It follows that 97 percent of the biosphere is thus *ocean* space. Yet, far into the twentieth century, basic knowledge about the scope and scale of even basic features of the sea was unknown. Discovery of the tallest peaks, deepest canyons, broadest plains, and longest mountain ranges on Earth awaited technologies that did not exist prior to the 1950s. Some questioned the existence of life in the deepest parts of the ocean until 1960 when two men confirmed the presence of numerous creatures, including a flounder-like fish, seven miles down in the Mariana Trench. A new kingdom of life, the Archie, microbial forms that synthesize sustenance and provide the basis of rich communities of life in the absence of sunlight, was not discovered until the late 1970s.

What else is out there, down there, that we need to understand?

As a child, it did not occur to me that life as we know it is utterly dependent on the presence of the ocean. I was unaware that the ocean drives climate and weather; that rain, sleet, and snow are mostly derived from clouds formed from water in the sea or that 70 percent of the oxygen in the atmosphere is generated by ocean-dwelling organisms. I did not know about the abundance of microbes in the ocean that shape planetary chemistry, driving the carbon cycle, the nitrogen cycle, the oxygen cycle, and much more. I was not alone. No one knew because they were among the discoveries yet to be made. New technologies, from sonar and global positioning systems to supercomputers and satellites, greatly increased the pace of gathering, analyzing, and communicating information. Most important, perhaps, we learned that there are limits to what we can take out of the sea and what we can put into it without dire consequences to us and the world as we know it. We now know we have the power to change the nature of nature. It is a concept contrary to the way people have heretofore regarded the natural world, especially the ocean.

Half a century ago, the ocean seemed so vast, so resilient, that nothing we do could cause harm. With this perspective in mind, Rachel Carson, famous for her 1962 classic, *Silent Spring*, wrote in her 1951 opus, *The Sea Around Us*:

> Eventually man . . . found his way back to the sea. . . . And
> yet he has returned to his mother sea only on her own
> terms. He cannot control or change the ocean as, in his
> brief tenancy on earth, he has subdued and plundered the
> continents.

Ironically, since the 1950s, new technologies and growing industrial demands for marine life, oil, gas, and minerals have caused unprecedented "plundering" that more than matches human impacts on the land. Hundreds of millions of tons of ocean wildlife have been extracted from the sea, including 90 percent of most large fish and many small species as well. Dredges have leveled thousands of miles of ocean floor and trawls have scraped it like monstrous bulldozers. Billions of tons of garbage, sewage, trash, and toxic chemicals have been deliberately dumped or inadvertently washed into the ocean. About half of the coastal mangrove forests, marshes, kelp forests, and sea grass meadows that bordered islands and continents in the 1950s have been destroyed by human activities. More than half of the shallow coral reefs have been "subdued," either destroyed or reduced to a state of serious decline. More than 400 low-oxygen dead zones have formed in coastal waters, and excess carbon dioxide discharged into the atmosphere is being absorbed by the sea and transformed into carbonic acid. A growing trend toward acidification of the planet's blue heart is the "terrible twin" of CO_2-induced global warming with consequences that will ultimately affect all life on Earth.

Although we may not have the power to control the ocean, there is no doubt that we are changing its basic nature.

We are not the only creatures to live through this exceptional era. Sea turtles can live for many decades, some for a century or more. Dolphins, manatees, walruses, grouper, lobsters, sturgeon, and sharks alive today may have been youngsters when the Beatles began serenading the world. Individual bowhead whales may have had their first glimpse of the ocean before the existence of motor-powered land, sea, air, and space craft. Fish sold in markets and restaurants as orange roughy could have hatched at about the same time that the great-great-great-great-great grandparents of today's children were born. Deep-sea corals dragged up from two thousand feet by those fishing for orange roughy began life when Egypt's pyramids were being built.

Even the youngest of these creatures may sense that the world has changed significantly during their lifetime, but they do not know why, and they do not know what to do about it. We do know why, and we do know what to do to reverse the alarming declines of the natural systems that keep us alive.

At a 2009 conference in Mexico, primatologist Jane Goodall explained that the DNA of humans and chimpanzees differs only slightly, and there is clear evidence that we share many physical, intellectual, and emotional attributes. But chimpanzees do not write books or gather in conferences to try to figure out what to do about global warming, or build rockets to travel into space, or travel deep in the sea to explore forms of life prospering far beyond the edge of their home territories. Dolphins don't either, nor do tunas or turtles or sharks.

～～～

WE ARE THE ONLY CREATURES on the planet with the power to alter the way the world works, and we are the only ones able to understand and solve the problems we have caused. Now, as never before, we are learning how dependent we are on the rest of the living world; as never again, we may have a chance to secure an enduring place for ourselves within the natural systems that sustain us.

One of the simplest and most important actions we can take is to restore and protect the living ocean.

Early in the twentieth century, concerns about the loss of wildlife and areas of natural, historic, and cultural significance on the land led to the development of a system of national parks in the United States. Some say it is the best idea America ever had and, fortunately, it was an idea that caught on. Nearly every country has protected at least some of its ancient natural heritage, now encompassing about 12 percent of the land globally. A fraction of 1 percent of the ocean has experienced similar care. But there is reason for hope.

Since the 1970s, many countries have established small but promising marine sanctuaries and reserves, more than 4,500 in all, and serious efforts are underway to declare large areas within national waters where even fish, lobsters, oysters, and other sea creatures will be safe. Depleted areas can never again be what they once were—or would have been without us in the mix. But in repeated studies, protected areas have greater diversity, the large animals achieve greater size than outside the reserves, and there is more biomass overall than in nearby exploited areas.

Some are aiming for protection of 12 percent of the ocean by 2012; others believe at least half of the ocean needs to be protected within areas of national jurisdiction and a comparable amount in international waters, the high seas, by 2020, to provide resilience and stabilize the effects of climate change. Whatever the numbers, it makes sense to do everything possible to avoid further degradation of the planet's blue heart. We should take care of the ocean as if our lives depend on it—because they do.

Caught in the Same Net

The Ocean and Us
Carl Safina

A lifelong and impassioned fisherman who grew up on Long Island, environmentalist Carl writes beautifully told stories—in his prizewinning books, Voyage of the Turtle, Eye of the Albatross, *and* Song for the Blue Ocean—*that have taken readers around the ocean world. The following journey is adapted from his 2010 book,* The View from Lazy Point.

LONG ISLAND, NEW YORK. When the tide pours from the bay into the Sound like this, fish—if there are any—concentrate in the narrow channel, waiting for smaller fish being swept into striking range. I choose a small lure that sinks rapidly and resembles a little fish swimming. I cast it out, reel it back.

Fishing is a meditation on the rhythm of a tide, a season, the arc of a year, and the seasons of a life. But what I most like about fishing is understanding a place well enough to find the fish. And how else would you know what's in all that deep, dark water?

The lure comes wiggling to my rod; I cast again. For those who don't fish, the ocean is just scenery. The beauty in fishing comes to the senses as a search for *connection* with deep-dwelling mysteries. I fish for nearness to the mysteries, and to reassure myself that the world remains. I fish to wash off some of my grief for the peace we've so squandered. I fish to dip into that great and awesome pool of power that propels these epic migrations. I fish to feel—and steal—a little of that energy.

You look out at that infinite span of water that gift wraps the planet and you say, "Catch dinner." The true act of fishing is attaining some sense of where, when, and how to begin searching for a fish. Weather, tides, moon phases, and seasons—in a circular, self-reinforcing way, fishing provides, and requires, a sense of place. As the years layer up, your mind sees all those adventures, friends, and meals. A string of notes on the strand of time makes life's music.

For all I appreciate about fishing, it's not much fun for the fish. One autumn I lost my appetite for the killing. I was on a friend's boat and we were jigging bluefish from a deep rip, and my heart just went out of it. This had been building for months. Then I looked over the side and saw thousands upon thousands of glittering anchovy scales drifting loose in the tidal current, mute evidence of the violent siege and chaos beneath our hull. I realized that if the bluefish and I could converse about appetites and predatory urges, we'd understand each other well. The anchovies would certainly have urged me back into the fray, since every bluefish I took meant dozens of anchovies rescued for the day.

I continue casting and reeling back. In my kind of fishing, there are two kinds of disappointments. One makes a hole in dinner plans. For that, vegetables suffice. The other punctures your heart. Many of the creatures that should be in a place at an appointed time and season come no longer. Menu substitutions might work for dinner, but not for the future of the world. I have watched animals that once thrilled me—like bluefin tuna and big sharks—struck to such staggering scarcity that, in my own time, fishing for them has transformed from celebration to transgression.

In 1985, my friends and I ventured my little eighteen-foot outboard boat fifteen miles south of Montauk, New York, at the easternmost tip of Long Island, to an area called the Butterfish Hole, and anchored in 150 feet of water. When I was sure the anchor had caught, I secured the line and glanced at my watch. Six a.m.

My friend John started throwing pieces of fish into the tide. I put a piece on a hook and instructed John's wife, Nancy, to strip sixteen arm-lengths of line from the reel, letting the bait drift out of sight, before applying the reel's brake. I began baiting a second line. At the instant I heard her click the brake into position, the rod bent double and line started shrieking off the reel while Nancy gamely hung on. We all looked wild-eyed into each other's youthful faces. Could there really be *that* many tuna here? Yes, there could.

By 8 a.m., nine tuna ranging from thirty to one hundred pounds jammed our big coolers. Other tuna were coursing awesomely through the blue water behind the boat, eating every piece of fish we threw. Back then it never occurred to us we'd ever need to go more than fifteen miles from shore. We thought that's where tuna lived because, well, that's where they lived. We had no way to foresee how much the world would change.

A year later, Japanese buyers arrived on the docks, and the globalized market hit home and ate our ocean empty. One morning offshore amidst a dense fleet of boats slaughtering large numbers of bluefin tuna, I heard someone get on the radio to suggest that maybe we all should leave a few for tomorrow. Crackling through the speaker came this reply from a sport fisherman: "Hey, nobody left any buffalo for me." Now, the great tuna runs off Long Island are in the past.

I keep casting for about half an hour. Nothing. Sunset yields to sundown. I'm about to quit when on a whim I try changing lures. I've been using a deep runner, so I switch to a surface lure.

I watch the lure sail into the deep dusk, plop down, and spread dark ripples in the flowing tide. I start retrieving, and since there's not quite enough light to see it, I listen as I begin chugging it across the surface. Chug . . . chug . . . *poosh!* I see a black splash. The line stretches taut and the rod dips as a fish—a good one—thrashes furiously to shake the lure loose. Still attached, it catches the current and frantically beelines away. I reel it closer, and it runs again. In a few minutes a bluefish is splashing at my feet, and I grab the line and slide it ashore.

This early in May, this bluefish comes as a surprise. It seems early by a couple of weeks. In two more casts, I catch two more bluefish and then stop fishing. An ample sufficiency is enough. Peepers are still calling into the spring air as I string the fish and begin walking home in dense fog.

〰〰

THE GRAPEVINE REPORTS that to the springtime beach has come a remarkable castaway: a dead whale. I go to the beach and look up and down the surf line. About a mile away, I see what looks like a black-hulled trawler wrecked on the beach.

In the sea, such a creature is impressive. But up close, this sixty-foot fin whale seems surreal. The whale's hulk lies marooned on its port side. Under the wide sky and with the backdrop and sound track of the immense sea whence it has just come, it is both in and out of its element.

Its tar-black skin is calico patched with pink sand abrasions from the surf swells that pushed it aground. Its mouth bites a bulldozer's wedge of beach sandwich. In life, the huge pleats of its distensible, Jonah-gulping throat ballooned like a pelican's pouch, engulfing a swimming pool of water, fishes, and krill. The tail flukes, pitched at a 45-degree angle, span about twice my body length. The tailstock connecting the body with the massive blades of its propelling tail seems sturdy as a tree trunk, but it also bears the sleekness of motion, attenuating to a wedge above and a wedge below, a double-edged splitting maul for shattering water as the whale swims. Or swam. The sun throws a lifelike highlight onto its open eye.

Blood and fluid ooze from a wound near the base of its pectoral fin, as though the percolating corpse is just another leaking tanker. Formerly, whales were the world's wells, civilization's chief source of oil, and we pumped the sea nearly dry of them. We appear to have learned little of whales and nothing of oil. Japan cannot get beyond their blood thirst for killing whales, nor we our oil addiction. The average American uses twice as much fossil fuel as the average Brit. Compared to 1970, we in the United States use half again as much energy; we've upped our vehicle miles driven by more than 175 percent and increased the size of our average new homes by half again. The United States burns more than 20 million barrels of oil a day, about the same as the industrial behemoths Japan, Germany, Russia, China, and India—*combined.*

I notice the whale's got a bruise across its back and a gash near its eye. And when the whale biologist arrives, she examines the oozing bruise and pronounces trauma; a ship has done this. We stand here encountering this ancient being simply because it encountered us first and tragically.

Indeed, the entire world has encountered us. Geologists place time on Earth into great bins and drawers called eons, eras, epochs, and so forth. These mark times when the planet changed its marquee. Each time the theater of life has opened the curtain on a new act—such as the first appearance of cells, the first multicelled organisms, the first animals with shells—and each time it has brought down the house with mass extinctions, catastrophic meteors, and cycles of ice ages, it has left a playbill in the rocks. All these ages later, geologists have named and labeled the boundaries of these nested bins and boxes of time. They name the last ice ages as the Pleistocene epoch. They call the time after them, starting roughly 12,000 years ago, the Holocene, meaning "whole new time." It includes all of civilization. And "whole new time" may be an understatement.

And in just this way, a funny thing has happened on the way to the future. In the year 2000, Nobel laureate Paul Crutzen suggested that the Holocene is—finished. Human domination has so changed the world as to constitute a new epoch: the Anthropocene, "the new time of humans." Can it be so? Has the time really come when people are *the* dominant force on the planetary surface? Although the idea of the Anthropocene remains debated by geologists, to this whale, it might have seemed obvious.

Scanning with my binoculars, I see that half a dozen net-dragging trawlers are giving early-arriving fish and squid a working over. Dozens of diving northern gannets are cratering the water behind the boats as much of the catch—fish that are too small or unwanted species—is shoveled overboard. The abundant waste seems at least a boon to birds.

But in the pretzel-textured logic of the Anthropocene, even the conclusion that food nourishes doesn't always hold. The easy bottom-fish junk food from the trawlers packs only half the calories of the herring gannets normally catch. Chicks need high-calorie food. Result: Due to abundant food from fishing boats, gannet chicks are starving. Scientists have also linked breeding collapses of various seabirds to fisheries depleting their normal prey. I've seen the gargantuan herring trawlers that rake the very same New England waters where gannets, whales, other seabirds, and tuna need those herring.

In a world of starving people, people still discard food. In a time dominated by people, seabirds starve by eating the fish people throw away. Waste like this, the inequity of haves and have-nots, overpopulation, and a world more tightly networked than it first appears all conspire to keep many poor, people and seabirds alike. Can we distinguish natural from artificial in the Anthropocene world? The migrations, the climate—when we look closely, all bear our thumbprint. People are using the world's fishes, forests, soils, freshwater, and other resources about 25 percent faster than the world can replace them. It means, basically, that the world would be broke if we weren't borrowing so heavily from the future.

MESO-AMERICAN REEF, BELIZE. Looking like a helium-filled peach, the moon floats free of the horizon. I slip into warm black water and begin swimming. When the ocean's motion begins massaging my progress and a swell rolls over my snorkel, I know I've reached the channel slope. I flick on my light. Its halo ushers me among the hulking shapes and shadows of massive elkhorn corals.

The seafloor is a field of their broken skeletons overgrown with seaweeds. But many living, or partly alive, coral colonies also stand here. The hope: These survivors might be disease resistant, signaling possible recovery from the epidemics.

Squid jet past my light beam; night is their time, too. As porch lights attract moths, my beam soon swarms with frenzied mysids and polychaetes and glass-clear larval fishes that whirl and spin too fast for me to examine closely.

I'm actually searching for something I've never seen. I'm examining the corals' tiny polyps for signs of pregnant swellings. My light beam begins filling with minute pink balls wafting from the polyps. Suddenly the reef is a fantasy ballroom, a blizzard. This blizzard falls *upward*. Dazzling fertility, magic clockwork. Soon the sea's underside is coated with drifting pink grains of bundled eggs and sperm. At the dark surface, the smell of them is thick and erotic, the smells of oils and sex.

In the morning, a couple of very tired scientists are still poring over microscopic new corals. Wiry and athletic and native-born to things aquatic, Susie Arnold grew up on Cape Cod. Her PhD advisor is Bob Steneck.

They show me how, almost as soon as a coral larva settles, its pill-shaped body flattens. Within hours calcium carbonate forms around the soft parts. What seemed wondrous in the night sea becomes miraculous by noon.

In the afternoon, we drop anchor in forty feet of water, an easy dive to the reef. Susie is counting baby corals. Bob points to his eye, meaning, "I want to show you something." He indicates several young corals a few inches across. On my pad, he writes, "Little seaweed here—more nursery habitat." Then just a few feet away, he pushes his fingers into a deep cushion of weeds, writing: "Lots seaweed—few nooks for baby corals." He pushes away weeds at the base of several young fist-sized corals, revealing white, dead coral skeleton.

In the airy lab, Susie examines fifty six-by-six-inch terracotta tiles she's brought up temporarily from the reef. The tiles are her research. Coral larvae settle on a tile and start growing. The tiles act like blank diary pages, letting the reef write its story.

On the table, the tiles display an astonishing community of baby sponges, bryozoans, baby urchins, minute snapping shrimp living *inside* minute sponges, copepods, amphipods, baby brittle stars—all battling for real estate. Suddenly Susie says, "Here's a great example of a young coral; take a look."

A small coral about half an inch across comes into focus. She adds, "All these colorful little sheet-like sponges, see them? All this fleshy sea-weed on the side of the tile? This little coral's gotta deal with all this. To make it, it'll have to outgrow all this stuff." She's finding high mortality; over 90 percent of baby corals die.

Susie muses, "When you look at a reef and see a lot of seaweed and it's kind of dark? That's, like, the last thing a baby coral sees before it dies."

Seaweeds create deadly shade. Seaweeds can carry infectious bacteria to corals or irritate coral polyps so they close—and starve. "The ways sea-weeds affect corals turn out to be complicated," Bob informs. "But none of them are good; they're all different variations of bad."

Susie, gazing into the microscope, adds, "It's a tough time to be a baby coral."

Corals probably don't care whether seaweed gets removed by fish, urchins, or a guy with a brush. What matters is that the reef must be frequently scrubbed.

By the early 1980s, with seaweed-eating fish depleted, the Caribbean's long-spined sea urchin, *Diadema antillarum,* assumed the role of major seaweed-grazer. In 1983, an urchin-killing epidemic appeared off Panama and, in just months, the Caribbean's urchins were devastated. "The reefs needed either grazing fish or urchins," Bob explains. "They could not withstand losing both." What had been high-rise coral reefs became seaweed rubble mounds.

There are other problems, Bob adds. Spiking water temperatures in the 1990s caused corals to lose their sugar-making algal partners, turn a bleached white, and die over large areas. Can corals adapt to warming seas, continually adapting their temperature tolerance? Life often finds ways of coping.

But even if corals outran warming, they'd still run into the pH problem. In seawater, carbon dioxide from burning oil and coal immediately forms carbonic acid by binding to, and locking up, carbonate molecules. This deprives animals like hard corals, clams, snails, and various plankton of the building material needed for making their calcium carbonate skeletons and shells. Their growth slows. Carbonate concentrations in the upper few hundred feet of the ocean have already declined about 10 percent compared to seawater just before steam engine times. "Already," Bob adds, "some corals are growing thinner, weaker walls."

And I've already talked to shellfish growers who are seeing their larval oysters dying when lower-pH seawater reaches their hatcheries.

Although some people still argue over whether warming will generally be good or bad (though it will generally be bad), there is no argument that acidification will be anything *but* bad for the things people care about, like shellfish and coral reefs and all the associated fish, turtles, seafood, tourism, and so on.

Corals have been through a high carbon dioxide world before. "But," Bob says, "it caused mass extinctions, and it took, I mean, *millions* of years for hard corals to reappear."

What has not been through these changes at all is civilization. Civilization arose as climate stabilized. We are saying farewell to that time.

As the sun sinks, the plump moon again rises, spreading its silver cloak upon the sea and the shadowed clouds, the sandy curve of shore, and the white gleam of surf on the reef edge. And I decide not to think and to just feel the night sea breeze.

SHISHMAREF, ALASKA. Belying its ferocious reputation as a deadly body of water, the Chuckchi Sea is laid down flat like a lion among lambs, gently licking the shoreline. The air feels thin, the sun direct. I push up my sleeves, enjoying beach weather a stone's throw from the Arctic Circle.

The Inupiat Eskimo community of Shishmaref (population 600) stands upon a sandy island, three miles long but just a quarter mile wide. Stanley Tocktoo, a man of medium build and copper skin, is the town's mayor. On a small bluff overlooking the sea, we talk over the growls of huge balloon-tired trucks delivering massive boulders to a crane; the crane is arranging the boulders into defensive beach armoring.

Earlier defenses—caged rocks and seawalls—the sea demolished. Now they're ratcheting up with boulders barged from elsewhere. I'm told this will cost $36 million. Thing is, nobody believes this can fix the problem. Everyone understands this fact: Shishmaref is doomed.

"Our people have lived right here for centuries," Tocktoo relays. "Now we're told this place has nine to fifteen years left."

In times past, a natural armor of sea ice extending from the shoreline prevented ferocious autumn storm waves from approaching town. Now, there's often no ice at all.

Tocktoo says, "Without ice, we lose land. One storm, northwest, seventy-miles-an-hour wind, we lost fifty feet of land. Never been like this before. Man, it's weird."

A few paces away, a house lies newly shattered on the beach, toppled just days ago from the crumbling bluff. "There was eighteen homes here." Only this toppled one remains visible. "My house washed away. It can do that."

And beyond Eskimos, beyond the Arctic, when millions of people living along the continental coasts start moving to higher ground as melting glaciers continue raising sea level worldwide, they'll crowd right on top of poor, already-crowded people, already clinging to wafer-thin margins of life. At risk from rising sea level: nearly 30 million in Bangladesh, more than 70 million in China, 12 million in Egypt, another 20 million in India, and more than 30 million others elsewhere, including the small island states.

It won't be pretty. Australia's Defense Ministry warns that although Australia should ease suffering caused by global warming, if conflict erupts, the country should use its military "to deal with any threats." National Defense University, an educational institute overseen by the U.S. military in Washington DC, explored the potential impact of a destructive flood in Bangladesh that would send hundreds of thousands of refugees streaming into neighboring India. In real life, India is already racing to build a 2,100-mile fence. Said Deputy Assistant Secretary of Defense Amanda J. Dory, while helping the Pentagon try to incorporate climate change into national security planning, "It gets real complicated real quickly."

KING GEORGE ISLAND, ANTARCTICA. Researchers Wayne and Sue Trivelpiece need to get food samples from chinstrap penguins nesting across the island near a place called Paradise Cove. They warn me it can be a challenging hike.

The first leg is a long coast walk. About a mile and a half later, we round a headland. Pushed here by an ice sheet not long ago, the ground stretches desolate to the distant hills. It's the moon with wind. Fierce gusts greet us, snapping our hoods against our heads. Ice is what Antarctica uses to freeze you; wind is what it uses to burn you.

"This landscape has changed so much," Wayne says. "When I first came here, that one peak was already sticking out of the glacier, but now you see about a hundred feet more of it. That's how much the ice has thinned."

We've been walking about three and a half hours when we crest a saddle across a ridgeline, earning the commanding brink of cliffs whose ledges fall away to pounding green sea foam. The scale is enormous in a way that landscape in peopled areas never seems. It's a Refresh button for the spirit, a place to feel wild in.

We stroll to a higher spot so Sue can show me the chinstrap colony. Suddenly, she says, "Wow. That's unbelievable. They're gone!" On several flat-topped ledges, there's a lot of guano and the ground is well trod— but without penguins.

From down to the right, around a little bend, we hear the remnants of this colony and find some chinstrap penguins upon a rock.

Sue, still flabbergasted, says, "Fifteen years ago, chinstraps nested all along these rocks, all the way down and all the way across."

Penguins eat the little shrimp-like animals called krill. And young krill, in their first couple of years of life, eat by grazing algae from the underside of sea ice. And the sea ice they need is shrinking.

"Air temperatures here," Wayne explains, "have risen about 10 degrees Fahrenheit (6 degrees Celsius) in the last forty years. Starting a few years ago, daily high temperatures in *winter* began averaging above freezing. As it's gotten warmer, it's been, like, two good years of ice; three years of almost no ice; two good years of ice; three, four, five years of almost no ice."

"Adult krill can live up to around seven years," Sue says, "so it took a while for them to really crash." That starves penguins. Chinstrap and Adélie penguins are both down by more than half in this region since the 1970s.

"The drop in penguin numbers coincided with very dramatic krill declines," Sue explains. In earlier years of their studies, about 40 percent of young chinstrap and Adélie penguins survived long enough to return as adults to breed. Recently, it's 10 percent.

"After hunting reduced whales by 90 percent," adds Wayne, "people in the fishing industry were saying, 'There's enough krill out here to double the total output of the world's fisheries.' Well, things have certainly changed."

Things have always changed. But now we're changing the world. Is rushing penguins off the stage something we want on humanity's résumé? About a dozen of the world's dozen and a half penguin species are declining sharply. Northern rockhopper penguins have declined 90 percent since the 1950s, a loss of a couple of million birds, equivalent to losing one hundred birds daily for the past half century. African penguins have declined from about 150,000 pairs around 1960 to

25,000 pairs today. Magellanic penguins are declining 1 percent per year. Even the magnificent emperor penguins are down by perhaps as much as half in the past fifty years, with extinction in this century a possibility.

I'd like to think that the bottom of the world is far enough from tailpipes and smokestacks that the animals can live unbothered by us. But I know better. And tonight's radio call with Palmer Station brings news from a Russian oceanographic ship: An iceberg estimated at a staggering 170 miles long by 25 miles wide—nearly the size of Connecticut—is breaking free and will soon be adrift.

〰〰

WE MAKE OUR LIVES in a world not of our making. We feel in a world that does not feel. Yet it's become a world in which our presence is felt. What attitude might confront such a world? An attitude of curiosity for the complex world? An attitude of admiration for the beautiful world? An attitude of gratitude for the improbable world? Of respect for the elder world? Of awe for the mystery? Of concern for consequences? If these attitudes guide action, we may not always be certain which choice is right, but we may travel a path that is wise.

We have made Earth ours. We are no longer voyagers. We are proprietors. We have put our name on time itself, changed the marquee, and declared in lights: *The Anthropocene Era, Starring Homo sapiens.* There's a lot at stake now.

Straining the cables of our planet's life-support systems despite clear warnings may be mere foolishness. But the unborn, who did not choose this path, will arrive saddled with all conceivable consequences. The poor likewise did not choose it, nor the other living creatures that, like us, strive to live and raise their young yet find their world besieged. And because we've created a situation that is not merely unsustainable but *unjust,* it crosses a line; it becomes a matter of right and wrong, a moral matter.

Albert Einstein said our task is to "widen our circle of compassion to embrace all living creatures and the whole of nature in its beauty." And so all paths converge: What serves the continuity of life is sacred. What serves the future serves us, too.

LONG ISLAND, NEW YORK. As I walk onto the beach just after dawn, I'm startled to see dozens of foot-long fish called bunkers flipping around on the wet beach. Something just drove them ashore. And I just missed a spectacular attack.

A big bluefish glides by over the sand in the surf's green water. I unfurl a long cast. Hardly has my lure splashed in when a fish grabs it and yanks my rod down hard while running seaward. It comes up frothing the surface, and when I see its wide broom of tail, I know I've got my keeper striped bass. Following their deep crash from overfishing in the 1980s, the striped bass's subsequent recovery is perhaps the world's best fisheries management success, a triumph of political discipline, a lesson in healing, and a great solace in a world so full of holes. That we could regain what we have abused is a story that not only instructs; it inspires. But it's no small matter, indeed, to go from letting bass or birds recover to taking the giant steps required to re-chill the poles, refill the seas with fish, save the tropics' forests and reefs, stabilize the ocean's chemistry, and secure agriculture against warming and drought. Nations must act, and soon. Time grows short at an accelerating pace.

Inspired by it all, I walk off the beach anticipating a delicious meal and a good day of work ahead, feeling this morning's espresso of adrenaline more pleasantly than any caffeine. Seeing that the oceans can still surge with abundance is what makes me happy.

Remembering the Ocean
Céline Cousteau

*Céline is one of four grandchildren of Jacques-Yves Cousteau.
Her family name in the ocean community—as well as in the
outside world—denotes a legacy. Even with her love for
and lifelong familiarity with the ocean, she finds herself
sometimes needing to maintain a constant link,
returning to the sea often for revitalization.*

BROOKLYN, 2009. I urgently needed to reconnect with the ocean.

City-bound for too long, I grabbed my voice recorder and sunglasses and hopped the Q train from Carrol Gardens to Brighton Beach, my quickest access to a small escape. I needed to see and hear the ocean.

When I arrived, elderly couples quietly strolled along the boardwalk or sat on scattered benches facing the ocean. The beach was otherwise deserted on a cool early winter afternoon. Walking through the damp sand, I made my way to the shore and sat on a post a few feet from the wintry Atlantic. Narrowing my eyes to slits behind my sunglasses, I took myself back to a sunny day on the Mediterranean. I could smell the drying algae washed up on shore and hear the mourning doves in the pine trees behind me. Closing my eyes even more tightly, completely blocking out the people around me wrapped in layers, I imagined a sun-warmed breeze blowing off the Caribbean, bringing with it the familiar smell of salt and sun.

The rushing of the gazelle-like limbs of a local running club bolting past brought me back to the reality that although I *was* on the edge of the ocean, I was still in New York and that the warm breeze was in fact a chilly wind. But the brief visit to the ocean side did what I hoped it would; like taking a deep breath of oxygen-rich air, it jump-started my thoughts and feelings. *The ocean. I can remember now.*

MONACO, 1980. The rocking boat is small and crowded. Rarely quiet, I am not asking questions now, simply waiting to be given more information. I'm excited by the idea of what's to come and a bit nervous about how well I will do. My long hair whips my face as I turn toward the wind. At my grandiose age of eight, I am already stubborn and have refused to let my mother cut more than a few millimeters of split ends, the result being that the wind now weaves my hair into a bird's nest. I look back at the tightly knit city riding the waves of the mountains. This is usually where I visit my grandparents during my summer holiday, which of course depends on where in the world they were that summer.

A few years before, we had lived a short distance away from them, my family—mom and brother—settling for a while in the south of France. From our home's terrace, we could survey the shimmering Mediterranean and watch the fishermen return to port from their pre-dawn excursions. Every day, I would walk from our cliff-side house down the winding path to school. On weekends, I would go down to the market to help choose our evening meal from the plethora of fresh catches laid out by all the smiling men smelling of fish. Twenty years later, I still occasionally visit our home here, grabbing short respites from the world. The same fishermen now display only a few scaly creatures, seemingly scattered as mere adornments on the little stands lining the port. Behind them, paint peels from the hulls of their once-proud wooden fishing vessels, looking weary much like the faces of the ships' captains. Instead of the local families with panniers who used to visit the market, it is now filled mostly with tourists crowding the small port, the bright colors of their new summer clothes contrasting incongruously against the peeling, weathered boats.

The small dive boat comes to a stop and I am brought back to the day's events when the anchor is thrown overboard. I listen attentively to my five-minute lesson before the cumbersome metal tanks are placed on my back, my mask fitted to my face, and the regulator placed into my mouth. I respond by nodding, "Yes, I can breathe, yes, the mask fits well, yes, I am okay, yes, I am ready!" A voice in my head echoes those last words, but they end with a question mark. I tell myself that all I need to do is stick close by and follow his lead.

My grandfather takes me by the hand and in a giant stride we step off the stern, fins momentarily slowing my entrance into the calm sea. Bobbing at the surface, trying to look and feel calm, my eyes bulge under my mask as I keep them fixed on his face. My index finger and thumb come together mirroring his okay sign and I point my head down, plunging through the surface, my hand still grasping his, my heart beating to a new rhythm.

I don't know when I let go of his hand. Maybe it was to point at one of the many purple and blue sea urchins dotting the rocks below, which mesmerize me and make me want to see them up close. On land I moved quickly, but here beneath the surface of the sea, the elements distort that intention. Like a clumsy firefly, I zigzag back and forth, wanting to see it all, wanting to touch it all. The dive gear on my back molds to my small frame as naturally as the backpack I wear to class.

That day the ocean welcomed me like a mother waiting for her child to come home from her first day of school. She was nurturing, patient, giving. She indulged me in my childlike enthusiasm and with gentle waves rocked me back and forth as I tried to prove that I had listened, that I knew how to suspend myself between the drops of water. New to the game, I would sink quickly and scramble back up toward the sky. But she did not mock me for doing it wrong; she simply held me up until I was ready to try again. When I turned to make sure I was not alone, he was always there, an arm's length away, watching and smiling behind his own mask, his familiar nose pressed against the glass.

This new world made its imprint on me immediately, engraving memories in each of my senses that would live quietly within me until

I was ready to come back for a next visit. She would always greet me with open arms, welcoming me home.

FIJI, 1998. While everyone else is napping, hanging out on the beach, hiking the trails, I sit in my lounge chair outside my cabin, hunched over my book, pencil suspended, eyebrows scrunched in the hope that my memory will store the words in their rightful place. I had dipped my toes in the sea earlier and knew how easy it would be to just jump in, to play. I look up at the glistening water, inviting me to come in, and let out a self-pitying sigh. I hear the waves gently lapping at the rocks on the shore. Like a sibling, the water is taunting me, knowing I still have homework to do. Even the birds seem to be laughing at me.

My mind drifts back to that first dive so many years ago. Much time has passed since, and I've come to this beach to make it official, to finally get the piece of paper that says I am qualified to float amongst drops of water. I wish he could be with me now, but my first guide to the ocean can no longer grasp my hand or smile at me as I glide through the water. It has only been a year since he left, and there is still so much we could have experienced together.

Five days later, when all the tests are passed, salt water having invaded my eyes and turned them red and dry, having proved that I understood and had control underwater, I dive in, official for the first time. Not far below the surface, I stop to relish just being there, suspended. I rediscover what had created such a sense of wonder so many years ago, and a smile distorts the seal of my mask.

During the afternoon drift dive, the current sweeps me past a magnificent wall heavily laden with coral, swarming with fish, colorful from every angle. In an attempt to find the little nudibranchs* amongst this panoply of decorative cover, I work hard against the current to stay in one place, holding on to a bare patch of rock with two fingers. The sense of wonder and excitement I feel is the same as it was over a decade ago when those colorful sea urchins beckoned me.

---

* Soft-bodied, shell-less marine opisthobranch gastropod mollusks noted for their often extraordinary colors and striking forms.

Like looking for hidden treats on Easter Sunday, I search behind the fans, peer into every little crevice, and peek behind darting fish. When I find one, I stare unabashedly at the bright colors, the stripes, the spots, and their sometimes frilly fringes. It's like playing a game of hide-and-seek with a sibling, except it's always my turn to seek. The ocean plays tricks on me, jokes with me, teases me, much like a sibling. This time, however, no one will jump out from behind the curtains to scare me.

I could keep playing this underwater game for hours, but when I look up, my fellow divers are riding the current, sweeping by me toward an unknown destination. I unclamp my two-finger hold and get swept back into the swift-moving waterway. The drift dive reminds me of life, full of determined moments of intense focus followed by times when going with the flow is the only way to go. There will always be surprises down current, things just as wonderful and awe-inspiring as the ones left behind—which is confirmed when we head to Shark Alley for our next dive.

CALANQUES, 2006. Every time I saw my grandmother, I knew fun was on the horizon. She had a mischievous twinkle in her eyes, as if she had her own little secrets in life and couldn't wait to bring me into the privileged circle of those who shared them. She would give me ten francs and send me to the port to buy myself an ice cream cone and then request a full report upon my return. Who had I seen? Were the boys handsome? What ships were coming in? And, most important, had I enjoyed myself? She used to tell me that a girl my age shouldn't spend all her time with an old lady, but I preferred her company to that of all others.

Sixteen years have passed since her ashes were thrown into the same waters I first submerged myself in. Years have gone by since this small girl held those ice cream cones tightly and watched the world go by, carefully transcribing each fresh memory so that I could recount every last detail for her about my afternoon at the port. The place I used to quietly sit and observe has today become a yacht-riddled parking zone.

I now step into the crystal blue waters dancing between the stark white cliffs of the Calanques near Marseille. I walk in to my knees and try to remain still, smiling, eyes open, attentive to what the photographer is asking me to do. But I cannot resist any longer and, despite the carefully applied makeup and only giving him a ten-second warning, I dive in headfirst. As I surface, the makeup runs down my cheeks, creating little black streams winding around like veins on my tanned skin. Gel and hairspray mix with salt water, turning my hair into a plastered mess. Everything feels normal again.

I dive down a few feet to the bottom to feel the smooth rocks. I absorb the salty water through my pores. The ocean is cold but invigorating, waking me up from a low hum of routine. I come back up, grinning, and quickly apologize to the photographer. He smiles, understandingly. His assistant walks toward me, not quite as pleased as I am with the moment, and wipes my face of the evidence of my sudden impulse. We work until the sun drops behind the cliff and my body starts to shiver. The wide, late-afternoon smile I've been wearing has not been forced for the camera but comes from a moment of peaceful contentment.

It struck me at that moment, when I listened to my instinct to dive into the sea, that I truly need the ocean. Not like one needs food or shelter, but more like one needs love. When I ravenously eat a slice of my mother's *tarte tatin,** indulge myself in a *far niente* holiday, or share a precious moment with a loved one, there is a similar sense of contentment. Filling myself to the brim with this feeling is not an everyday occurrence. Perhaps I did not want to remember what it felt like to immerse myself in the salty waters because I was protecting myself from feeling its absence.

Sometimes I visit the ocean in my dreams, and sometimes I see my grandmother. Sometimes I forget them both so that I don't miss them. But they are always there. They won't let me forget. I peek at the memories hiding inside the crevices of my mind. Other moments are captured in the stillness of black-and-white photos or told through people who have shared the moments with me. Sometimes I visit the ocean in the day and float on her waters, lungs full of air, as I watch the clouds go by. On other days, I dive deeper and submerge myself, the sun's rays

* Traditional French caramelized apple pie baked upside down.

shining through the blue water, the dancing streams creating fairytale creatures. I try to remember every detail in case anyone should ask me to recount what I have seen.

UGANDA, 2009. Sitting in a doorway in the heart of Africa, I watch the rain cascade down onto the thirsty Ugandan soil. As I wait for it to pass so that I can join the farmers in their fields to record their story in words and pictures, I daydream about the ocean. To tell her story I must remember it first, which requires an exercise of memory, pulling on the senses the ocean has created through the moments I have shared with her.

The ocean has many personalities. She is welcoming, kind, and nurturing. She can also be angry, sad, rebellious, mischievous, and playful. She suffers, gives, takes, rejects, and fights back, and then gently rocks you to sleep. She takes care of us and, in return, we must protect her when she is vulnerable.

The ocean is part of a bigger story whose woven threads connect us all. Like individual members of a family, the ocean is something different for each of us. Like a unified family, we face the same future, for ocean is life, breathing with every tide. Ocean is home, and though we might not be there with her all the time, she is always there when you need her. She will never let you forget.

Illuminating the Life of the Deep
Edith A. Widder

*Edie is a deep-sea biologist, one of the most experienced
in the world. Her field of expertise is the part of the
ocean we know very little about . . . its deep.*

In the darkest depths of the sea, I have seen the light. It is a light produced by life itself, a light that may yet reveal the hidden secrets of our
troubled ocean.

Bioluminescence is a ubiquitous phenomenon among the myriad
creatures of the sea, a purposefully orchestrated flash of biologically
produced chemicals of the kind we see on land in the summer night's
glow of the firefly. It was my fascination with all things bioluminescent
that induced me to enclose myself in an experimental deep-sea diving
suit and descend through the darkness of the Santa Barbara Channel one
evening in 1984 to witness it firsthand. It was a dive that would forever
change the way I look at our underwater world.

As I descended through the depths, tethered to the surface inside my
bulky bubble-headed diving suit, I was completely unprepared for the

beautiful show to come when, at 880 feet below the surface of the sea, I turned out the lights. While I bobbed gently up and down like a tea bag on its string, I was engulfed in explosions of light, swirling and streaming like the wildly chaotic stars in Van Gogh's *Starry Night*. What I didn't know then was that I was the cause of that silent fireworks display. The movement of my suit was mechanically stimulating those emitting the lights. Many of the displays looked like puffs of blue smoke—the result of an animal releasing its luminescent chemicals into the water. I now know that the lights I saw that evening from inside my protective bubble were the living displays of defense. Just like the ink cloud released by an octopus or squid or the blinding burst of a flash bulb in the face, they were the means of escape in a dark world prowled by predators.

There was no going back. From that day forward, I had to understand the meaning of all this living light emanating from the dark. But to understand the light, I would first have to become an ardent observer of it. In doing so, I would join a historical parade of deep-sea explorers whose first task of learning the underwater world was to get there.

∿∿

NOT SO LONG AGO, it was assumed that nothing could survive the crushing pressures and cold darkness of the deep sea. But in 1861, a cable raised from the bottom of the Mediterranean Sea came up encrusted with corals and other life forms, revealing that life at extreme depths was not only possible but flourishing. Eleven years later, the first major oceanographic expedition was launched with the voyage of the HMS *Challenger,* which over three and a half years circumnavigated the globe while using trawls, dredges, sediment samplers, and soundings to explore the ocean's depths. The descriptions of their findings and the organisms they collected filled fifty volumes and founded much of the developing field of marine biology.

Trawls and dredges remained the primary tools of exploration until well into the twentieth century when a zoologist named William Beebe and an engineer named Otis Barton teamed up for a magnificent adventure. Instead of dragging deep-sea animals up into their world to study them, Beebe and Barton traveled down into the animals' world to observe them in their natural habitat. To protect themselves from the crushing pressures of the deep, Beebe and Barton encased themselves in a steel sphere. The bathysphere, as it was called, had walls one and a half inches thick with a cockpit less than five feet wide and a steel cable connecting it to the surface. In 1934, Beebe and Barton squeezed themselves into this tiny elevator and descended more than a half mile, where the pressure on the sphere surpassed 1,300 pounds per square inch.

Peering out the porthole, Beebe found a mysterious world teeming with fantastic creatures. He described such oddities as stalk-eyed dragonfish and saber-toothed viper fish studded with jewel-like light organs called photophores. Some of the creatures were unknown from the collections of the net trawls. One was a nearly tailless fish measuring two feet long, which Beebe named the pallid sailfin, *Bathyembryx istiophasma,* "a Grecian way of saying that it comes from deep in the abyss and swims with ghostly sails." Another fish he described with five "unbelievably beautiful lines of light, one equatorial, with two curved ones above and two below. Each line was composed of a series of large, pale yellow lights, and every one of these was surrounded by a semicircle of very small, but intensely purple photophores." He named this creature the five-lined constellation fish, *Bathysidus pentagrammus.* Beebe's descriptions were detailed enough for drawings to be made, but neither fish has been observed since. Are they still lurking in the dark depths awaiting discovery by stealthier means? The bathysphere was dead quiet compared to modern platforms that generate copious acoustic and electronic noise, and Beebe expressed surprise at the number of large fish he observed unlike any seen in his many trawls from the same waters. Perhaps larger fish can evade our nets and subsea vehicles just as giant squid have done.

It would be another quarter century before ocean exploration carried Beebe's pioneering bathysphere dives to new depths. On January 23, 1960, the bathyscaphe *Trieste* carried Don Walsh and Jacques Piccard to the deepest known place in the ocean. In a sphere with walls five inches thick, to withstand pressures exceeding 16,000 pounds per square inch, Walsh and Piccard piloted the *Trieste* to the bottom of the Mariana Trench in the western Pacific, some 35,800 feet down. After nearly five hours and seven miles of descent, the explorers spent only twenty minutes on the bottom before beginning their ascent. But before leaving, Piccard saw fish outside the tiny porthole, proving that life was possible in the deepest reaches of the sea.

Perhaps even more incredible, Piccard claims he saw a flatfish with eyes. What possible reason for eyes on a creature of such extreme depths, except for seeing light? And where would that light have come from but from life itself? Piccard's observations have since stood as proof to the claim that bioluminescence occurs throughout the depth and breadth of the ocean.

In the following decade, some fifty manned submersibles were launched, none designed to reach such depths as the *Trieste* but all more maneuverable and inviting the myriad discoveries to come. Foremost among this deep-seafaring fleet was the *Alvin*, a three-person research submersible most famous for a 1977 discovery that shook the very foundations of biology. Exploring the Galapagos Rift off the coast of Ecuador, *Alvin*'s crew came upon a fantastic sight. At a depth of 8,200 feet, where fissures in the seafloor were spewing shimmering hot water, they found a thriving community featuring never-before-seen giant tube worms with bloodred plumes, dense clusters of foot-long clams, and chalky-white crabs. Later it was discovered that this bizarre deep-sea community was founded not on the sun-charged energy of photosynthesis—until then presumed to be the source of all life on Earth—but on bacteria feeding on the hydrogen sulfide issuing from the hot-water vents. The sea-vent discovery added exclamation to the obvious, of just how little we knew of the denizens of the deep and how much more was yet to be learned.

In the 1980s, submersibles began exploring the mid-water vastness between the sunlit surface and the deep-sea floor, the largest and least explored habitat on Earth. Johnson-Sea-Link (JSL) submersibles, named after their inventor, Ed Link, and their financer, Seward Johnson Sr., featured a five-inch-thick acrylic sphere accommodating a pilot and scientist, followed by a bus-like two-passenger pod. JSLs were originally designed for transporting divers down to the limits of scuba depths. Once at depth, the dive chamber was pressurized to ambient pressure, allowing the divers to swim out without wasting any of their precious air or bottom time getting down to their work site. It was an efficient means of dealing with what was a highly inefficient working scenario:

After just four minutes at 600 feet, a diver would need a mind-numbing twenty-seven hours of decompression to recover.

Link soon upped the scientific efficiency of his submersible, replacing the human arms of scuba divers with those of robotics, remotely operated limbs fitted with a variety of tools, including a claw, a benthic scoop, and cable cutters. There was a "critter-getter" that vacuumed samples through a hose on the robotic arm and, most important, there were eight wastebasket-sized Plexiglas cylinders with sliding lids. With these tools in the hands of a skilled pilot, JSL-transported scientists could collect delicate soft-bodied fauna known as the jelly plankton. What had long been rendered mutilated blobs of mucus in sampling nets and trawl buckets now appeared in life as a bizarre menagerie of gossamer creatures displaying all manner of delicate and diaphanous forms. The ecological importance and sheer abundance of the "jelly web" were yet more revelations about how little we knew of the marine world.

∿∿∿

IT WAS THROUGH THE JSL'S FISHBOWL IN REVERSE—with the fish on the outside and the observers on the inside—that I came to appreciate fully the unexplored universe of the deep sea. My favorite place in all the world would become a place three thousand feet down, my favorite moments those as I readied myself to make the half-hour ascent to the surface. Those moments would start when we turned out the lights, first the headlights illuminating the world outside and then all the little red indicator lights inside our sphere. Therewith followed the sensation of floating in utter blackness, impervious to the straining of our eyes. Then, opening the valves to the ballast tanks and activating the vertical thrusters, our ascent would begin, instantly transporting us into the eye of a fireworks display.

From out of the thrusters streamed blue points of light, flashing and glowing like embers swirling up from an icy campfire. Tiny puffs of blue smoke mingled with bursts of blue sparks from a Fourth of July sparkler. Blue neon lines raced around in tight figure eights and loop-the-loops. And just when it seemed we had reached the breathtaking limits of the living display, a string of blue Japanese lanterns would suddenly drape itself across the top of our vessel. Glowing brilliantly, the chain would stretch into a parabola until finally breaking, sending streamers of light fluttering into the sub-generated current. This luminescent display so lit our little world that we could read the gauges inside the cockpit by living light.

Seeing this side of the undersea world as so few others have, I am reminded of both its wonders and its fragility. As our primitive view of the ocean's complexity has evolved, so has our realization of what threatens it.

In 2004, the U.S. Commission on Ocean Policy published its landmark report detailing the deteriorating condition of our oceans. The litany of offenses was a long and depressing list. It detailed how the ocean has been looted and stripped to put luxury food items on our tables while filling with an ever-increasing inventory of toxins and trash.

The report reads as a painfully sad story of loss of habitats, of life forms, and of clean water. Along our coasts, precious nurseries of the ocean have been systematically eliminated.

Beaches, where for millions of years turtles have come to lay their eggs in the darkness, have been paved over and lit with blinding lights. Mangrove havens for larval fish have been destroyed and replaced with seawalls. Destructive foreign organisms have invaded with our help, suffocating blooms of algae feed on our pollutants, and the muck of society's runoff smothers sea grasses and oyster beds. The list runs on.

The fish that once sustained villages of people who pulled nets in small boats have been lost to a modern armada of factory ships serving a ravenous world community of 6.7 billion people, plying the seas with nets so enormous that their catches are measured in hundreds of tons. In the past half century, more than 90 percent of the biggest fish have been removed from the ocean. And as we remove the fish, so do we remove their habitat. Trawlers drag nets across the bottom of the ocean, scraping and flattening everything in their paths. I have visited such places in submersibles. I have witnessed kingdoms of corals—some more than a thousand years old—and magnificent gardens of fish and invertebrates obliterated by the single pass of a trawl net.

All this is to say that we are in a race—not only to halt the destruction but to learn what is there before it is heedlessly demolished. To that end, I have envisioned bringing eyes into the ocean to every undersea wonderland, revealing the beauty and mystery for all to admire, appreciate, and ultimately protect. With engineers, scientists, and technicians at Harbor Branch Oceanographic Institution, the Monterey Bay Aquarium Research Institute, and the Ocean Research & Conservation Association, we have begun deploying underwater cameras on the ocean floor, lit by red light invisible to marine organisms, watching the life of the sea as never before. We are moving beyond those days when with my mere presence I once frightened the bioluminescent masses into revealing themselves. And once again, I am looking to the marvel of bioluminescence to lead the way.

<p style="text-align:center">~~~</p>

BIOLUMINESCENCE IS THE SEA CREATURE'S ANSWER to navigating the blackness of its environment to find mates, evade predators, and locate prey. Bioluminescence has even been fashioned in the form of a burglar alarm, an adaptation I discovered invaluable for my own scientific designs.

Certain prey species, caught in the clutches of a predator, emit a brilliant, eye-catching display of light. It is a bioluminescent call for help, analogous to the blaring horns and flashing lights of an automobile's antitheft alarm. The display may attract the attention of a nearby predator that will attack the attacker—a police officer, if you will—thereby sending the burglar fleeing and affording the prey its chance to escape.

One of my favorite burglar alarms is that of the deep-sea jellyfish *Atolla*. These beautiful jellies, which range in size from bottle cap to large dinner plate, reflect crimson red when seen under white light. But in the dark, their bioluminescence shines a brilliant icy blue. Depending on the stimulus, they can produce a variety of displays, but the burglar alarm is the most spectacular. It is a pinwheel of light that swirls around the bell in radiant waves bright enough to attract predators more than three hundred feet away.

I wondered if such a display might make an effective lure, a way to attract predators to the camera, beyond the familiar scavengers that more typically converge on food bait. To test this hypothesis, we built an optical lure made out of sixteen blue lights embedded around the perimeter of a round jellyfish-shaped mold.

I wanted to test the lure at a deep-sea oasis, a biological hot spot in the depths of a barren seascape where large predators likely patrolled. I found such a spot in the northern end of the Gulf of Mexico. At the bottom of the Gulf lay an undersea lake, a pool of hyper-salty water attracting a strange and rich community of creatures, including snails, sponges, shrimp, starfish, eels, and fish—the perfect oasis.

We loaded the camera on the JSL submersible and carried it down to the brine pool. Dropping through two thousand feet of water, we watched the penetrating sunlight change from azure to indigo. By the time we reached one thousand feet, the light had faded to a faint blue blur overhead; by twelve hundred feet, there was the gradually dimming shade of gray; by eighteen hundred feet, all was dark.

We found the pool at twenty-one hundred feet. It loomed up out of the darkness in our headlights, more fantastic than I had imagined. The underwater lake was bounded by a well-defined shoreline and a surface of water underwater. Our sub made waves that lapped against the brine pool's shoreline. We found a flat spot on the seafloor and, with the sub's robotic arm, positioned the camera by the edge of the pool. We placed a bait bag in front of the camera along with our electronic jellyfish lure and left our invention to do its work.

Two days later, having recovered the camera from the ocean floor, I was in the ship's dry lab scanning through the video we had just collected. I was at last looking through a secret window into the deep sea, one through which we were not shouting and screaming and scaring everything away but one through which we were peeking, unobserved, like a bird-watcher in an underwater blind.

I had scanned the first four hours of the recordings and, to the un-trained observer, it looked like pretty dull stuff, featuring fish swimming around being fish. But to me it was the thrill of a lifetime, peeking beneath the waves to watch the ocean's deepest, most mysterious inhabitants behaving as they do day to day under cover of darkness. These fish were not running away from blinding lights and whining thrusters. These fish were swimming lazily, some heading straight for the camera and the red light that illuminated the scene, light that was apparently invisible to them. As giddy as I was from these incomparable images, I was not prepared for what came next.

I pressed the down arrow to activate the next sequence and suddenly there was an enormous squid filling the screen. My shipmates heard me shouting all the way up on the bridge. People came running. I ran the sequence over and over again. It was a squid stranger than any of us had ever seen. As it turned out, it was stranger than *anybody* had ever seen; not even the experts at the Smithsonian Institution, who later reviewed the recording, recognized it. This would turn out to be a squid defying placement in any known scientific family, and it was drawn in by the burglar-alarm display, appearing on the screen just eighty-six seconds after the electronic jellyfish was activated for the first time.

How many more such creatures live hidden in the depths? How many among the fast swimmers and ultrasensitive designs of the sea have evaded our slow-moving nets and blinding, deafening subs? There is so much we don't know about life in this, by far the largest habitat on our planet.

We are now watching the underwater world anew, as unobtrusive observers, completing the ultimate dream of the deep-sea explorer: to see without being seen, to unveil the blackest unknown in the truest of lights. And with that light, I see a new hope dawning for the life of our oceans, an opportunity to reveal both the incomparable beauty and the devastating destruction beneath the waves, and ask you, the observers, "Is this worth saving?"

Sea-Struck
Liz Clark

Four years and 15,000 miles ago, twenty-something surfer and sailor Liz set out from California to circumnavigate the planet, slowly, aboard her forty-foot ketch, Swell. *She writes to us from a small island in French Polynesia, where she'd stopped off for repairs—and a perfect surf break. Throughout her voyage, she has also been taking a firsthand look at how the ocean is changing and how it is changing her.*

I've been sea-struck for as long as I can remember. Dangling my feet over the bowsprit of my father's sailboat before I'd lived even a decade, I recall a visceral, undeniable attraction to the sea. It mesmerized me as the water rushed below, stirring, flowing, shifting, surging, crashing, creeping, washing. Each ripple just a small expression of its unfathomably greater entity. Where these ripples met the land, I discovered surfing, immersing myself in a more physical relationship with seaborne energy. The salt water soothed, healed, and tested me. But even as my dedication to wave riding intensified, I would gaze out past the sets, where the unbroken horizon invoked a sense of unlimited possibility. The wildness of the open sea still had me hopelessly enchanted. But I knew that playing on that playground was no game. The sea was self-regulating; only those willing to test their wits with the utmost of attention and respect survive. But afflicted with this "sea-sickness," my options were to suffer stifling disappointment for having never tried or attempt to live out my vision of a life at sea despite the unavoidable risks.

After fourteen years spent dreaming about setting sail to unknown destinations and two more of rigorous hands-on preparation, I had done nearly all I could do to ready myself and my vessel for the prospects of sea adventure. It was the unknown, the risks, and the challenges ahead that both petrified and delighted me. Despite my overwhelming uncertainties, I set sail in October 2005, headed south from Santa Barbara, California. The following excerpts from my voyage journal are a glimpse into my personal love story with the ocean.

BAJA CALIFORNIA, FEBRUARY 2006. We rounded the bluff and Punta San Carlos with daylight to spare. Rights peel down the long point toward the dozen colorful shacks of this northern Baja fishing village, breaking up the endless landscape of tan, yellow, and beige. My crew of two and I scurried to untie the boards, peel off our salt-crusted foulies, and shimmy into our wetsuits. A leap into the cold sea washed away the accumulated salt, grime, and anxiety of the past week. I paddled toward shore, marveling at the tests the sea had already given me just since leaving San Diego. I'd nearly run aground on an uncharted shoal at the mouth of Bahia San Quintin when a sizable wave had broken 150 feet off the bow. The depth gauge dropped to twenty feet, then nineteen, eighteen before I made a jarring turn to starboard away from the high spot. A few mornings later, I wiggled the throttle of the engine into neutral and turned over the key. Nothing. Wiggled it again. Nothing. Subsequently, I dove into my first test of mechanical savvy. After losing a day to the "neutral safety wire" mystery, we continued gliding down the coast until a warm, volatile wind came howling off the land. A gust pinned *Swell* completely over on her side when the tail of the jackline was sucked into the roller-furling winch. After I cut it free with my rigging knife, the boat righted herself and I pulled down the sails, hands trembling with adrenaline. Aside from these incidents, we'd skirted hundreds of lobster traps, avoided submerged reefs, and battled nausea.

As I paddled my surfboard toward shore that evening I doubted my ability as a captain. Although the waves were hardly extraordinary, each glide felt like a miracle, granting me momentary reprieve from the pressure and fear of learning to be the captain of my sailboat, along with succeeding to live out my dream. For that moment, I indulged in the familiarity and comfort of surfing. I appreciated even the simplest elements of wave riding—extra consciously placing my feet, not wasting an inch of the wave's push, and letting the cold whitewater plow over me to flush my nose and mouth and ears. This was the same sea that I'd crossed to arrive there; I just needed time to get familiar with it in its other context. When the sun hung low and orange above the horizon, I glanced across the bay. There was *Swell,* bobbing faithfully atop the smooth neon colors, bathed in a golden halo of the sun's final rays. The image nearly took my breath away. There was salt on my lips and a burn in my shoulders. I was in my dream but wide awake.

TUAMOUTU ATOLLS, DECEMBER 2007. I was a wreck of nerves as I followed the Spanish-flagged *Octobasse* out of the lagoon on my first attempt at an upwind passage against the South Pacific's trade winds. The wind was already howling, and I repeatedly asked myself why I was leaving the comfort of the atoll's lagoon for an upwind hell bash. I sighed and flattened the headsail as tight as possible; I was committed.

Every six to seven hours, we tacked strategically, but by nightfall, the wind and seas were increasing. *Swell* bucked and bashed, bombs of water exploding under the hull as I fought against the flow of the sea and wind. Waves washed across the deck, and the cabin floor looked like a nautical yard sale as various items worked themselves loose in the jarring seas. The chain plates squealed, every one of the boat's joints moaned, and I was seasick.

"What am I doing?" I thought to myself. "I'm scared, uncomfortable, and putting unnecessary strain on my precious floating home." I spoke with *Octobasse* every few hours over the radio, elaborating on my concerns and feeling small and weak against the push of this angry sea.

The following morning, in a fog of nausea, anxiety, and discomfort, a squall hit *Swell* with unprecedented fury. Its dark line approached dauntingly, and I scurried on deck to pull down more sail. I was almost in tears when the blast of wind and rain arrived. But as the wrath enveloped us, a strange thing occurred. The combination of pelting rain and fierce wind in the glittering morning light showed me a face of the sea I had never before seen. A brilliant white layer of illuminated raindrops and windblown spray iced the sea's surface. I stood tethered to the cockpit, feeling the pelt of the cool rain on my bare skin, hypnotized by this ferocious splendor. The moment's beauty shook me from my pitiful state. I beamed back at the sea with gratitude for this subtle morning lesson. I realized that once again, there were hidden rewards for stepping out of my comfortable boundaries. *Swell* heeled and lurched, but we were completely in control. In that instant, my fear vanished.

LINE ISLANDS, REPUBLIC OF KIRIBATI, APRIL 2008. I donned my mask, snorkel, and fins; tied the bowline of the dinghy to my right ankle; and plopped over the side at the mouth of the lagoon pass. The tug of the current was already evident as the seafloor passed quickly below me. I dove to the limit of my rope and held my breath, suspended in aqueous flight with the rush of the incoming tide.

The corals came alive with color and texture as I swam deeper. Schools of rainbow runners, tuna, jack, and barracuda dipped and veered in synchronized frenzies. I couldn't decide where to look; like driving down the main strip of Las Vegas for the first time, there was too much to take in all at once. A large Wahoo passed above amidst a school of silvery flanked baitfish that flashed here and there in rhythmic orchestras of light. Below me was no less spectacular; the reef was laden with detail and abuzz with an incomprehensible variety of teeny fluorescent-lined gobies, wildly striped surgeonfish, wide-eyed squirrelfish peering out from rock caves, and angelfish with upturned noses. An eel glared at me, jaw agape, as I was whisked past his front door. I pushed internal "cruise control" and just let my eyes drift from one splendor to the next, imagining that I was an invisible particle of organic material suspended in this pulsating vein of sea. Never had I witnessed an undersea ecosystem in such fervent blossom!

As I rose to the surface for a breath, I thought back to the choked and deserted reefs I'd explored along the coasts of Mexico, Central America, and the more populated parts of French Polynesia. I remembered cringing as the construction team at a resort in Bora Bora rammed a new pillar into the reef to hold up another row of over-the-water bungalows. I thought back to the piles of plastic that lined the bays outside of Panama City and the streams of pollution that drained from the city gutters into the sea. I recalled the rotten smell of California's coast after the rains and surfing in sewage and runoff. Everything we do on land eventually affects the sea.

With another breath, I plunged below again. I looked left, and a lionfish flitted his elaborate fan of fins within a tight gap in the reef. An octopus curled and camouflaged against the coral. I looked ahead just in time to nearly collide with a hurried troop of yellow-trimmed sweetlips. Anemone fingers flowed in watery wafts, and the corals, oh the corals! Soft, hard, fingered, smooth, purple to lime-green, they stacked vertically upon each other like colorful piles of dirty dishes in a kitchen sink. I yielded to a pack of four prowling gray sharks swimming up-current. A few rogue blacktips whipped by, too, and then a beady-eyed nurse shark resting on the bottom.

More fish, more gliding, more colors! A school of jacks, a giant wrasse, and a needlefish whizzed by as the current increased where the mouth of the pass narrowed. As I surfaced, a great manta appeared ahead. As I ascended to his level, he lifted one wing up while the other arced down. I recognized the fragility of the underwater world around me. I feared the fate of these creatures and that of humanity if we fail to find a balance that preserves the earth and ocean that support us. The turbulence increased as the seafloor rose and the tidal rush mixed with the water inside the atoll. I surfaced in a dizzy buzz. I had sailed this far for just this reason: to see places where, for now, nature reigns.

PASSAGE FROM THE LINE ISLANDS TO FRENCH POLYNESIA, JUNE 2008. The weather was manic, blowing thirty-five knots all day without a cloud in sight. Around sunset, a thick forest of towering thunderheads sprang from the sea. I was nine days and 1,000 miles into the 1,500-mile passage back to Polynesia. Even without this bizarre weather, it was my most challenging passage yet, forcing me to sail against the prevailing winds nearly the entire way.

On this moonless night, no horizon was visible. I could make out only varying hues of black all around. *Swell* skirted before an approaching thunderhead, feeling only trailing swirls of its disturbed air. For a moment, it looked clear ahead, but wait! What's that!? To my left, I witnessed the darkness thicken. I altered our course and reefed the sails yet again. The cloud mutant bloated and mushroomed to what must have been a thousand feet straight up. There was no hope of escape as it bore down on us with unprecedented vengeance. Lightning sliced down, momentarily illuminating the face of this demon. I froze in terror. Short, strained breaths and panic came over me. There was nothing I could do. The air grew eerily thick and still. *Swell* wallowed limply with no wind in her shortened sails. I clutched the mainsheet with paranoia. I wanted to close my eyes, to disappear, to be anywhere but there. I was nothing but a speck of helpless flesh, minute and powerless. I mumbled prayers unintelligibly, twitching and fidgeting in fear of what was next.

In another instant, the monster slapped us with the swiftest, fiercest paw of wind I'd ever felt. *Swell* was pinned for what felt like a minute on her starboard side. I cried out for my father, but he couldn't hear me. No one heard me. Lightning struck just a boat length away, then the sky shook and I froze and cowered as the *Craaaaaaaaaaaaaaaaaaaaaaaaaaaack* of the thunder penetrated my bones.

The warm sea poured into the cockpit as I frantically released the mainsheet. Once the initial blow had diminished, *Swell* slowly righted herself. Then came the rain. But this wasn't normal rain; this was a sky of water, its fall deafening. The wind subsided as the cloud moved past us. My body trembled wildly. I tasted blood in my mouth and rubbed my tongue where I'd bit through the inside of my lip. The lightning repeatedly cast its ghostly light on the scene as the monster raged westward to remind me that this hideous moment was real. I gathered myself enough to squint ahead into the clearing night sky. A small patch of stars hinted hope, but more lightning flashed a few miles off. Tears flowed down my cheeks, mixing with my soaked skin, but I made no noise of crying. I looked at my watch. It was only 10 p.m.

"If I can get through this night," I thought, "I can do anything."

MARQUESAS ISLANDS, SEPTEMBER 2007. On a glorious day at sea in the South Pacific, I delighted in the realization that I truly enjoyed being alone. I hadn't always been excited by the prospect; in fact, solitude had previously petrified me. I'd inched my way toward becoming a solo sailor over the first part of my voyage.

But I found myself alone there, wedged into the aft corner of *Swell's* cockpit, carefully making a handmade fishing lure between gazes at the vast, majestic blue. *Swell* slipped slowly through the dynamic brilliance at a mere three and a half knots, sails plump with wind. I had no firm destination and no need to be anywhere but exactly there. Without anyone to remind me of my human status, I floated in the clouds overhead and dissolved into the rhythmic splashing of the hull through the water. The moment was timeless. Looking out from where I sat, it could have been 1300 BC or AD 30 or 1991 and it would have looked the same: peaks of blue sea, tall puffs of clouds, the sun, and wind all running west together.

One thing I have learned to love about being on the ocean is that it never judged me. It seemed never to care what I was wearing, how my hair looked, or whether I was clean or dirty. It didn't mind when my voice cracked on the high notes of a song or if I didn't pluck my eyebrows or if my joke wasn't that funny. I looked around with gratitude and admiration for the great body of water around me. It had given me so much, taught me patience, humility, integrity, peace, and grace. It had made me feel vulnerable but also powerful beyond my wildest dreams. It had given me a chance to find out who I really was. On the sea alone, I was free to be exactly me. And on that particular afternoon, alone in the heart of the South Pacific, I couldn't remember ever having felt more content.

One Stroke at a Time
Roz Savage

Management consultant cum open ocean rower, Roz has taken sea-level observation to a new level, having rowed solo across the Atlantic and, by last December, halfway across the Pacific. When at sea, she battles day by day with whether she loves—or hates!—the ocean.

The sun beat down from a cloudless equatorial sky. The ocean was like a mirror, the first time I had seen it this flat in the 104 days I had been at sea. The heat was intense and, with no breeze to whisk it away, the sweat ran down my back in rivulets. I stopped rowing for a moment to glug down some water, but it was warm, tasted of plastic, failed to refresh. I yearned for an ice-cold drink, preferably one with bubbles and alcohol.

I was tired. The year before (2007), I had rowed three thousand miles from San Francisco to Hawaii in ninety-nine days; now I was about to make landfall on Kiribati in October 2008, having put another three thousand miles behind me.

These last few miles were potentially the most dangerous of the voyage. If not being rowed, ocean rowboats are very much at the mercy of the wind, waves, and currents. The previous two nights, I had barely slept as I skirted past a couple of small outlying atolls, waking up every hour or so to squint at the screen of my GPS to make sure I wasn't drifting toward shipwreck on a reef. A few times, the wind had shifted and I'd had to return to the oars to put a comfortable margin of safety between my boat and potential disaster.

I was closing in on the tiny island of Tarawa, the capital of Kiribati, a scattering of small coral reef atolls lying one degree north of the equator. Kiribati has two main distinguishing features: It is in the first time zone west of the international dateline, and it will also be one of the first nations on Earth to fall victim to climate change as sea levels continue to rise around the globe. It's possible that this fragile nation clinging to the edge of the world will become uninhabitable within the next fifty years, its water supply contaminated by salt water even before the low-lying islands disappear beneath storm surges and rising seas as extreme weather events become more frequent.

At this moment, it was my own survival that was uppermost in my mind, however. I forced down more of the hot, plasticky water and rowed on. Even after rowing 3,000 miles, I had been pushing hard these last few days and was nearing the end of my resources. My head went down and I focused on just the next ten strokes, then the next ten, then the next ten.

Many tens of strokes later, I finally crossed the line of latitude parallel with the southern tip of Tarawa. Too drained even to let out a whoop of joy, I collapsed backward off my rowing seat and lay semi-reclined on the deck, my shoulders leaning against the hatch of my forward cabin. I had done it. Two stages of the Pacific down, one to go. But I wasn't ready yet to start thinking about the final stage that would take me from Kiribati to Australia.

I thought back to where I'd come from. Less than a decade before, I had been working in a London office cubicle, dissatisfied and unhappy, uncertain why all my friends seemed to find their all-too-similar lives quite acceptable and I could not. In search of an answer, one day I sat down and wrote two versions of my own obituary, the one I wanted and the one I was heading for. They differed dramatically, and I could see that a major course correction was needed.

I stumbled into ocean rowing and, ever since, the ocean has proved a harsh but effective teacher. It has given me time alone to think. It has taught me the value of simplicity. It has reminded me that we humans are inextricably bound to this fragile planet, and any notions we may have that we are above or beyond nature are dangerous delusions. At the same time, she has shown me how an ordinary human being can achieve the extraordinary, by presenting me with challenge after challenge, pushing me to what I thought was my limit, only for me to discover that when I have no choice I can go beyond those boundaries and achieve more than I would ever have dreamed possible.

IT WAS IN HOPES OF FINDING GREATER WISDOM that I first set out across an ocean, and I have learned many things during more than three hundred days spent in the watery wilderness. Others before me have found retreat in the desert, in the mountains, in a cave, or in a monastery. For me, the starting place of my slow struggle toward enlightenment was the uncomfortable seat of a small rowing boat built for one.

I thought back to this a few nights before the end of my voyage from Hawaii to Kiribati. I was within a few miles of the equator, and it was a hot and sticky night, nearly unbearably stuffy in my cabin. I was suffering from a nasty heat rash, as I had done for much of the crossing, and the itching was driving me crazy. I craved to feel a cool, fresh breeze on my skin.

I hauled my bedding out from the small cabin and onto the deck, pushing my sleeping bag, blanket, and cushion into the shallow trough between the runners of my rowing seat and snuggling down into a cozy nest. I knew it probably wouldn't be long before a rainsquall arrived, but it was worth the effort, even if only for an hour or two. I lay there contentedly, luxuriating in the relative coolness of the night air, rolling onto my back to look up at the stars.

There are few places on Earth better to view the night sky than from the middle of an ocean. As your eyes get used to one patch of sky, you notice stars beyond stars, fainter ones hiding behind their brighter counterparts and then more.

Contemplating the heavens makes me feel both very small and yet immense at the same time. We humans tend to live with an illusion of separateness, thinking that we are separate from each other as individuals and that we are separate nations, divided by oceans, all separate from nature. But the reality is that we are all united by our dependence on this planet, on this ocean.

~~~

THERE IS NOTHING LIKE TWENTY-FOOT WAVES to remind you of the puniness of humans. During my early days crossing the Atlantic, I felt the ocean was trying to teach me a lesson and that if I could only grasp what she was trying to teach me, all would be transformed, anticipating some kind of Hollywood ending. It took me awhile, during which I indulged in all kinds of bizarre and superstitious behavior, to try to cajole the ocean into a better mood, before I realized that the ocean was not trying to teach me anything. The ocean is not a sentient being, capable of rearranging its behavior for my personal edification. It is supremely and magnificently indifferent. Waves merely obey the laws of science; there is no magic trick that would allow me to circumvent those laws. I just had to do what a rower does: take one stroke at a time and allow the ocean to carry on doing what oceans do.

Some people love the ocean. Some people fear it. I love it, hate it, fear it, respect it, resent it, cherish it, loathe it, and frequently curse it. It brings out the best in me and sometimes the worst. Its sheer vastness and depth never cease to amaze me, and yet my focus is often reduced to just the wave ahead. Although I have now spent over three hundred days cumulatively on the ocean, I don't think I will ever feel truly at home there.

My journey from San Francisco to Hawaii took me about a million oar strokes. I could have easily stood beneath the Golden Gate Bridge on that first cold, dark night in May 2007 and said to myself that one oar stroke wouldn't get me anywhere. But instead, I chose to take a million tiny actions. Put them all together and they got me across 3,000 miles of ocean. There were times when I struggled, times when I wondered what the hell I was doing, times when I wanted to be anywhere else but on that tiny, tippy, uncomfortable little boat. There were times when I had to persuade myself to take just another ten strokes, another ten, another ten.

But I had a vision of what it would feel like to arrive at the end of my journey and know it had all been worthwhile, and that vision kept me going, one stroke at a time. That feeling of achievement when I reached my goal was the best feeling in the world. If I could bottle it and sell it, I would make millions.

Perhaps the most powerful thing the ocean has taught me is that we don't need to be afraid of the future because every one of us has it in our power to shape it. That even the smallest actions count. Not only does every tiny action matter, but in the long run, it is the only thing that matters. It is how this rather small, not-so-young woman manages to row across oceans—by taking one stroke at a time.

PART II

LOSING IT

Climate Change and the Ocean
An Interview with
President Mohamed Nasheed, the Maldives

Forty-two-year-old President Nasheed is the first democratically elected president of the island nation of the Maldives, home to 350,000 people in the Indian Ocean off the tip of Sri Lanka. A former human rights activist and journalist, he was jailed and tortured by his predecessor. Today he is one of the most outspoken politicians in the world on the impact of climate change and its impact on all coastal areas, especially the Maldives.

Jon Bowermaster: How immediate is the problem of climate change and rising seas in the Maldives today? What evidence are you seeing?
President Nasheed: Climate change is not a distant or abstract phenomenon in the Maldives. The effects of climate change are being felt today. One third of inhabited islands in the Maldives are suffering from coastal erosion, which is exacerbated by climate change. Fishermen are complaining that weather patterns have become unpredictable, and warmer and more acidic seas threaten our coral reefs. If the world fails to curb carbon dioxide emissions, and global temperatures continue to soar, these problems will worsen over the coming decades.

JB: Have sea levels risen already?
PN: The Environment Ministry calculates that sea levels in the Maldives are rising by 0.7 mm per year, which is around the global average. The big

fear, however, is that this rise in sea level accelerates as climate change starts to accelerate even more toward the end of this century. This is a concern not just to the Maldives but to all low-lying areas around the world.

A one-meter rise in sea levels, which some climate scientists warn will happen if nothing is done to reduce carbon pollution, would be devastating for the Maldives. Such a rise would also inundate other low-lying countries such as Bangladesh and the Netherlands and seriously threaten many of the world's coastal cities. We must not allow this to happen.

JB: Soon after your election, you announced plans to look for higher ground to move your people to. Where are you looking, and how is the search going?
PN: Nobody in the Maldives wants to leave home. The government is doing everything we possibly can to remain here. We are improving sea defenses, such as seawalls, revetments, and embankments. We are working to improve the coral reefs and coastal vegetation, which are our islands' natural defense mechanisms. And we are exploring new building designs, such as building houses on stilts so they withstand storm surges and floods.

The bottom line, however, is dry land, and if the world allows the climate crisis to turn into a catastrophe, then future generations of Maldivians will have no choice but to seek new homes on higher ground. I believe it is right to have this conversation today so we can start to plan for the problems tomorrow may bring.

Last year, I suggested we should start saving a portion of our tourism revenues in a Sovereign Wealth Fund to help future generations cope with climate change. Ultimately, this fund could be used to help people leave. Again, I stress that this is not a problem unique to the Maldives. We are merely the first people who are talking out loud about these issues. If we ignore the warning signs and continue blindly down a business-as-usual polluting path, then it will not just be Maldivians looking for a new home but also the good people of London, New York, and Hong Kong.

JB: In your travels around the Maldives, do you find that most people understand the seriousness of climate change and its potential impact on them?
PN: People living in Malé and other urban areas are quite knowledgeable about the environment, particularly young people. In more remote

parts of the country, people see that erosion is increasing. They know that the fish catch is more irregular, and they understand that coral reefs are stressed. Maldivians know there are environmental problems that affect their daily lives and that these problems are linked to global climate change.

JB: You've also proposed that the Maldives will become the first carbon-neutral country on the planet. How is that going, and have you set a time line?
PN: We have a plan to make the Maldives carbon neutral in ten years. At the heart of this plan lies a commitment to renewable energy. One hundred fifty-five 1.5 MW wind turbines, coupled with half a square kilometer of solar panels and a backup biomass plant, would produce enough green energy to power the country. Aviation is trickier. Until airlines can switch to biofuels, there is little the Maldives can do other than offset the pollution caused by international tourist flights by investing in carbon-reduction schemes elsewhere.

Our carbon-neutral plan is on track. This year, the government has started working with a number of international energy companies to build wind farms, which we hope will provide the bulk of our electricity. We are also working with the government of Japan on a $10 million solar project to install photovoltaic panels on schools and government buildings in and around the capital.

JB: You recently convened an underwater meeting of your entire cabinet. Whose idea was that? Some in the press called it a stunt—which is not always a bad thing when you're trying to draw attention to important issues.
PN: It was a cabinet decision to conduct the underwater meeting. We estimate that over 1 billion people watched, heard, or read about the underwater cabinet meeting. Although it was a bit of fun, it underscored a serious message. I hope the meeting raised people's awareness about the dangers climate change poses to the Maldives and the rest of the world. I hope that some of those people go on to ask their own politicians what they are doing to help solve the climate crisis. It is only when people start holding leaders to account, when politicians start losing elections over environmental issues, that they will treat climate change with the seriousness it deserves.

JB: How many feet above sea level is your bedroom? Office?
PN: The president's office is about six feet above sea level.

JB: What can bigger nations do to help lessen contributions to climate change, which will adversely affect island nations first?
PN: To save the Maldives—and the rest of the world—we need to halt climate change. It is as simple, and as complicated, as that. And to halt climate change, we must listen to the advice of those who know best. Not politicians but climate scientists.

Scientists used to be concerned about climate change. But after the massive loss of polar ice two years ago, that concern turned to alarm. Scientists realized that global warming was happening more quickly and on a larger scale than they had anticipated. Wherever scientists looked—high-altitude glaciers, hydrological cycles, and the spread of mosquitoes—they found change happening decades ahead of schedule. Average global temperatures have risen by about 2 degrees Celsius (about 4 degrees Fahrenheit) since the Industrial Revolution, but this has been enough to tilt the world's climate off balance.

In January 2008, James Hansen, one of the world's leading climatologists, published a series of papers showing that the safe limit for carbon dioxide in the atmosphere was at most 350 parts per million (ppm). Anything higher than that limit, warns Hansen, could seed "irreversible, catastrophic effects" on a global scale. At the moment, the amount of carbon dioxide in the atmosphere is 387 ppm and rising. Reducing the amount of carbon in the atmosphere to 350 is our best chance of preventing global temperatures from rising even further.

Sadly, most politicians have chosen to ignore these warnings and still talk about limiting temperature rises to 4 degrees Celsius (7 degrees Fahrenheit). But a 4-degree temperature rise would not stop climate change. Rather, 4 degrees will sink the Maldives, melt Greenland, and devastate the Amazon rain forest. Four degrees would also turn most of the Mediterranean into desert. We must not allow that to happen.

We all need to stop polluting the atmosphere with greenhouse gases, which we know are poisoning our world. And we need to start using the renewable resources we all have in abundance to power the planet, namely, the sun, the sea, and the wind.

JB: Many of the things causing climate change are created far from the shores of the Maldives. Do you hold the big industrial nations responsible for a problem now dramatically facing your country?

PN: Blaming others for causing the climate crisis is not necessarily the best way to solve it. What's done is done. We want to focus on the future, not on the past. The industrialized nations have the greatest changes to make in terms of transforming their economies toward carbon neutrality. But developing nations also have responsibilities. If we want to reduce carbon pollution in the atmosphere, developing nations cannot pursue the same dirty development path that the West did. We must embrace renewable energy and green growth. Developing countries are relatively poor, however. To my mind, it makes sense that Western nations, which have the money and technical resources, should help poorer, developing nations go green. It is in everyone's interest that richer countries play this leadership role while also transforming their own economies.

JB: In the face of the growing consensus that our seas will rise, perhaps more quickly than we now expect, how do you maintain your apparent sense of optimism?

PN: I believe in humanity and human ingenuity. I do not believe that humans are suicidal or that the path ahead is insurmountable. I believe that the winners of the twenty-first century will be those countries that jettison dirty fossil fuels for renewable energy and green technologies. These pioneering countries will free themselves from the unpredictable price of foreign oil. They will corner the market in the green industries of the future. These countries will also have greater moral authority and political clout on the world stage. The Maldives has committed to carbon neutrality, but our efforts alone will not stop climate change. We need other nations to come on board and commit to carbon neutrality. Politicians rarely act unless their electorates push them to do so. In that regard, I would invite everyone living in a country that has not signed up to carbon neutrality to ask their elected representatives why they are dragging their feet on the most important issue in human history.

Plastic Ocean
Our Oceans Are Turning into Plastic . . . Are We?
Susan Casey

*Captain Charles Moore, who ten years ago discovered what has
popularly become known as the Great Pacific Garbage Patch,
returned there during the summer of 2009. He anticipated
there would be more plastic swirling in the gyre, but he
reports finding more than twenty to thirty times as much.
Journalist Susan Casey's insightful report anticipated
that growth . . . and predicts its consequences.*

Fate can take strange forms, so perhaps it does not seem unusual that
Captain Charles Moore found his life's purpose in a nightmare. Unfor-
tunately, he was awake at the time and 800 miles north of Hawaii in the
Pacific Ocean.

It happened on August 3, 1997, a lovely day, at least in the beginning.
Sunny. Little wind. Water the color of sapphires. Moore and the crew
of *Alguita,* his fifty-foot aluminum-hulled catamaran, sliced through
the sea.

Returning to southern California from Hawaii after a sailing race,
Moore had altered *Alguita*'s course, veering slightly north. He had the
time and the curiosity to try a new route, one that would lead the vessel
through the eastern corner of a 10-million-square-mile oval known as
the North Pacific subtropical gyre. This was an odd stretch of ocean,

a place most boats purposely avoided. For one thing, it was becalmed. "The doldrums," sailors called it, and they steered clear. So did the ocean's top predators: the tuna, sharks, and other large fish that required livelier waters, flush with prey. The gyre was more like a desert—a slow, deep, clockwise-swirling vortex of air and water caused by a mountain of high-pressure air that lingered above it.

The area's reputation didn't deter Moore. He had grown up in Long Beach, forty miles south of Los Angeles, with the Pacific literally in his front yard, and he possessed an impressive aquatic résumé: deckhand, able seaman, sailor, scuba diver, surfer, and finally captain. Moore had spent countless hours in the ocean, fascinated by its vast trove of secrets and terrors. He'd seen a lot of things out there, things that were glorious and grand, things that were ferocious and humbling. But he had never seen anything nearly as chilling as what lay ahead of him in the gyre.

It began with a line of plastic bags ghosting the surface, followed by an ugly tangle of junk: nets and ropes and bottles, motor-oil jugs and cracked bath toys, a mangled tarp. Tires. A traffic cone. Moore could not believe his eyes. Out here in this desolate place, the water was a stew of plastic crap. It was as though someone had taken the pristine seascape of his youth and swapped it for a landfill.

How did all the plastic end up here? How did this trash tsunami begin? What did it mean? If the questions seemed overwhelming, Moore would soon learn that the answers were even more so and that his discovery had dire implications for human—and planetary—health. As *Alguita* glided through the area that scientists now refer to as the Eastern Garbage Patch, Moore realized that the trail of plastic went on for hundreds of miles. Depressed and stunned, he sailed for a week through bobbing, toxic debris trapped in a purgatory of circling currents. To his horror, he had stumbled across the twenty-first-century leviathan. It had no head, no tail. Just an endless body.

"Everybody's plastic, but I love plastic. I want to be plastic." This Andy Warhol quote is emblazoned on a six-foot-long magenta and yellow banner that hangs—with extreme irony—in the solar-powered workshop in Moore's Long Beach home. The workshop is surrounded by a crazy Eden of trees, bushes, flowers, fruits, and vegetables, ranging from the prosaic (tomatoes) to the exotic (cherimoyas, guavas, chocolate persimmons, white figs the size of baseballs). This is the house in which Moore, fifty-nine, was raised, and it has a kind of open-air earthiness that reflects his '60s activist roots, which included a stint in a Berkeley commune. Composting and organic gardening are serious business here—you can practically smell the humus—but there is also a kidney-shaped hot tub surrounded by palm trees. Two wet suits hang drying on a clothesline above it.

This afternoon, Moore strides the grounds. "How about a nice, fresh boysenberry?" he asks, and plucks one off a bush. He's a striking man wearing no-nonsense black trousers and a shirt with official-looking epaulettes. A thick brush of salt-and-pepper hair frames his intense blue eyes and serious face. But the first thing you notice about Moore is his voice, a deep, bemused drawl that becomes animated and sardonic when the subject turns to plastic pollution. This problem is Moore's calling, a passion he inherited from his father, an industrial chemist who studied waste management as a hobby. On family vacations, Moore recalls, part of the agenda would be to see what the locals threw out. "We could be in paradise, but we would go to the dump," he says with a shrug. "That's what we wanted to see."

Since his first encounter with the Garbage Patch nine years ago, Moore has been on a mission to learn exactly what's going on out there. Leaving behind a twenty-five-year career running a furniture-restoration business, he has created the Algalita Marine Research Foundation to spread the word of his findings. He has resumed his science studies, which he'd set aside when his attention swerved from pursuing a university degree to protesting the Vietnam War. His tireless effort has placed him on the front lines of this new, more abstract battle. After enlisting scientists such as Steven B. Weisberg, PhD (executive director of the Southern California Coastal Water Research Project and an expert in marine environmental monitoring), to develop methods for analyzing the gyre's contents, Moore has sailed *Alguita* back to the Garbage Patch several times. On each trip, the volume of plastic has grown alarmingly. The area in which it accumulates is now twice the size of Texas.

At the same time, all over the globe, there are signs that plastic pollution is doing more than blighting the scenery; it is also making its way into the food chain. Some of the most obvious victims are the dead seabirds that have been washing ashore in startling numbers, their bodies packed with plastic: things like bottle caps, cigarette lighters, tampon applicators, and colored scraps that, to a foraging bird, resemble baitfish. (One animal dissected by Dutch researchers contained 1,603 pieces of plastic.) And the birds aren't alone. All sea creatures, from whales down to zooplankton, are threatened by floating plastic. There's a basic moral horror in seeing the pictures: a sea turtle with a plastic band strangling its shell into an hourglass shape; a humpback towing plastic nets that cut into its flesh and make it impossible for the animal to hunt. More than a million seabirds, 100,000 marine mammals, and countless fish die in the North Pacific each year, either from mistakenly eating this junk or from being ensnared in it and drowning.

Bad enough. But Moore soon learned that the big, tentacled balls of trash were only the most visible signs of the problem; others were far less obvious and far more evil. Dragging a fine-meshed net known as a manta trawl, he discovered minuscule pieces of plastic, some barely visible to the eye, swirling like fish food throughout the water. He and his researchers parsed, measured, and sorted their samples and arrived at the following conclusion: By weight, this swath of sea contains six times as much plastic as it does plankton.

This statistic is grim for marine animals, of course, but even more so for humans. The more invisible and ubiquitous the pollution, the more likely it will end up inside us. And there's growing—and disturbing—proof that we're ingesting plastic toxins constantly, and that even slight doses of these substances can severely disrupt gene activity. "Every one of us has this huge body burden," Moore says. "You could take your serum to a lab now, and they'd find at least 100 industrial chemicals that weren't around in 1950." The fact that these toxins don't cause violent and immediate reactions does not mean they're benign: Scientists are just beginning to research the long-term ways in which the chemicals used to make plastic interact with our own biochemistry.

In simple terms, plastic is a petroleum-based mix of monomers that become polymers, to which additional chemicals are added for suppleness, inflammability, and other qualities. When it comes to these substances, even the syllables are scary. For instance, if you're thinking that perfluorooctanoic acid (PFOA) isn't something you want to sprinkle on your microwave popcorn, you're right. Recently, the Science Advisory Board of the Environmental Protection Agency (EPA) upped its classification of PFOA to a likely carcinogen. Yet it's a common ingredient in packaging that needs to be oil- and heat-resistant. So although there may be no PFOA in the popcorn itself, if PFOA is used to treat the bag, enough of it can leach into the popcorn oil when your butter deluxe meets your superheated microwave oven that a single serving spikes the amount of the chemical in your blood.

Other nasty chemical additives are the flame retardants known as polybrominated diphenyl ethers (PBDEs). These chemicals have been shown to cause liver and thyroid toxicity, reproductive problems, and memory loss in preliminary animal studies. In vehicle interiors, PBDEs—used in moldings and floor coverings, among other things—combine with another group called phthalates to create that much-vaunted "new-car smell." Leave your new wheels in the hot sun for a few hours, and these substances can "off-gas" at an accelerated rate, releasing noxious by-products.

It's not fair, however, to single out fast food and new cars. PBDEs, to take just one example, are used in many products, including computers, carpeting, and paint. As for phthalates, we deploy about a billion pounds of them a year worldwide despite the fact that California recently listed them as a chemical known to be toxic to our reproductive systems. Used to make plastic soft and pliable, phthalates leach easily from millions of products—packaged food, cosmetics, varnishes, the coatings of timed-release pharmaceuticals—into our blood, urine, saliva, seminal fluid, breast milk, and amniotic fluid. In food containers and some plastic bottles, phthalates are now found with another compound called bisphenol A (BPA), which scientists are discovering can wreak stunning havoc in the body. We produce 6 billion pounds of that each year, and it shows: BPA has been found in nearly every human who has been tested in the United States.

We're eating these plasticizing additives, drinking them, breathing them, and absorbing them through our skin every single day.

Most alarming, these chemicals may disrupt the endocrine system—the delicately balanced set of hormones and glands that affects virtually every organ and cell—by mimicking the female hormone estrogen. In marine environments, excess estrogen has led to Twilight Zone-esque discoveries of male fish and seagulls that have sprouted female sex organs.

On land, things are equally gruesome. "Fertility rates have been declining for quite some time now, and exposure to synthetic estrogen— especially from the chemicals found in plastic products—can have an adverse effect," says Marc Goldstein, MD, director of the Cornell Institute for Reproductive Medicine. Dr. Goldstein also notes that pregnant women are particularly vulnerable: "Prenatal exposure, even in very low doses, can cause irreversible damage in an unborn baby's reproductive organs." And after the baby is born, he or she is hardly out of the woods. Frederick vom Saal, PhD, a professor at the University of Missouri at Columbia who specifically studies estrogenic chemicals in plastics, warns parents to "steer clear of polycarbonate baby bottles. They're particularly dangerous for newborns, whose brains, immune systems, and gonads are still developing." Dr. vom Saal's research spurred him to throw out every polycarbonate plastic item in his house and to stop buying plastic-wrapped food and canned goods (cans are plastic-lined) at the grocery store. "We now know that BPA causes prostate cancer in mice and rats and abnormalities in the prostate's stem cell, which is the cell implicated in human prostate cancer," he says. "That's enough to scare the hell out of me." At Tufts University, Ana M. Soto, MD, a professor of anatomy and cellular biology, has also found connections between these chemicals and breast cancer.

As if the potential for cancer and mutation weren't enough, Dr. vom Saal states in one of his studies that "prenatal exposure to very low doses of BPA increases the rate of postnatal growth in mice and rats." In other words, BPA made rodents fat. Their insulin output surged wildly and then crashed into a state of resistance—the virtual definition of diabetes. They produced bigger fat cells and more of them. A recent scientific paper Dr. vom Saal coauthored contains this chilling sentence: "These findings suggest that developmental exposure to BPA is contributing to the obesity epidemic that has occurred during the last two decades in the developed world, associated with the dramatic increase in the amount of plastic being produced each year." Given this, it is perhaps not entirely coincidental that America's staggering rise in diabetes—a 735 percent increase since 1935—follows the same arc.

This news is depressing enough to make a person reach for the bottle. Glass, at least, is easily recyclable. You can take one tequila bottle, melt it down, and make another tequila bottle. With plastic, recycling is more complicated. Unfortunately, that promising-looking triangle of arrows that appears on products doesn't always signify endless reuse; it merely identifies which type of plastic the item is made from. And of the seven different plastics in common use, only two of them— PET (labeled with #1 inside the triangle and used in soda bottles) and HDPE (labeled with #2 inside the triangle and used in milk jugs)—have much of an aftermarket. So no matter how virtuously you toss your chip bags and shampoo bottles into your blue bin, few of them will escape the landfill—only 3 to 5 percent of plastics are recycled in any way.

"There's no legal way to recycle a milk container into another milk container without adding a new virgin layer of plastic," Moore says, pointing out that because plastic melts at low temperatures, it retains pollutants and the tainted residue of its former contents. Turn up the heat to sear these off, and some plastics release deadly vapors. So the reclaimed stuff is mostly used to make entirely different products, things that don't go anywhere near our mouths, such as fleece jackets and carpeting. There-fore, unlike recycling glass, metal, or paper, recycling plastic doesn't always result in less use of virgin material. It also doesn't help that fresh-made plastic is far cheaper.

Moore routinely finds half-melted blobs of plastic in the ocean, as though the person doing the burning realized partway through the process that this was a bad idea and stopped (or passed out from the fumes). "That's a concern as plastic proliferates worldwide, and people run out of room for trash and start burning plastic—you're producing some of the most toxic gases known," he says. The color-coded bin system may work in Marin County, but it is somewhat less effective in sub-equatorial Africa or rural Peru.

"Except for the small amount that's been incinerated—and it's a very small amount—every bit of plastic ever made still exists," Moore says, describing how the material's molecular structure resists bio-degradation. Instead, plastic crumbles into ever-tinier fragments as it's exposed to sunlight and the elements. And none of these untold gazillions of fragments is disappearing anytime soon: Even when plastic is broken down to a single molecule, it remains too tough for biodegradation.

Truth is, no one knows how long it will take for plastic to biodegrade, or return to its carbon and hydrogen elements. We only invented the stuff 144 years ago, and science's best guess is that its natural disappearance will take several more centuries. Meanwhile, every year, we churn out about 60 billion tons of it, much of which becomes disposable products meant only for a single use. Set aside the question of why we're creating ketchup bottles and six-pack rings that last for half a millennium and consider the implications of it: Plastic never really goes away.

Ask a group of people to name an overwhelming global problem, and you'll hear about climate change, the Middle East, or AIDS. No one, it is guaranteed, will cite the sloppy transport of nurdles as a concern. And yet nurdles, lentil-size pellets of plastic in its rawest form, are especially effective couriers of waste chemicals called persistent organic pollutants, or POPs, which include known carcinogens such as DDT and PCBs.

The United States banned these poisons in the 1970s, but they remain stubbornly at large in the environment, where they latch on to plastic because of its molecular tendency to attract oils.

The word itself—nurdles—sounds cuddly and harmless, like a cartoon character or pasta for kids, but what it refers to is most certainly not. Absorbing up to a million times the level of POP pollution in their surrounding waters, nurdles become supersaturated poison pills. They're light enough to blow around like dust; to spill out of shipping containers; and to wash into harbors, storm drains, and creeks. In the ocean, nurdles are easily mistaken for fish eggs by creatures that would very much like to have such a snack. And once inside the body of a bigeye tuna or a king salmon, these tenacious chemicals are headed directly to your dinner table.

One study estimated that nurdles now account for 10 percent of plastic ocean debris. And once they're scattered in the environment, they're diabolically hard to clean up (think wayward confetti). At places as remote as Rarotonga, in the Cook Islands, 2,100 miles northeast of New Zealand and a twelve-hour flight from Los Angeles, they're commonly found mixed with beach sand. In 2004, Moore received a $500,000 grant from the state of California to investigate the myriad ways in which nurdles go astray during the plastic manufacturing process. On a visit to a polyvinyl chloride (PVC) pipe factory, as he walked through an area where railcars unloaded ground-up nurdles, he noticed that his pant cuffs were filled with a fine plastic dust. Turning a corner, he saw windblown drifts of nurdles piled against a fence. Talking about the experience, Moore's voice becomes strained and his words pour out in an urgent tumble: "It's not the big trash on the beach. It's the fact that the whole biosphere is becoming mixed with these plastic particles. What are they doing to us? We're breathing them, the fish are eating them, they're in our hair, they're in our skin."

Though marine dumping is part of the problem, escaped nurdles and other plastic litter migrate to the gyre largely from land. That polystyrene cup you saw floating in the creek, if it doesn't get picked up and specifically taken to a landfill, will eventually be washed out to sea. Once there, it will have plenty of places to go. The North Pacific gyre is only one of five such high-pressure zones in the oceans. There are similar areas in the South Pacific, the North and South Atlantic, and the Indian Ocean. Each of these gyres has its own version of the Garbage Patch as plastic gathers in the currents. Together, these areas cover 40 percent of the sea. "That corresponds to more than a quarter of the earth's surface," Moore says. "So 28 percent of our planet is a toilet that never flushes."

It wasn't supposed to be this way. In 1865, a few years after Alexander Parkes unveiled a precursor to manufactured plastic called Parkesine, a scientist named John W. Hyatt set out to make a synthetic replacement for ivory billiard balls. He had the best of intentions: Save the elephants! After some tinkering, he created celluloid. From then on, each year brought a miraculous recipe: rayon in 1891, Teflon in 1938, polypropylene in 1954. Durable, cheap, versatile—plastic seemed like a revelation. And in many ways, it was. Plastic has given us bulletproof vests, credit cards, slinky spandex pants. It has led to breakthroughs in medicine, aerospace engineering, and computer science. And who among us doesn't own a Frisbee?

Plastic has its benefits; no one would deny that. Few of us, however, are as enthusiastic as the American Plastics Council. One of its recent press releases, titled "Plastic Bags—A Family's Trusted Companion," reads: "Very few people remember what life was like before plastic bags became an icon of convenience and practicality—and now art. Remember the 'beautiful' [sic] swirling, floating bag in *American Beauty*?"

Alas, the same ethereal quality that allows bags to dance gracefully across the big screen also lands them in many less desirable places. Twenty-three countries, including Germany, South Africa, and Australia, have banned, taxed, or restricted the use of plastic bags because they clog sewers and lodge in the throats of livestock. Like pernicious Kleenex, these flimsy sacks end up snagged in trees and snarled in fences, becoming eyesores and worse. They also trap rainwater, creating perfect little breeding grounds for disease-carrying mosquitoes.

In the face of public outrage over pictures of dolphins choking on "a family's trusted companion," the American Plastics Council takes a defensive stance, sounding not unlike the NRA: Plastics don't pollute, people do.

It has a point. Each of us tosses about 185 pounds of plastic per year. We could certainly reduce that. And yet—do our products have to be quite so lethal? Must a discarded flip-flop remain with us until the end of time? Aren't disposable razors and foam packing peanuts a poor consolation prize for the destruction of the world's oceans, not to mention our own bodies and the health of future generations? "If 'more is better' and that's the only mantra we have, we're doomed," Moore says, summing it up.

Oceanographer Curtis Ebbesmeyer, PhD, an expert on marine debris, agrees. "If you could fast-forward 10,000 years and do an archaeological dig . . . you'd find a little line of plastic," he told the *Seattle Times* last April. "What happened to those people? Well, they ate their own plastic and disrupted their genetic structure and weren't able to reproduce. They didn't last very long because they killed themselves."

Our oceans are turning into plastic . . . are we? Wrist-slittingly depressing, yes, but there are glimmers of hope on the horizon. Green architect and designer William McDonough has become an influential voice, not only in environmental circles but also among Fortune 500 CEOs. McDonough proposes a standard known as "cradle to cradle" in which all manufactured things must be reusable, poison-free, and beneficial over the long haul. His outrage is obvious when he holds up a rubber ducky, a common child's bath toy. The duck is made of phthalate-laden

PVC, which has been linked to cancer and reproductive harm. "What kind of people are we that we would design like this?" McDonough asks. In the United States, it's commonly accepted that children's teething rings, cosmetics, food wrappers, cars, and textiles will be made from toxic materials. Other countries—and many individual companies—seem to be reconsidering. Currently, McDonough is working with the Chinese government to build seven cities using "the building materials of the future," including a fabric that is safe enough to eat and a new nontoxic polystyrene.

Thanks to people like Moore and McDonough and media hits such as Al Gore's *An Inconvenient Truth,* awareness of just how hard we've slapped the planet is skyrocketing. After all, unless we're planning to colonize Mars soon, this is where we live, and none of us would choose to live in a toxic wasteland or to spend our days getting pumped full of drugs to deal with our haywire endocrine systems and runaway cancer.

None of plastic's problems can be fixed overnight, but the more we learn, the more likely that, eventually, wisdom will trump convenience and cheap disposability. In the meantime, let the cleanup begin: the National Oceanic and Atmospheric Administration (NOAA) is aggressively using satellites to identify and remove "ghost nets," abandoned plastic fishing gear that never stops killing. (A single net recently hauled up off the Florida coast contained more than 1,000 dead fish, sharks, and one loggerhead turtle.) New biodegradable starch- and corn-based plastics have arrived, and Wal-Mart has signed on as a customer. A consumer rebellion against dumb and excessive packaging is afoot. And in August 2006, Moore was invited to speak about "marine debris and hormone disruption" at a meeting in Sicily convened by the science advisor to the Vatican. This annual gathering, called the International Seminars on Planetary Emergencies, brings scientists together to discuss humankind's worst threats. Past topics have included nuclear holocaust and terrorism.

~~~

THE GRAY PLASTIC KAYAK floats next to Moore's catamaran, *Alguita,* which lives in a slip across from his house. It is not a lovely kayak; in fact, it looks pretty rough. But it's floating, a sturdy, eight-foot-long two-seater. Moore stands on *Alguita'*s deck, hands on hips, staring down at it. On the sailboat next to him, his neighbor, Cass Bastain, does the same. He has just informed Moore that he came across the abandoned craft yesterday, floating just offshore. The two men shake their heads in bewilderment.

"That's probably a $600 kayak," Moore says, adding, "I don't even shop anymore. Anything I need will just float by." (In his opinion, the movie *Cast Away* was a joke—Tom Hanks could've built a village with the crap that would've washed ashore during a storm.)

Watching the kayak bobbing disconsolately, it is hard not to wonder what will become of it. The world is full of cooler, sexier kayaks. It is also full of cheap plastic kayaks that come in more attractive colors than battleship gray. The ownerless kayak is a lummox of a boat, fifty pounds of nurdles extruded into an object that nobody wants but that'll be around for centuries longer than we will.

And as Moore stands on deck looking into the water, it is easy to imagine him doing the same thing 800 miles west, in the gyre. You can see his silhouette in the silvering light, caught between ocean and sky. You can see the mercurial surface of the most majestic body of water on Earth. And then below, you can see the half-submerged madhouse of forgotten and discarded things. As Moore looks over the side of the boat, you can see the seabirds sweeping overhead, dipping and skimming the water. One of the journeying birds, sleek as a fighter plane, carries a scrap of something yellow in its beak. The bird dives low and then boomerangs over the horizon. Gone.

Message in a Bottle
Adventures Aboard the Plastiki
David de Rothschild

When Thor Heyerdahl sailed his balsa wood raft Kontiki *across the Pacific Ocean from Peru to French Polynesia in 1947, he was trying to prove that the settlement of the region emanated from South America. By contrast, the voyage of David's boat, the* Plastiki, *is a journey all about innovation. The 60-foot ocean-going sailboat, constructed entirely from plastic bottles and a uniquely engineered material called SR-PET, will carry him and his team across the Pacific, from California to Australia, in an effort to draw the world's attention to the fact that the same ocean is now home to vast acres of man's detritus.*

Ever since the Industrial Revolution in the eighteenth and nineteenth centuries, it seems the barometers of success and modernity within society have been measured by our interaction, or rather lack of interaction, with the natural world. The formula appears to be simple: The more we package, mechanize, and force nature into the background, the more developed and evolved our society will become. What we produce and consume has become a representation of our values and identities.

The almost automated desire to take nature and manipulate it to meet this formula—to create a more linear, predictable, controllable commodity out of it—is constantly being taken to new extremes. We are even creating experiences that can best be described as manufactured landscapes like Japan's Sea Gaia Ocean Dome, the world's largest artificial beach (thankfully now closed). It made for a pristine paradise with perfectly groomed sand made of crushed white marble, a permanent blue sky, and constant 30°C (86°F) temperature—all of which existed just 300 meters from the real ocean.

Tragically, it's now conceivable that we have reached a point at which whole generations are no longer aware of or in touch with the true, raw, and unadulterated natural world. Nature is often no longer perceived as natural unless it comes in a glossy plastic package with an instruction manual.

For most, this "nature deficiency disorder," this blurring between artificial and real, seems so perfect, so convenient. However, it's this convenience, coupled with a voracious appetite for one-time-use plastics, that is now hurtling back toward us as an ever-growing and devastating set of plastic fingerprints on our natural world. It's not well known that since Leo Hendricks unveiled the first fully synthetic, moldable hard plastic called Bakelite to the American Chemical Society in 1909, except for a very small percentage that has been incinerated, every single molecule of plastic ever manufactured still exists somewhere in our environment.

The most apparent and shocking is the plastic waste that can now be found scattered across the surfaces and the depths of our planet's oceans. It's beyond tragic to articulate.

For me the stark reality of the situation kicked in back in 2006 when, during the research and planning stage for my next Adventure Ecology expedition, I came across a UNEP publication titled "Ecosystems and Biodiversity in Deep Waters and High Seas." The report pointed out that on or below every square mile of our ocean, there were 46,000 pieces of floating marine debris and that the problem was particularly acute in certain areas. From ocean trenches in the Atlantic to floating particles across the farthest reaches of the Pacific, synthetic polymers are on the rampage; as much as 90 to 95 percent of the total amount of marine debris is plastic, leaving less than 10 percent made up of slowly degrading materials such as timber and glass through to more hazardous and hard-to-clean-up medical, industrial, and raw-chemical sewage-related waste. And unlike organic compounds, plastic doesn't biodegrade.

Plastic is impervious to enzymatic breakdown. It's literally jamming up the code of nature. Which means the very durability that makes plastic so useful to humans also makes it incredibly harmful to all the natural life cycles in every ecosystem worldwide. The effects of these manufactured materials on the vitality of fish, marine mammals, and birds alike are twofold.

One is the actual ingestion of plastic, as in the case of the majestic and now endangered albatross. The Laysan albatrosses that nest on Kure Atoll and Oahu, Hawaii, get it the worst. They are mistakenly swapping squid, fish, and krill for floating plastic items such as fishing line, light sticks, and lighters. *Scientific American* quoted Lindsay Young of the University of Hawaii, summing the problem up perfectly: "There were so many small plastic toys in the birds from Kure Atoll . . . that we could have assembled a complete nativity scene with them." It's estimated that of the 500,000 albatross chicks born every year on Midway, almost half of them die from consuming plastic fed to them by their parents. One was found to have 306 pieces of plastic inside its belly.

But even more ominous is the second major issue regarding the spreading plastic plague, toxicity transference.

In the open ocean, plastic photo-degrades, which means it absorbs the sun's photons and begins to break into simpler and simpler compounds without ever actually disappearing. The tiny pellets that result are called mermaid tears or nurdles. Because of plastic's open molecular structure, mermaid tears sponge up fat-soluble compounds like PCBs, DDT, and a host of herbicides and pesticides present in the ocean in diluted quantities. Plastics also have a nasty affinity for oil; just think of the permanent ring left behind in a food container after storing spaghetti sauce.

The transference occurs as small amounts of these chemicals work their way up the food chain from the filter feeders all the way through to the fish fingers on the kitchen table. All over the world, children and adults alike are unwittingly exposing themselves to low levels of toxicity. Plastic is an odorless and tasteless parasite.

But if killing all forms of marine life and now, potentially, us humans, isn't reason enough to react, there is more. Plastic and other marine debris are smothering beaches as well, especially those in the path of the swirling garbage patch. Currents that drag garbage into the gyres also shoot it out to surrounding landmasses. The nineteen islands of the Hawaiian archipelago, including Midway, for instance, receive massive quantities of trash, some of it decades old. Some beaches are buried under five to ten feet of refuse, and others are riddled with fine granules of plastic or "plastic sand."

In October 2006, the U.S. government established the Northwestern Hawaiian Islands Marine Monument as an attempt to quell the rising tide of debris. Congress passed legislation to increase funding for trash removal and ordered several government agencies to expand cleanup efforts. This could prove to be an important step if it leads to governments focusing more attention on a problem that, although dire, has received serious scientific focus only since the early 1990s.

That said, the people who are studying the issue continue to point out the overall lack of viable solutions. Trawling the oceans for trash is impractical in terms of budget and logistics, and it would ultimately harm plankton and other marine life. Even if it was safe for sea creatures, cleaning up the north Pacific gyre alone involves clearing a section of ocean that spans the area of a continent and extends one hundred feet below the surface. Maybe more feasible and exponentially more effective is managing the waste on land, where fully 80 percent of ocean debris originates in the first place. (The rest comes from private and commercial ships, fishing equipment, oil platforms, and spilled shipping containers.)

But what's crazy about this situation is that it simply doesn't have to be this way!

If we can shift a common perception of plastic from waste to a valuable resource, we can slow, and in some places even reverse, the alarming environmental damage occurring around the planet. Meeting this challenge doesn't even need to be a chore. It can be an adventure, an honest-to-goodness, swashbuckling adventure. The kind that gets you out of your car, your office, or your bed and into nature, so you understand exactly, even viscerally, what it is you're trying to save.

There has never been a better example of using adventure to inspire, engage, and change perceptions of an existing reality than Thor Heyerdahl's exploits in the South Pacific. In 1947, the Norwegian adventurer set out to prove that pre-Colombian indigenous people from South America could have populated the Polynesian islands by migrating—no fewer than 4,300 miles—by boat. Heyerdahl and his crew traveled to Peru, where they constructed a balsa wood raft, using only those materials and knowledge that would have been available before European influence. Six adventurers clambered aboard the boat they called *Kontiki* and sailed it across the Pacific to test Heyerdahl's theory of oceanic migration.

The raft made it; his theory did not. But the *Kontiki*'s story line created one of the most compelling and captivating adventures of the last century. It danced across the imaginations of multiple generations, sowing the sense of excitement and freedom that comes with following one's dreams.

Heyerdahl's adventure was sitting foremost in my mind in late 2006 as I struggled to come up with a compelling method to illustrate one of the most significant and unnecessary man-made environmental, and now health, issues of our time. There had to be a way to stem this plastic plague, a plague that's ultimately been driven by our overconsumption, misuse, lack of recapture, and inefficient design.

As I walked to the Adventure Ecology offices one morning, I was pondering the question: What do we have in our time that's readily available, as plentiful as balsa wood, and could be used to construct a craft for a journey that would both highlight all the messages mentioned here and test a theory à la the *Kontiki* in the open ocean? The answer was literally at my feet. Plastic bottles.

Modern society produces piles upon piles of plastic bottles. And although the United States leads the world in the consumption of bottled water, it is truly a global phenomenon. According to the Beverage Marketing Corporation, worldwide consumption reached 41 billion gallons of water in 2004, an increase of 57 percent in just five years. We chug and chuck, chug and chuck, day after day, month after month.

The plastic water bottle epitomizes the absurdity of our throwaway society. Each and every day, Americans consume 70 million bottles of water. That adds up to nearly 9 billion gallons of water annually at a cost of approximately $11 billion, despite the fact that both the purity and taste of water flowing from the taps in our homes and workplaces are of equal or better quality. An even crueler irony is that according to the nonprofit research organization Pacific Institute, it takes two liters of water to manufacture a one-liter plastic bottle. And the energy used during the life cycle of a single-use plastic bottle, from making the bottle itself to filling, shipping, chilling, and finally disposing of it, is equivalent to filling it one-quarter full with oil. Far from being natural or even virtuous, as many consider it, bottled water is the poster child for wasteful indulgence.

So the next step in thinking was logical. We need to redesign, revalue, reduce, reuse, and ultimately rethink our use of plastic so that it can contribute to solutions rather than compounding the problems. And with a respectful nod to the *Kontiki* and its audacious, attention-grabbing voyage, the *Plastiki* expedition was born!

The goal started out as sailing across the Pacific, from San Francisco to Sydney, to shine a global spotlight on the plight of our oceans and marine life at the hands of plastic debris. However, realizing the enormity of the problem, it became apparent that if our expedition was ever going to capture hearts and minds as well as foster the creation of solutions, we couldn't just sail on any old vessel.

To this end, a simple yet compelling concept was developed: Construct a boat entirely out of two-liter plastic bottles, recycled waste products, and innovative materials. We thought that if *Plastiki* could showcase smart designs that rethink the waste polluting our seas as a resource, but not only à la Heyerdahl, the vessel could garner media attention on behalf of our imperiled oceans, and the project would be an opportunity to develop solutions that could help revalue waste materials, like how we use them, what we use them for, and, most important, how we dispose of them. We were hoping for a good chance to stem, finally, the rising tide of plastics.

But when the dream left my head and became the adventure that it is today, we were suddenly faced with a number of major hurdles. We were trying to build a boat that not only had to be capable of crossing our largest ocean but also had to do so using unconventional and, for the most part, untested materials!

From the outset, we wanted to create a boat that would perform and be visually iconic but also constructed with plastic bottles that were fully intact, meaning without being melted or ground up. Why? One, they had to serve a purpose rather than just act as an aesthetic to emphasize their usefulness. And two, using the bottles in their original form made it possible for us to up-cycle them at the end of the voyage. We wanted to transform them into items with higher value, such as polyester fleece, to send a very clear message in a bottle.

To achieve this, we needed a design by which seawater would actually flow through and around the bottles. A core tenet of boatbuilding is to keep the water out, and here, we were inviting it in. But with the aid of visionary architect Michael Pawlyn, we harnessed some principles of bio-mimicry to devise a solution. The seed structure of a pomegranate was perfect inspiration for creating plastic-bottle pontoons.

The vessel went through a number of design iterations and material changes along the way. It evolved from being a trimaran with a dominant central hull to a catamaran with the pod-like cabin suspended on a platform between two hulls. In the conceptual stage, the main form of propulsion was a kite sail, and it's still our intention to use it as backup propulsion. However, the vessel finally ended up with two conventional masts and recycled sails but in a very unusual arrangement.

Throughout the design and building process, there were many points at which our success hinged on our ability to adapt quickly to the unpredictable outcomes of using experimental materials. Our first major breakthrough occurred when we figured out that by pressurizing individual bottles, we could use them to maintain the boat's buoyancy. They would also resist water pressure and wave action. We considered bundling long strands of bottles for the superstructure, but due to an overall lack of longitudinal stiffness, we quickly realized we needed to find a suitable material to make the skeleton of the boat.

We began by looking at bamboo, which stayed within the theme of the *Kontiki* expedition, but decided an all-plastic vessel was more fitting for our needs. A bout with recycled plastic lumber proved it wholly inappropriate due to its density and lack of stiffness. Over time, the troubles we faced during our search for the right material pushed us toward the path of least resistance. It was a path that was going to see us melting down all the bottles and losing the imagination-grabbing iconic image that we were trying so hard to preserve.

With outright stubbornness and determination, we stayed true to the vision of our dream. But to do it, we had to engineer a new product dubbed self-reinforcing polyethylene terephthalate (SR-PET), which is a proprietary plastic evolved from plain old PET plastic. Had we taken the easy route, we would have lost the biggest breakthrough for the *Plastiki* project and, more important, a possible real-world solution for our plastic problem. Simply put, the structural skeleton of the *Plastiki* as well as the majority of the boat is made entirely out of the same plastic used in soda and water bottles, the same material that ends up in our oceans! The two could coexist within the same waste cycle and feed into each other's production. Just as long as the plastic flows back into factories, not our backyards and coastal waters, it would be a model referred to as "closed loop."

Our accomplishments have generated hope within us that the *Plastiki*'s design and innovative materials will help create market value for postconsumer plastics and spur industry-wide change. Maybe we can inspire the first steps to reversing the effects of manufactured waste in the material world.

THREE YEARS HAVE PASSED since that initial idea, and since then, I have learned and shared many lessons.

The expedition has tried to focus on more than the destination. Our journey and way of viewing the process created a platform for smart thinking and a place where everyone acknowledged nobody is as smart as everybody. We strived for cultivating a community of thought leaders, designers, engineers, and scientists who recognized their roles as part of one holistic system in which every individual action creates a reaction. And that now more than ever, we need to stop and realize the devastating impact of our ever-increasing human fingerprints.

Together is the only way we can move forward and create the necessary solutions for our oceans and our planet, so we can stop apologizing to the million seabirds and 100,000 marine mammals unnecessarily killed and to the children of today and tomorrow who are already asking, "Why isn't anyone reacting?"

For some, answering that question means lobbying companies and communities to find alternatives to plastic packaging. Or it might entail getting governments to expand recycling programs and accommodate bio-plastics in the marketplace. I advocate all of these actions.

But the *Plastiki* is looking to inspire something larger—a sea of change, if you will, in how we view waste and how we integrate it back into the web of life. This starts first off with recognizing there isn't a place called "away" and involves nurturing and directing inquisitiveness toward inventing smart ways to design and use everyday materials. We took the plastic bottle, which in so many ways symbolizes all that's wrong with Dumb Planet 1.0 ways of thinking, and turned it into a platform of hope by showing it can be an effective and useful resource.

With *Plastiki,* we are not just about voicing problems; we are also about articulation and action toward solutions. With a little curiosity, imagination, and time to innovate a plastic bottle to become a boat, and that boat to forge its way into the collective imaginations of people everywhere, who knows what else is possible? One day, maybe, we could dream for more than just the survival of our ocean.

Barging Down to the Sea
Farming the Ocean Without Regret?
Brad Matsen

Aquaculture: Is it good or bad, evil or necessary?
The debate over fish farming rages as the world's demand
for fish grows and the resource suffers. During the past decade,
worldwide aquaculture production of salmon, shrimp, tuna, cod,
and other marine species has grown by 10 percent annually,
its value by 7 percent a year. In the United States, aquaculture is a
$1 billion business annually, headed to $5 billion by 2025. Yet there
are associated sustainability and pollution problems that accompany
all fish farming. Brad suggests that properly managed aquaculture
has a future but that proper management is hard to find.

Every spring since 1972, salmon born in hatcheries on the Snake River have embarked on their downstream migrations to the Pacific Ocean aboard barges at Lower Granite, Lower Monumental, Little Goose, and McNary dams. Hustling crews wearing white hardhats load the fish in round-the-clock extravaganzas of concrete raceways, pumps, pipelines, and floodlights. At night, the scene is reminiscent of the technoscape of the spaceship landing in the film *Close Encounters of the Third Kind*, remote, well lit, organized, and urgent. On each two-day trip down the Snake and into the Columbia River aboard the peach-colored steel barges, millions of young salmon hover in a netherworld of bubbling tanks, tended by a couple of people to net the few dead floaters and see to the diesels that run the aeration systems. Without the barges, most of the millions of fish that survive the trip downriver would otherwise have been killed in the turbines and spillways of the dams. Before the salmon fry are loaded on the barges, their adipose fins are clipped so every hatchery fish is easy to identify when caught by sport and commercial fishermen or taken for eggs in the hatchery at the end of its homeward spawning run. Few wild fish, adipose fins intact, remain. Some consider the Army Corps of Engineers Juvenile Fish Transportation System to be an aquacultural triumph. Others see it as outrageous hubris that cannot be sustained.

I rode one of those barges down the Columbia in the late 1990s. The trip was a confusing manifestation of hope, both repulsive and comforting like the life-support machinery in an intensive-care ward. We had dammed the waterways that were crucial to the existence of salmon and yet were keeping the runs on the respirator by throwing energy and ingenuity at the reality of their demise. The endless demands for electricity and irrigation water in the runaway economy of the Pacific Northwest kindled the cultural will to build more than 130 dams on the Columbia watershed, and our well-intentioned natures compel us to compensate for the obvious loss of fish habitat. The men and women who run the hatcheries, load the barges, keep the pumps running, and feed the fish come to their chores with the satisfaction of most rescuers. But, please. Bringing fish to sea on barges?

It is impossible to discuss the relationships between human beings and their food without considering an overwhelming truth: When I was born in 1944, there were 2.5 billion people on Earth. When I rode that barge down the Columbia at the end of the twentieth century, we numbered just over 6 billion. Meanwhile, as Thomas Malthus predicted a hundred years before my barge trip, food production to sustain all those people has increased at a far less vigorous rate. We learned how to wring the most out of soil to boost production on land (though not without what we now know to be catastrophic consequences), forestalling Malthus's gloomy forecast for a few decades. We also increased the amount of food we took from the sea by simply fishing more and more. Then, in the late 1980s, we discovered that the amount of protein we can harvest for food from the ocean has topped out at about 130 million tons. No matter how much horsepower and ingenuity we expend in our fisheries, that's all we're going to get. Finally, we have come face-to-face with the consequences of too many people competing for a finite amount of food.

"More than anything else, we're going to have to change the way we think of the sea," Jane Lubchenco told me a few years ago. She is now leading the National Oceanic and Atmospheric Administration (NOAA), the overseer of U.S. fisheries policy, and has been studying the relationship between humans and the sea for most of her life. "Things are fundamentally different on Earth from ever before in its history chiefly because of the enormous explosion of human population. Fishing and the ocean must be viewed in a broader context of the changes that are happening in the world at large, and we have to look at the human population problem head-on. Nobody doubts that resources are finite anymore. We all know we are part of nature rather than in charge of it. Now, how do we learn from the past and do better in the future? The best thing we can do is to understand the system perspective, not just look at individual stocks, species, and economic relationships."

Understanding the system perspective about food from the sea was relatively easy when most people ate nothing they didn't kill or grow themselves and the consequences of abuse, when it occurred, were quickly obvious. If early inhabitants on the Pacific Coast took too many salmon from a stream near where they lived, they starved a few years later. Now, in the richer developed nations on Earth, those feedback loops aren't so easy to interpret and usually have fewer short-term consequences. No salmon on the Columbia River? No problem—order the pork chops. Or grow more salmon.

It's a mythic story of pioneer ingenuity and the Wild West. The Americans built their first hatchery for Pacific salmon in 1872 on the McCloud River in California; the first hatchery in Canada was on the Fraser River at Bon Accord, near what is now a suburb of Vancouver. Japan imported modern salmon hatchery methods and technology from the United States and Canada beginning in 1889. Soon after, salmon eggs from the Pacific Northwest were shipped as far away as Australia and New Zealand. Hatcheries for egg production and enhancement of natural runs were so successful that the dam builders, including the Army Corps of Engineers in the United States, counted on them to heal the rivers. In the 1930s, when Grand Coulee Dam destroyed every inch of spawning habitat in the 1,000 miles of the upper Columbia River, people wrote songs about building dams, creating fish, and our dominion over nature.

Hatcheries remained largely the business of government fish-growing and dam-building agencies until the 1970s, when Alaskans voted to allow what they called private, nonprofit hatcheries. Most people refer to this kind of salmon making as "ranching." You hatch the fish in controlled conditions with far greater than natural survival rates, turn them out to pasture—the ocean—and wait for their return in summers to come. The idea was to transform the unpredictable annual variations of some of the runs into dependable—domesticated?—runs. The salmon pass through the open waters to give commercial and sports fleets the first shot at them (and, not incidentally, gain political and financial support for the hatcheries) and then harvest the rest right at the hatcheries to meet expenses and take eggs for the next crop.

That's the idea, but a few bold scientists suspect the high expectations for salmon ranching will fall to the truth in an old adage: *Nullum gratuitum prandium.* There is no free lunch. Regardless of their origins, salmon compete for food in rivers, bays, and ocean, and in 1993, only fragments of the expected runs of both wild and ranch pink salmon returned to Prince William Sound, home of the world's biggest hatcheries. We also have to worry about wild salmon interbreeding with hatchery fish, which may reduce their ability to survive. If a female hatchery pink salmon spawns with a wild male pink salmon, for instance, succeeding generations of that union will inherit only part of the precious genetic code of the wild. Because early life in a hatchery is easy living for a salmon, all those survival traits, powerful physiology, and ancient instincts are not fully tested and selected. Hatchery salmon are weaker salmon.

At about the same time the perceived success of hatcheries and ocean ranches peaked in the mid-1970s, a professor at the University of Washington was refining the tools and methods for the next step in the direction of domestication: salmon farming. Dr. Loren Donaldson figured out how to rear trout and Atlantic salmon from womb to tomb in captivity, and Norway, the most salmon-desperate nation in the world, snapped to attention. The Europeans had long since overfished and over-populated their watersheds, and Norway had battalions of out-of-work fishermen sitting on the beach. With Donaldson's breakthroughs, they saw a way to put everybody back to work. Marine trout and salmon farms were controlled by local banks, their boards of directors had to include fishermen, and the Norwegian government began a worldwide marketing campaign. By 1980, global production of farmed salmon was a modest 25,000 tons, out of a total salmon pack of about 700,000 tons. By 1993, the Norwegians had been joined in force by Canadian, Irish, Scottish, Chilean, Japanese, Russian, American, New Zealand, and Australian farmers and were producing about 250,000 tons each year out of total world production of about 800,000 tons. In 1998, farmed salmon production exceeded wild salmon landings for the first time. In 2007, 65 percent of the world's salmon were reared in marine farms.

In just thirty years, salmon farms have proven to be as problematic as dammed rivers, hatcheries, and barges. The market has collapsed several times when a disease or a plankton bloom that kills salmon but doesn't hurt human consumers invaded whole coastlines of pens. Tons of salmon ended up on the market at the same time, the glut drove down the price, and everybody lost money. Commercial fishermen loathe the farms because they compete directly with the wild or hatchery salmon they catch and sell. Environmentalists loathe the farms because they dump enormous loads of fecal contaminants and uneaten food into surrounding waters, much of which is laced with antibiotics essential to keeping fish alive in crowded conditions. Hundreds of thousands of escapees from salmon farms over the years are competing with wild fish for food. On the waterfronts of the Pacific coast, pickup trucks sport bumper stickers that declare "Real salmon don't eat pellets," a reference to the universal farmed-salmon food called the Oregon Moist Pellet, a protein-fiber morsel akin to chicken feed. I've also seen "Friends don't let friends eat wild salmon."

More profound, some opponents of salmon farming point out that abundant farmed salmon selling at a few bucks a pound in supermarkets in the United States, Canada, Europe, and Japan sends the wrong message about the feedback loops on which sustained food production depend. If we are eating low-cost salmon, their reasoning goes, it is impossible to banish the cultural notion of dominance that allows us to dam the rivers and pollute the watersheds essential to the life cycles of wild salmon. If the consequences of watershed and habitat destruction don't reach our dinner tables, we will not act to correct those abuses.

The absurdities of salmon barges and the ultimate consequences of cheap farmed salmon pale by comparison to the abuses of some of our other attempts to farm the sea. In Ecuador, a marine shrimp farming boom began in the early 1960s and between 1975 and 1985 that South American nation led the world, producing revenues of $225 million a year and creating 150,000 jobs. Unfortunately, building the shrimp farms destroyed thousands of acres of mangroves that are irreplaceable rearing areas for countless other species. *Nullum gratuitum prandium.* The shrimp companies were making plenty of dough, but the coastal people who had lived well on fish, bivalves, and wild shrimp for centuries weren't doing so well.

Still, we persist. Humans have been cultivating food in the sea for as long as they have been hungry, and the dream remains tantalizing to us. Three thousand years ago, the Greeks noticed that their piles of discarded oyster shells produced new oysters, which meant they didn't have to leave the safety of home to get a meal even after they ate most of the wild oysters in front of their villages. Even further back than that, farmers all over what is now Asia knew that carp and catfish grew fat in the runoff ponds of their farms, so they set aside some of their ponds for nothing but fish growing.

Despite the folly of barging salmon down the Columbia, growing them in pens, and hacking down the Ecuadorian mangroves (among the many other aquacultural abuses), a lot of people remain optimistic that we are clever enough to grow and harvest aquatic protein sustainably. In New Brunswick, Canada, a fisheries biologist named Thierry Chopin, for example, is trying to mimic natural systems to raise salmon instead of trying to dominate them.

"There is no doubt that the world's fisheries are in trouble," Chopin told me. "And now we know that aquaculture has serious issues, too. Obviously, we have to figure out the right kind of aquaculture." According to Chopin and a growing number of aquaculture visionaries, the right kind of aquaculture is either growing fish in integrated multi-trophic aquaculture (IMTA) farms that sustain the coastal habitat rather than stressing it or growing the fish in offshore pens.

Chopin and his colleagues in New Brunswick rear Atlantic salmon (*Salmo salar*) in pens alongside rafts of blue mussels (*Mytilus edulis*) and cultivated ropes of kelp (*Saccharina latissima* and *Alaria esculenta*). "The mussels go after the particulates in the water from uneaten food and fecal matter; the kelp goes after dissolved nitrogen, phosphates, and other nutrients that would throw the coastal system out of balance. We're thinking now of trying sea cucumbers and polychaete worms to take care of everything that makes it to the bottom."

Like hog farmers marketing everything but the oink, Chopin sells not only salmon and mussels for food but kelp for processing into cosmetics and feed for fish instead of using fish meal or oil from land plants and for direct human consumption as pickles, salads, and soups.

"Selling kelp is difficult in the U.S. and Canada, but in China and Japan, many kinds of kelp and seaweed are traditional food sources," Chopin said. "Multi-trophic aquatic farms are nothing new. The Japanese and Chinese were doing it centuries ago but, like everyone else, they were seduced by higher value species and they kind of lost their way."

Chopin was a speaker at a seaweed symposium in Kobe in 2007. When the Chinese and Japanese organizers invited him, he asked them what he could possibly have to tell them that they didn't already know. "We used to know a lot about multi-trophic farms," they replied. "But we forgot."

The most significant barrier to farming the sea rationally is that investors make more profits more quickly with monoculture than with multi-trophic aquaculture. "Seaweed and bivalves easily regulate the systems," Chopin said. "But the world has gone for fish, fish, fish because it is more valuable in the short term."

Although Chopin and others work at solving the puzzles of profitable multi-trophic farms, a lot of the wise guy money is looking at heavy industrial operations to build and maintain sea farms well offshore where deep-ocean circulation banishes many of the problems of contamination from penned fish. Salmon, cobia, mahimahi, cod, tuna, and other high-value species are where the real money is in sea farming, so the offshore pens are drawing a lot of interest.

The Blue Revolution, as some call the move into offshore sea farms, is not without its problems and opponents. The World Wildlife

Fund (WWF) cautions against foreseen and unforeseen consequences if deep-ocean sea farms proliferate.

"As with other types of aquaculture, one of the key controversial issues related to offshore farming is minimizing the impact farming has on sensitive habitats (e.g., marine-protected areas and ocean sanctuaries), endangered species, and other flora and fauna," WWF told the U.S. Congress during debate on national offshore sea farm policy. "Similar to other types of aquaculture, there also are concerns that species raised in offshore aquaculture facilities would spread diseases to other fish, high levels of fishmeal and fish oil would be needed to feed the fish, and the water would be polluted by chemicals used at the facilities. Offshore aquaculture is such a new field that there are not enough scientific data available to assess whether its impacts are more or less severe than the impacts associated with near-shore aquaculture."

NOAA Administrator Jane Lubchenco said that if her agency moves forward with new regulations for offshore farms, they would have more safeguards. After years of watching the barges lumber down the Columbia, industrial overfishing, and all the other missteps in our attempt to take food rationally from the sea, she is instinctively cautious. At her confirmation hearing, Lubchenco did not mince words. "Scientists and policy makers," she said, "have not yet identified the 'right conditions' under which marine aquaculture is sustainable."

If we can't figure out a way to make marine aquaculture sustainable, our only viable option for producing enough protein to stave off the Malthusian catastrophe is coming ashore, and we don't have that right yet, either. Most of the world's aquaculture already comes from onshore ponds and tanks, chiefly in Asia and Africa. In most large-scale aquatic farms on land, pollution of fish and shrimp from heavy metal, mercury, and other toxic incursions produces its own set of potential disasters to the human ecosystem.

"We have been thinking like rich people," said Hillary Egna, director of the Aquaculture Collaborative Research Support program at Oregon State University. Egna and her colleagues have been working for decades to reduce poverty and end hunger through rational aquaculture. "We want to grow salmon, shrimp, and other high-value species in high-input, high-maintenance systems. In the rest of the world, they're eating catfish, tilapia, and carp grown in freshwater with minimal additional food in small farms, usually with very little impact on the rest of the environment. As long as we keep toxic pollution under control, those operations work very well when they are ramped up to industrial scales."

Egna has two tenets that she believes should be the aquaculturists' equivalent of the physicians' Hippocratic oath:

1. Don't fight nature.
2. Have a market.

I would add:

3. It's the water, folks. To get aquaculture right, we just have to take care of the water. The rest will work out fine.

Acid Test
Lisa Suatoni

*Ocean acidification, caused by carbon dioxide
dumping into the seas, is the evil twin of global warming,
which similarly affects the planet's atmosphere. Lisa is a scientist
with the Natural Resources Defense Council and is among just a few
who can easily define its causes, effects, and possible solutions.*

There is a disturbing discussion in scientific journals these days about the future of coral reefs, those large stony structures that ring the undersea world built by a myriad of shell-forming organisms the size of the tip of your finger. Scientists are debating when, this century, reef-building corals will begin to dissolve. That's right, coral reef ecologists are trying to predict in what decade the stony metropolis that houses the colonial animals that we call corals will begin to crumble. Estimates range from 2050 to 2100, partly because the chemical threshold at which reefs shift from net growth to net dissolution will vary depending on location. The loss of corals from coral bleaching and diseases is already leading to the "flattening" of reefs, and experts agree that continued ocean acidification will accelerate that problem.

Coral reefs, as we know them today, have existed for 65 million years. Why then are their calcium carbonate skeletons suddenly at risk?

The answer is clear: The oceans are rapidly becoming more acidic. Ocean acidification, or the declining pH of the world's ocean waters, is the second and less known impact of rising atmospheric carbon dioxide concentrations (the first, of course, is global warming).

The phenomenon is simple chemistry. As we generate excess carbon dioxide by burning fossil fuels, much of it accumulates in the atmosphere, where it causes climate change. However, about a quarter of that CO_2 ultimately ends up in the sea. And when carbon dioxide dissolves in sea-water, it becomes an acid. The massive influx of CO_2 into the sea is difficult to comprehend, currently proceeding at approximately 1 million tons per hour. In terms of mass, that's like dumping 24 million Volks-wagen Beetles into the sea each day. Since the start of the Industrial Revolution, the seas have absorbed 500 billion tons of CO_2, increasing the average acidity by 30 percent.

A primary concern about rising ocean acidity is the threat to shelled organisms. As ocean acidity increases, the availability of carbonate, a raw material for shell building, declines. This depletion results in slower growth rates and weaker shells in a large proportion of the organisms studied. If acidity gets high enough, ocean water becomes corrosive, and shells grow more slowly or literally dissolve. Such an extreme physiological challenge could lead to species extinctions. If carbon emissions continue to rise unabated, the result will be global osteoporosis, harming not only commercially important shellfish such as lobster, crabs, and mussels but also key species in marine food webs. Marine ecologists are especially worried that disappearances of important species such as plankton at the base of the food chain could trigger ripple effects up the food chain, compromising the stability and productivity of the very food webs on which we depend.

However, rising oceanic CO_2 poses a problem far beyond shelled organisms, and new threats are still being discovered. When rising carbon dioxide levels in the sea are coupled with declining oxygen levels— a separate trend driven by global warming—breathing may become more difficult for many organisms. This synergy between ocean acidification and global warming has scientists redrawing maps of existing oceanic dead zones and projecting appreciably larger regions in the ocean that are deficient in oxygen and inhospitable to many forms of life. Ocean acidification may even affect such seemingly unrelated issues as ocean noise. Because sound travels farther as pH declines, the cacophony of ocean noise from shipping, sonar, and oil and gas exploration will likely intensify, posing an even greater challenge to marine mammals that communicate and navigate by sound.

Although marine scientists have been studying the biological impacts of ocean acidification for only a short time, evidence is accumulating that recent acidification may already be affecting marine life around the world (though concurrent changes in ocean temperature make diagnoses difficult). For example, Pacific oysters on the West Coast of the United States have not successfully reproduced in the wild since 2004 due to high larval mortality. On an island off Washington State, seaweed is supplanting mussels on the rocky shore. Scientists believe that rising ocean acidity may have tipped the ecological balance between these intertidal competitors in favor of the algae. On the other side of the planet, a coral species in Australia's Great Barrier Reef has shown a 14 percent decline in calcification since 1990, and body weights of a species of plankton in Antarctica are now 30 to 35 percent lower than they were historically.

Forecasting the future chemistry of the seas is straightforward compared to predicting future climate scenarios. Mathematical models show that if we continue to burn fossil fuels as we are now, average surface water acidity will more than double by the end of the century compared to pre-industrial times. Well before that, however, large regions of the oceans will become corrosive to some shelled organisms. For example, scientists predict that, within decades, the Arctic will become corrosive to organisms that form their shells of the kind of carbonate known as aragonite. For the Antarctic, the same will be true by mid-century. Similarly, regions of upwelling, where deep cold water rises to the surface, will regularly begin to deliver corrosive waters onto many continental shelves.

If these changes occur, marine scientists expect to see biological impacts well beyond simple shell impairment. Incidences of stress, reproductive failure, and changes in community makeup are expected to multiply. These and other biological impacts may be wide-ranging but are still poorly understood. Will we lose species? Which ones? What effect will ocean acidification have on marine ecosystems and our ocean economy? Reading the scientific literature, it is clear that researchers have just begun to chisel away at these questions and that the exact contours of the problem remain unknown.

However, what is clear is that tropical reef-building corals are especially vulnerable and may well be the oceanic "canaries in the coal mine" of a high-CO_2 world. Numerous studies on a variety of corals show a common response of decreasing calcification rates with rising acidity, eventually leading to erosion. What happens to a "homeless" coral, or a "reef-less" coral community, is not entirely clear; extinction of coral species is a real possibility. Despite some uncertainty, it is clear that coral reef ecosystems are on the brink of a major transformation. The dissolution of stony corals and consequent loss of the reef's architectural complexity will lead to a less rich and less productive marine community. When you add the further impacts of global warming, overfishing, habitat destruction, and polluted runoff, experts agree that the future of coral reefs looks grim.

The potential loss of coral reefs illustrates how ocean acidification, like global warming, can be not only an environmental issue but an economic, security, and ethical one as well. Currently, coral reefs generate billions of dollars annually in tourism, provide shoreline protection from storms and flooding, and supply food for tens of millions of people worldwide. The impending socioeconomic impacts loom large.

Although the scale of ocean acidification may appear overwhelming, there are solutions. And there are actions we can take. The only way to stop ocean acidification is to stabilize our carbon dioxide emissions. (In other words, there is not enough Alka-Seltzer in the world to neutralize this problem.) We need to power our lives without emitting huge quantities of CO_2. Each of us can make choices in our own lives that will help, but we can bring about a clean energy future only through national policy that caps carbon emissions and creates permanent incentives for renewable energy and efficiency.

In addition, we can help the ocean defend itself by making sure its systems are as healthy as possible. Just as people with compromised immune systems are more likely to die from common diseases such as pneumonia and flu, so stressed marine organisms are the first to succumb to "diseases" such as ocean acidification.

Coral Reefs in Crisis
Abigail Alling

*Abigail has studied coral reefs around the planet and,
as a member of Biosphere 2, lived for two years sealed inside an
enclosed mini-world constructed in the Arizona desert, where she
managed and monitored a million-gallon reef system. She currently
lives aboard and works from a research ship engaged in
marine conservation programs in Southeast Asia.*

I visualize coral reefs as a sparkling jewel, the colors of the rainbow, circling the equatorial regions of the ocean like a ring, a vibrant and busy ecosystem whose organisms are experts at capturing beams of sunlight to express fantastic forms of life, an underwater biome that has specialized in creating photosynthetic organisms such as algae, plankton, and zooxanthellae as compared to trees, grasses, and other plants.

This image is the quintessence of a reef, but most reefs look nothing like this anymore. Instead, they have been dynamited, fertilized by all forms of excess waste and pollution, overfished to species extinction or the decimation of populations, suffocated by erosion, and sickened by a rising fever known as global warming. Today a dull ring circles the equatorial regions of our planet; our biosphere is sick, and the decline in the health of corals is an expression of this illness.

My initial oceanic experience was sailing a twelve-foot dingy in the cold waters of Maine. It didn't take long to discover that I loved it, the lick of salt water on my lips, the wind in my hair, and the feeling of flying across water with my sails tucked and my hands grasping the tug of the tiller. Immediately, I dreamed of exotic lands and realized a longing to follow dolphins out to the sea and learn what was beyond the horizon. This initial calling eventually carried me to all the world's oceans and face-to-face with joy as I gazed at the beauty and radiance of life and grief as I witnessed its destruction by human activity everywhere.

In 1981, when I joined a newly formed Indian Ocean marine mammal sanctuary initiative, I was ignorant about such indifference, especially of the worldwide decimation of fish populations. Our home for those years was a small thirty-three-foot boat based out of Trincomalee Harbor, a large natural bay on the east coast of Sri Lanka where we lived alongside pygmy blue whales; sperm whales; beaked whales; and pilot, risso, pygmy, and false killer whales as well as spinner, spotted, bottlenose, striped, and common dolphins. We had arrived at the Mecca for cetaceans and were dazzled by the diversity and wealth of sea, land, and culture.

It was there that I first began to track the bycatch of marine mammals in Sri Lanka, and by 1984, I had estimated that 38,000 marine mammals were killed wastefully each year. For another decade, a fisherman friend of mine kept records of the overall daily catch, and he reported to me that with each passing year, fewer and fewer marine mammals were taken and the amount of fish caught a year was plummeting. When we met again in 2004, he said that no dolphins had been caught in these nets for more than a decade and only a handful of boats were used for fishing. Trincomalee was a coral reef coast and, as we stood on the beach talking, I could hear dynamite exploding. Frustrated fishermen had resorted to dynamiting the reefs to "catch" their fish.

One of the most tragic scenes I know is seeing a reef destroyed by dynamite or cyanide fishing. The extent of such fishing is not well known because it occurs usually offshore from small boats, but I have seen evidence of it during our voyages not only in the Indian Ocean and Southeast Asia but also in some parts of Melanesia and Polynesia.

My first encounter with dynamite fishing was off the coast of Sulawesi in 2001 when we found ourselves in the midst of repeated blasts that rocked our 120-ton ship! We popped our heads up the hatch and saw a small 16-foot boat about a half mile away that must have set off the bomb. By the time we reached the area with our diving gear, we observed a few dead fish along with fragments of living reef; the fishermen had scooped up most of the fish and hastily retreated. Although dynamite fishing is illegal, it is a cheap way to secure a quick catch of reef fish.

Cyanide fishing is a similar technique, by which potassium cyanide is released onto the reef, killing the fish and leaving a chemically scarred area that remains inhospitable to reef organisms for years to come. I have recently seen such a scarred reef in the Anambas Islands (South China Sea), and what was most striking about the damaged area was the total lack of life. Nothing was growing on the place that was touched by the chemicals, not even algae.

Usually when a coral reef is sick or when it dies, the corals are replaced by red, brown, and green algae, and when this happens, the reef changes from a coral garden into an algae garden. The presence of large macro algae suggests large concentrations of available nutrients. Although corals are not able to use large amounts of nutrients, algae will grow rapidly and colonize the reef like weeds in a garden. "The solution to pollution is dilution" was normal practice in the early 1980s when I was a graduate student. Ecology was only beginning to be recognized as a science and even the word *biosphere* was a foreign word needing explanation. The ocean and nature in general were viewed as an unlimited resource, not only teeming with life but large enough to absorb our wastes.

It was in this general milieu that a project called Biosphere 2 emerged in the early 1980s. A 3.15-acre miniature biosphere sealed off from Earth in the Arizona desert by steel below ground and a glass and steel space frame above ground, Biosphere 2 was the first self-sustaining and evolving world ever created by humans, and I was one of the lucky few to live inside for two years. Because it was a very small "world," it cycled rapidly, and we learned quickly to be accountable for our actions because one mistake could result in the contamination of our drinking water or atmosphere. We experienced the necessity of becoming active participants within an increasingly complex and coherent living system. It was delightful to understand this inside world, to appreciate the synergy of life, and to live day to day with the pleasure of being part of something larger than ourselves. We learned firsthand about the challenges of being a "planetary community" as we struggled to live together in one world and leave behind, where appropriate, our own individual cultures and viewpoints that stood in the way of this process. We had an accelerated chance to adapt rapidly and become stewards of our biosphere while using our minds, the most powerful tool available, to do work and solve problems that seemed impossible.

At the completion of the experiment, I desired to apply this experience to life at "home" on planet Earth. In the spirit of this wish, I soon found myself on an airplane looking out the window back at the receding Mexican landscape. It was 1998 and my eyes melted into the gorgeous sparkling blue of the Caribbean Sea. Almost like a cartoon, my gaze came to a sudden halt and closed in on the black water surrounding Cancun! "Wow! That is sewage spreading out from the city into the ocean," I exclaimed out loud. Cancun has no waste treatment law other than pumping raw sewage deep into the limestone coast where the black water oozes through the rock and eventually into the marine coastal environment. A fellow traveler looked at me and said with disgust that her son had been playing in the lagoon behind the hotel where they were staying and had seen feces floating in the water. She had packed up and left.

The lack of wastewater treatment is not unique to Mexico; it is a phenomenon occurring worldwide. Even countries that treat wastewater chemically are contributing to the nutrient overload. Wastewater, in general, is a fabulous nutrient resource that is wasted when not used, and it becomes toxic to environments in excess, often resulting in the death of ecosystems such as coral reefs and lagoon sea grass beds. One result is that the coral reef coast of Mexico is suffering from exactly this kind of nutrient overload. Coral gardens are slowly becoming algal gardens because algae are very good at taking up the excess nutrients.

Even off the remote island of Kitava in Papua, New Guinea, we witnessed a reef suffering from an overgrowth of algae smothering the corals. In this particular location, there is only one house on the beach adjacent to the reef, and the amount of sewage from it is not enough to affect the reef. However, just a few miles offshore is a large shipping lane with tankers steaming back and forth day and night in a deep pass with strong ocean currents. A tide brings this offshore water to the Kitava reef, washing it daily with water from faraway places. This is where the algae must be getting the nutrients to grow so well. The villagers are not contaminating their reef, but they are experiencing a loss of the reef's biodiversity due to contaminants from far away.

The United States has one reef system on its mainland that begins in the Dry Tortugas, runs along the Florida Keys, and continues north into the greater Miami metropolitan area. It has been decimated by land-based sources of pollution, including treated and untreated wastewater and urban, suburban, farming, and agricultural runoff, all of which flood the Florida coast. Repeated studies of these reefs have shown that just 3 to 5 percent of their living coral cover remains today. This is one of the most documented reef systems in the world, yet there is very little said about it publicly; imagine what is happening in areas far out of sight.

It's quite powerful to actually witness a reef being killed; it is a help-less experience, one I experienced last year during a dive along an undeveloped coastline on the west coast of Lombok, Indonesia. The dive began well, but when we came around the corner and got into the lee of the coast, the water became still and the reef quiet. Soft corals were bent toward the sand, dripping with sediment that covered the entire organism. A thick clay and silt layer of soil lay over the reef and its large boulder corals like a gray-brown blanket. Three lionfish floated motion-less in the still water, their eyes staring out at the eerie sediment wasteland. A few other fish appeared here and there, but that was it. My fellow divers and I looked at each other as bewildered as the lionfish. One of us finally signaled, "Let's go up." There, just inland, was the answer: Tractors were plowing the land, trees had been felled, and a swath of soil had been laid bare in preparation for a large construction project.

The runoff from construction and deforestation makes it to rivers or to the water's edge where it runs into the sea and settles out of the water column. When this happens in tropical seas, the sediment falls like a gentle snow onto the coral colonies, suffocating the coral (which is a small animal) and starving it as well as preventing sunlight from reaching the small algae, known as zooxanthellae, that live in its tissue.

Some island cultures prefer to mine coral rock (either living or dead coral) to use in constructing houses, roads, and jetties. On remote islands where cement for such uses is very expensive, locals see reef rock as free building materials. In the Maldives and other low-lying tropical coastal communities, this has had drastic ramifications, though, because the removal of the reef rock removes underwater walls key to helping prevent surging seas from swallowing coastlines. I dove on the reef of Ghizo, in the Solomon Islands, soon after the April 2, 2007, tsunami, and the familiar underwater coral landscape we had been surveying since 2000 looked like a computer simulation, as if an underwater hurricane had swept through, mowing down coral formations and turning them over all in the same direction. After seeing a reef turned upside down like that, it is easy to appreciate how a healthy reef will protect its adjacent coastline by slowing down oceanic storms and even tsunami waves.

Some coral reef islands have been wiped out intentionally by nuclear testing. The first thermonuclear device was detonated in 1952 by the United States in Micronesia at Elugelab Island in Enewetak Atoll. This island was vaporized along with its reef. To our dismay, we learned that many islands had been used for such practice in the Pacific Ocean, including the Kiribati Islands where our friends in Ghizo were from. They described how their entire village had been relocated to the Solomon Islands just three days after a big black cloud appeared near their island; within days after the cloud's appearance, they became ill and their cows died after drinking in a nearby watering hole. Similar testing was carried out on remote coral reef islands in the 1950s and 1960s not only by the United States but also by the United Kingdom, Russia, France, and China. (France continued its nuclear tests in French Polynesia until 1996.)

In December 2004, my phone rang, and it was a friend aboard our ship in the Kiribati Islands, detailing an alarming discovery that the corals surrounding the atoll of Kanton Island were dead. "Dead?" I answered, thinking it was not like her to speak so emotionally. It wasn't until I saw her video of the corals that I realized the impact of what had happened. We downloaded NOAA's sea surface temperature data and deduced that the reefs had suffered from unusually high and persistent water temperatures for seven months, from August 2002 to March 2003. The mysteriously warm waters had left the remote and beautiful coral reef ecosystem and its lagoon dead.

We had been monitoring offshore coral reefs for nearly a decade and had noticed some degree of bleaching corals at nearly every location but had never witnessed a field of table corals killed all at once due to a temperature event. When corals bleach, there is a rapid change in the color of the coral tissue to white because the minute algae living in the tissue migrate from the coral due to a change in temperature or the environment that they cannot tolerate. Because a coral animal needs these zooxanthellae algae in its tissue for food and oxygen, it will die unless the circumstances change and the algae return. For exactly those reasons, climate change has become the greatest threat to coral reefs today.

Increasing amounts of greenhouse gases in our atmosphere, particularly carbon dioxide, have led to global warming, as well as ocean acidification (a process whereby the pH of the water is shifted from an alkaline state toward an acidic one). Interestingly, these two processes were critical management issues inside Biosphere 2 because of its high levels of atmospheric carbon dioxide. In expectation of this cycle, we had included a reserve of calcium carbonate (limestone rock) because it absorbs carbon dioxide in the ocean and thus keeps the pH from falling. Corals form calcium carbonate as part of their life cycle and produce a rock substrate that is a natural buffer regulating ocean pH. Hence, it's critically important to manage atmospheric carbon dioxide levels as well as maintain healthy living reef systems.

Our best method for minimizing the overall production of carbon dioxide inside Biosphere 2 was to keep the system cool in order to slow down its metabolism. A biosphere is one large breathing system in which plants and algae produce oxygen, and all living organisms, including the teeming activity of microbial fauna in soils, respire carbon dioxide. Slowing the metabolism of an organism by cooling it down works the same for a biosphere, and thus the amount of daily carbon dioxide released is decreased. This process is a perfect example for what is sometimes referred to as "runaway climate change" whereby an increase in the temperature of the biosphere will increase the amount of carbon dioxide respired, which will contribute to a rise in global temperature.

Another threat to reefs that is accelerated by global warming is a phenomenon known as red tide. I have seen such an event only once, off the coast of Sumatra, when the sea turned the color of Coca-Cola due to millions of tiny red-brown phytoplankton per millimeter of water. The high surface water temperature and calm seas had provided an ideal soup for the bloom to occur, but where was the added nutrient coming from? Red tides can occur naturally, but both pollution and global climate change have increased their intensity, frequency, and duration. Although red tides will eventually pass and the waters clear, coral reefs may be left decimated by a prolonged incident because the phytoplankton obstructs the sunlight from reaching the coral colonies. During this time, other reef organisms may be suffocated due to the lack of oxygen in the water, and toxins emitted by the algae can affect the central nervous system of fish, resulting in their death.

When I saw this red tide, it took me back to a moment at Biosphere 2 about six months before the system was permanently sealed. The reef tank was intact, some of the coral reef organisms were already in the "ocean," and pumps were cycling currents, waves, and tides. Construction workers were harnessed on steel struts overhead while caulking and screwing the glass to frame structures. In the middle of the cacophony of activity, it rained a quick Tucson summer desert rain. I didn't think much of it and went about my business until about thirty minutes later when a colleague called by radio to say the ocean, which had a visibility of about thirty feet, had turned a dark pea green. This was my first experience with acid rain and the extreme rapid-response characteristic unique to coral reefs.

At the moment of rainfall, nitrogen and phosphorous-laden rain poured into the ocean and algae began to take up the nutrients, quickly replicating over and over again with all the newly available food. Pollution, whether organic such as sewage or inorganic such as the industrial smog in acid rain, is a common word usually used to describe various concentrations of nitrogen, phosphorous, and potassium. These are the basic elements used in fertilizers because usually these molecules are scarce and a limiting source to plants. A coral reef is an ecosystem that depends on the concentrations of these elements being nearly nonexistent. Thus I realized I was watching algae in the small ocean gorge on acid rain fertilization and threaten the rest of the coral reef's health.

Remarkably, though, the Biosphere 2 coral reef also illustrated a very hopeful message about the capacity of life to evolve. This particular reef was collected from Akumal, Mexico. It was transported in six tractor trailers and transplanted four days later into a covered steel tank in the mountains of Arizona. These corals had traveled to a temperate region where sunlight disappeared into seasonal snowstorms; migrated out of the pressure of the ocean depth to 3,900 feet above sea level; survived nearly 1,000 miles from the nearest salt water biome; and relied on technology to remove nutrients, create currents and waves, and maintain water temperature. The reef successfully survived for three years in this alien world, with 986 coral colonies of which 87 were babies found growing on the reef or the walls of the tank. It was proof that if you give life a chance and simulate necessary environmental parameters, living systems can adapt. For this biosphere, technology was designed and used to enhance life, not to harm it, which is a profoundly appropriate worldview deserving much further contemplation.

When I exited from Biosphere 2, I did so knowing that coral reefs were an indicator biome for the health of the oceans as well as the health of Earth's biosphere. It was this realization that birthed the Biosphere Foundation's "Coral Reef Satellite Mission," a global stewardship program designed to create the most advanced underwater observation program from space and one that would be visible to everyone via the Internet as the satellite traversed the seas. We envisioned this as the first of many space observation programs that would engage us in the visual exploration of our biosphere and, thankfully, it is now becoming possible because of collaborative programs such as Google Earth. The future of conservation will be more effective because it is increasingly possible to view the biosphere as a whole as well as zoom into its every detail. Through this process it is possible for anyone accessing the Internet to become familiar with thinking globally.

Put another way, each of our individual actions makes a difference because we are all connected to a larger synergic network of life. Corals are the ocean's early warning beacons, signaling a drastic change in the biosphere. If coral reefs are dying worldwide, then the health of the ocean must also be in decline. What can we do in the face of such devastating knowledge? A first step may be simply to fall in love with the fact that we are part of our ocean biosphere. Although this may sound like a simplistic solution, it is at the heart of a growing global disconnect that we are experiencing regarding the planet's loss of life. In that embrace, we will care to learn more, find solutions to otherwise daunting challenges, and become active participants contributing to a healthy biosphere. As we used to say in Biosphere 2 with a sparkle of newfound realization: "If our biosphere is well, then we are well."

Estuaries, Where Human and Nature Meet

John Cronin

*A former commercial fisherman and legislative aide, John served
for seventeen years as the pollution-fighting Hudson Riverkeeper,
inspiring the creation of 200 Waterkeeper programs worldwide.
At Beacon Institute and Pace University, he advocates technology
and policy innovations for the protection of rivers and estuaries, the
critical and imperiled links between our communities and the ocean.*

I was twenty-five when I first I boarded a real boat, a twenty-three-foot wooden, flat-bottomed, barge-like fishing vessel powered by a workhorse Johnson outboard located in a well forward of the stern. It was part of a small fleet, operated by the late Ron Ingold, that fished a row of stake nets in the Hudson River beneath the George Washington Bridge. In 1976, Ron was one of more than one hundred commercial fishermen still working the river.

While nighttime Manhattan blazed in the east, Ron and his crew fished to beat the tide. In a mad rush, gillnets, rings, buoys, lines, American shad, and river trash came flying over the transom in the expert leathered hands of the three fishermen with whom I shared the boat. The working crew should have numbered four. I had come to help with the haul but was useless, too green around the gills in the unfamiliar swirl and sway of the tidewater Hudson.

As the river waves increased, the air freshened with the smell of the sea. My mood brightened in the way only those fragrant waters can provoke. Then I thought the better of it. Raised just five miles upriver in the City of Yonkers, I was accustomed to odd nighttime odors—biscotti from the stacks of the Stella D'Oro factory on 237th Street in the Bronx, coffee from the Maxwell House plant on the Hoboken waterfront, mystery gases from myriad refineries in New Jersey. What exotic substance was being emitted nearby that mimicked the ocean's singular scent?

The incessant rolling of the river was maddening. There was no apparent reason for it. The evening was pleasant and fair, little breeze, no wakes from other boats. For an hour, I stayed quiet about this peculiarity, not wanting to draw more attention to my ever-sickening self. But annoyance got the better of me.

"Is it always like this?" I asked Ron peevishly.

"What did you expect from the ocean?" he answered.

I was in the bottom of the boat. Alarmed we had drifted into the Atlantic, I poked my head above the gunwales. Washington Heights, NY, was diagonally across. Edgewater, NJ, was right where we had left it. The bridge that connected the two flickered above. No, this was still the river.

But not really. Here the Hudson blends seamlessly with the Atlantic Ocean to form one of the planet's most unique ecosystems: an estuary.

Estuary is not a term that trips lightly off the tongue. It has a biologically suggestive sound, but human, like a vestigial organ located somewhere between the islets of Langerhans and the alimentary canal. I don't know whether Ron knew of the word. I was raised in a city on the estuary and never knew of it.

One way to understand an estuary is by its generic definition: a partially enclosed aquatic ecosystem where freshwater from rivers mixes with salt water from the sea. But I suggest you look up examples of estuaries and extract the essence for yourself. The lower 154 miles of the Hudson River is an estuary. So are Tampa Bay in Florida, Cook Inlet in Alaska, and the Tigris–Euphrates delta system in Iraq. To the unwary observer, it would be difficult to find four water bodies that less resemble each other.

Most of the world's population lives near estuaries. Most of the world's major cities, such as Los Angeles, London, Tokyo, and Calcutta, are located on estuaries. The geopolitical names of estuarine waters are better known than the fact that they are estuaries or are home to estuaries: Columbia River, Galveston Bay, San Francisco Bay, and Puget Sound; the Thames, Seine, Yangtze, Ganges, and South Africa's St. Lucia. There are too many estuaries on the planet to name or count.

Although the design and functioning of each estuary are singular and can be arcane, they have essential things in common. The bottom lies below sea level, allowing the tide to roll in. The freshwater that feeds the estuary flows overland, through tributaries and down rivers, from underground springs and aquifers, and from the sky above, diluting the ocean salt. An estuary's lowest reach is as salty as the sea. Move away from the ocean and the waters become brackish and then fresh in the farthest inland reaches. Were it not for all the freshwater draining from its watershed, what we call an estuary would simply be an arm of the sea.

This dynamism is the heart and soul of an estuary. One American Indian name for the lower Hudson was Muhheakantuck, loosely translated as "waters always in motion." This is an apt description. An estuary's ever-changing tides and currents constantly re-suspend sediments and food, energizing its incredible biological productivity. Freshwater perch and ocean sturgeon, young and adult, thrive at once in its rich nutrient soup.

American shad tell their own estuarine story. This largest member of the herring family is my role model, spending all its life following its ideal climate. Shad favor temperatures of 55 to 61 degrees Fahrenheit (13 to 16 degrees Celsius). They thrive in the coastal waters off Florida in winter and around Canada's Bay of Fundy come summer. The remainder of the year, they orbit between those poles on the warming and cooling isotherms of the Atlantic Ocean. Their physical appearance suggests a life at sea: a deep, narrow body, 24 to 30 inches in length, built for long-distance swimming, with a distinctive blue-green iridescence along the back and a silvery white underside.

In April, adult shad that hatched in the Hudson split off from the oceangoing population. Driven by a chemical trigger that roughly translates into an acute sense of smell, they find their way home after thousands of miles at sea. They take no time to feed during their upriver journey, and who can blame them? They are on their way to spawn 100 miles north in the river's freshwater reaches around Kingston, NY, and beyond.

When their eggs hatch, the larvae slosh their way to the lower estuary along the flooding and ebbing currents of the tidal Hudson. By the time they are juveniles, sometime from late August to September, young shad are physically ready for the nourishing, brackish waters of the lower estuary, where the river is shallow and broad, the food, sunlight, and plant life bountiful. When hearty enough, they head south for the saltier regions nearer the river's mouth and, finally, to the ocean itself. Five to six years later, they return as mature adults to their original spawning grounds to perform the same ritual of reproduction as their forebears. In all, a remarkable piece of ecological choreography, repeated for millennia on the Hudson and virtually every available inland tidewater on the coast.

The hero fish of many American estuaries is the striped bass. On the Atlantic coast, the Chesapeake, Delaware, and Hudson are its chief indigenous home waters. Migrating bass can range in near-shore ocean waters from Alabama to Nova Scotia. A Pacific fishery was established in 1879 with the introduction into California waters of 132 young bass transported by railroad from the Navesink River in New Jersey. They were likely Hudson River juveniles; that is the estuary nearest the Navesink with a spawning population. By the turn of the century, a West Coast commercial striper fishery was booming. In 1910, a record seventy-eight-pound striped bass made its way into the San Francisco fish market. Stripers have been stocked in other nations, including Ecuador, Iran, Latvia, Mexico, Russia, South Africa, and Turkey. The discovery that stripers can survive year-round in freshwater has inspired conservation agencies and fishing clubs to stock them in lakes and reservoirs well outside the species' natural range.

The striped bass has been both bellwether and lightning rod. Battles between commercial and sport fishermen over its status are legendary. Once the basis of a thriving commercial fishery, the striper has been declared a game fish in most waters, and few commercial fisheries remain. Fluctuations in the coastal striped bass population have in turns been attributed to overfishing, agricultural and feedlot runoff, industrial pollution, habitat destruction, acid precipitation, and power plant intakes.

The striper has been the star of environmental battles on the Hudson. Its protection figured in the defeat of a proposed pumped storage hydro-electric facility at Storm King Mountain and the Westway Highway project in lower Manhattan and caused the investment of tens of millions of dollars of fish-saving equipment at the Indian Point nuclear plants in Buchanan, NY. Controversies over its conservation on both coasts have highlighted the conflicts that arise between federal and state agencies and sport and commercial fishermen over management plans to protect the multimillion-dollar fishery.

Because they spend the majority of their lives at sea and spawn in freshwater, American shad and most striped bass are considered anadromous. Some other anadromous species are sturgeon, salmon, blueback herring, alewife, and smelt. Catadromous fish live in freshwater and return to the ocean to spawn. The American eel leaves its estuarine home and travels to the Sargasso Sea off Bermuda to spawn in late winter and early spring. The European eel, which is seriously endangered, performs the same migration, but European estuaries are its home. Amphidromous fish, like the bull shark, migrate between fresh and salt mainly to feed. Anadromous, catadromous, and amphidromous fish are of interest to biologists because of their migrations and a physiology that allows them to inhabit the disparate environments of marine and freshwater.

Estuarine systems, their marshes, wetlands, tributaries, and backwaters, are a Noah's ark of flora and fauna, home to resident and migrating animals, all manner of waterfowl, crustaceans, mammals, amphibians and reptiles, exotic plant life, and a range of rare, threatened, and endangered species. Their biodiversity presents seeming disparities, but those are the rule. Eric Lind, director of the Constitution Marsh Audubon Center and Sanctuary in Garrison, NY, reports that the short two-hundred-yard tidal reach of Indian Brook, a Hudson River mountain tributary that flows to Constitution Marsh, attracts species as wildly divergent as brown trout, blue crab, stone fly, sea lamprey, green frog, and striped bass, all this just upstream from the wild rice, mummichog, muskrat, menhaden, snapping turtle, alewife, cattail, and Virginia rail that are among the animal and plant life that inhabit or use the tidal marsh itself.

DESPITE THEIR IMPORTANCE, estuaries were once so obscure as to make their existence debatable. In a famous incident in the legendary Storm King case in the 1960s, Robert H. Boyle, naturalist and author of *The Hudson River: A Natural and Unnatural History,* was not allowed to testify that the lower Hudson is an estuary, although any schoolchild could have stuck a stick in the mud near Storm King Mountain and reported to the judge that the river rose and fell four feet with the tides four times per day.

Today, thanks in large part to environmental organizations and agencies, lesson plans, websites, books, and academic courses teach that estuaries are where rivers meet the sea, where salt water meets freshwater, where inland meets the tide. Just as important, estuaries are where human and nature meet, with profound consequences for each.

To my way of thinking, a description of the Hudson River estuary would be incomplete if it did not include the full river, the 13,500-square-mile watershed that surrounds it, and the communities built along it. This is an old land, constructed of granite and mud by water and ice. It heaves and flows with eons of nature's drama and millennia of human settlement. The river's bottom is a crack in the continent carved by a glacier 300 million years ago. It continues as the Hudson Canyon for 450 miles, cutting into the ocean floor and reaching a depth of over 2 miles below sea level. Pick a spot in any town anywhere on the estuary's edge along the river's final 154 miles and watch the tide force its way inland twice each day and retreat.

The Hudson River estuary has two high and two low tides each day, rising and falling three to four feet. This is not a uniform condition. When the tide is high at the George Washington Bridge, it is low at the city of Hudson, a former whaling port 100 miles inland, and mid-tide at the Federal Lock and Dam at Troy, the head of tide. Gradually, that pattern reverses over the next six hours. Further, the time of the tides occurs almost an hour later each day. If you could slice the lower half of the Hudson lengthwise and stand at the necessary vantage, its surface would describe an elongated wave ever in motion, ever changing.

In the river's southernmost miles, the scent of the sea can be evident though no sound or sight of surf is near. Upriver, coastal storms can bury the east and west shores beneath a foot of water, reminding deep inland communities that they too are kin to the salt. The 1991 Halloween Nor'easter swept automobiles from Manhattan's FDR Drive and swamped shoreline railroads more than 50 miles north, a preview of what climate change and rising sea levels may portend for coastal communities.

If the river's lower half is an arm of the sea, its upper 161 miles, above Troy, are an arm of the wilderness that reaches down from the Adirondack Mountains, a province of the Appalachians and cousin to the Canadian Laurentians. Strictly speaking, this section of river is not part of the estuary, but the estuary would be radically different without it. The upper Hudson is the bulk of the watershed, and the 140-mile Mohawk River empties into this nontidal stretch, delivering the estuary's largest supply of freshwater. This mix of inland and shore, mountain and ocean, is repeated throughout the Hudson's lore and literature.

The very nature of an estuary, its tides, configuration, navigability, local fisheries, and connection to the sea, helps form the history, decisions, and lives of its people. Fishers, swimmers, and paddlers on the estuaries fed by the Bay of Fundy in New Brunswick, Canada, measure their day by the coming and going of dramatic twenty-foot tides. In England, there is a recognized dialect called Estuary English. The Hudson's connection to the sea and long inland reach made the Erie Canal possible and revolutionized American east–west commerce.

Along the shores and on the waters of estuaries, civilizations were grown, cultures were established, commerce was begun, and nations were built. But this fast became a one-way relationship. Estuaries and the rivers that feed them were also convenient dumping grounds for commercial and domestic wastes, easily exploited fisheries in protected waters, natural global ports that prompted uncontrolled commercialization, and fertile lands that supported intensive agriculture. They were a seemingly unlimited source of water for manufacturing, power production, and public supplies, spurring sprawl and runaway growth.

We built highways, diverted waters, drained marshes, filled shallows, and dammed rivers. We constructed villages that became towns and towns that became cities. Aesthetically attractive coastal lands were developed for residential, recreational, and vacation use. The 1972 Coastal Zone Management Act encourages American states to restrict their coasts to "water-dependent" uses, in keeping with their traditional development.

In response, most states created coastal rules that allow, if not encourage, hotels that "depend" on water views and condominiums that "depend" on docks.

There is no place where the human struggle with its environment has played out so dramatically for so long. If all rivers lead to the sea, they must travel through estuaries first. And if our oceans depend upon the organisms, nutrients, and energy produced by neighboring land-masses and waters, estuaries are the delivery system for that life and sustenance. But this most intimate of connections between the human community and the oceans also became a delivery system for the fruits of our imprudence.

At the same time, estuaries are harmed by human activities that threaten the sea. Ocean acidification, climate change, and sea level rise, for example, can take their toll on estuaries first, threatening migrating species and the salt–fresh balance of their habitat and endangering fisheries, property, and public water supplies. Some ecosystems will get hit from both ends, source and sea, and even from the sky above. On Mt. Marcy, the highest point in the Adirondack Mountains where the Hudson River has its source, acid precipitation has decreased the natural production of some tree species in the watershed by as much as 80 percent.

Yet we must remind ourselves that we did not set out to ruin the planet's most unique aquatic ecosystems. We ignore world history if we believe that the alteration of our coastal zone is a modern phenomenon. An early lesson well known to elementary school children is the Fertile Crescent, the Tigris–Euphrates delta, the cradle of civilization, an eco-logical paradise of such grandeur the Book of Genesis placed it in Eden. There grew the first river civilization that laid down roots rather than wander. The Mesopotamians diverted water for irrigation, drained wet-lands, and redesigned shorelands. They built the first global center of trade and commerce and provided an early example of how humans alter the natural world to match their pursuits. Eleven thousand years later, in the shadow of Saddam Hussein's regime and the Iraq War, the once magnificent "land between two rivers" became a war zone in its own right, a terminal nightmare of bombings, damming, diversions, and habitat destruction and of the persecution and forced relocation of the Ma'dan people, the "Marsh Arabs."

But it requires neither war nor a dictator gone mad to bring these sensitive ecosystems and their cultures to the brink. Chesapeake Bay, once America's fish basket, has suffered devastating declines in its classic produce such as oyster, striped bass, and blue crab. On the San Francisco Bay estuary, a ubiquitous public education program posts signs on bay-side piers to warn the public of fish contamination. On the Neuse River estuary in North Carolina, a yearly plague of fish kills numbering in the tens of millions has become an ecological disaster and a public health threat.

In 1987, the New York State Senate and Assembly boasted in legis-lative findings that the Hudson "is the only major estuary on the east coast to still retain strong populations of its historical spawning stocks," and created a special management program to protect it. Over the next fifteen years, at least six major fish species went into precipitous decline. Atlantic sturgeon was banned from capture and sale because the coastal stock became so depleted. The commercial fishery for American shad is about to be closed due to a crashing population. And an official state warning established in 1975 advising the public to refrain from eating most Hudson River fish due to PCB contamination still stands.

Although they are unique and highly specialized ecosystems, estuaries do not enjoy comprehensive protection. Compared to ocean habitat, this should be easy. Oceans depend on difficult-to-enforce treaties, inter-national cooperation, and political coercion; estuaries are subject to the laws of their home nations. But estuaries often define the borders of countries, provinces, and states, creating regulatory and political skir-mishes. American estuaries depend on a patchwork of federal and state laws, administered by scores of agencies, authorities, and programs that collectively oversee coastal management, commerce, navigation, fish and wildlife protection, dams and canals, spills, and pollution discharges.

The 1972 Clean Water Act is the closest the United States comes to a comprehensive policy on water. Its purpose is "to restore and maintain the physical, chemical, and biological integrity of the nation's waters," on its face, a mission tailor-made for the nation's estuaries. It also directs "the President through the Secretary of State" to assist other nations in achieving "the improvement of water quality to at least the same extent as the United States does under its laws."

Key to the achievement of these domestic and foreign policies was a program of pollution control, technology innovation, research and development, and construction of facilities aimed at "eliminating the discharge of pollutants into the navigable waters by 1985" and achieving an "an interim goal of water quality which provides for the protection and propagation of fish, shellfish, and wildlife and provides for recreation in and on the water . . . by July 1, 1983."

Yet, at this writing, more than 200,000 facilities still have permits to discharge pollutants into American waters, most urban sewage treatment plants overflow raw human wastes into nearby waterways during significant rain events, 19.5 million Americans are made ill by drinking water each year, almost 1 billion people on the planet live without potable water, and at least four children per minute die from diseases caused by water pollution in the developing world. A National Estuary Program created by the Clean Water Act grants federal funds to study a few politically favored estuaries but provides no significant protections. Inland and coastal fisheries are beleaguered in the United States and all over the world and fish contamination is rampant. For example, a 2009 study by the U.S. Environmental Protection Agency found mercury-tainted fish in every water body the agency investigated.

And so, in a bizarre twist that turns water protection on its head, the Clean Water Act still retains as its current primary domestic and foreign policy goals: elimination of water pollution *twenty-five years ago* and restoration of fish, shellfish, and wildlife *twenty-seven years ago*. No new goals have been established to replace the old, failed ones. The law is adrift in a sea of regulatory programs that have no plan or direction. Innovation is stalled. There are no incentives for American industries or public facilities to perform better than the minimum requirements of the law. And comprehensive protection of innumerable estuarine ecosystems receives little to no special consideration.

For as long as the Clean Water Act's goals remain expired, estuaries are managed by a disorganized assemblage of laws, and domestic and foreign agencies fail to address coastal protection cooperatively and comprehensively, America's and the world's estuaries can count on a continued flow of tens of millions of pounds of pollutants per day and escalating damage to fish, shellfish, wildlife, and their habitats.

ON A SUNNY MAY MORNING IN 1981, I climbed out of my pickup truck camper, parked on Bob Gabrielson's Burd Street Dock in Nyack, NY, and breakfasted on leftover blackfish. Just four weeks earlier, I had resigned my job in the state legislature, moved into the old black Ford, and driven south to join Bob's commercial fishing crew for the full shad season.

It was a dry spring. Because of the increased salt in the estuary, all manner of ocean fish were making their way into the lower river. In addition to blackfish, we regularly saw flounder, sea robin, starfish, and jellyfish. The previous evening, we picked up a young Atlantic sturgeon, about ten inches in length. A rubber band was wrapped around its midsection, an uncommon but known phenomenon on the river. I would see it again on a different baby sturgeon two summers later off Garrison, NY.

Just beneath the band, the sturgeon's body was severely constricted and the flesh was raw, a certain target for deadly infection and fungus. At some point in its short life, the fish had swum into the carelessly tossed band, which became caught on the rough-skinned body and remained while the sturgeon grew.

Sturgeon are a lens into the past. They are often called living dinosaurs. Their lineage dates back 200 million years. Boyle described them well in his Hudson River book: "They have long, leathery snouts on the front of the head, while the bottom part is soft and white with a vacuum cleaner–type mouth that can hang down like the sleeve on an old coat. The eyes are small and glistening, like threatening peas, and the hard body is almost crocodilian, armed with five longitudinal rows of sharp shields, or scutes." There are twenty-six species worldwide, all with similar physical characteristics, all imperiled.

Just a few miles from our nets, on the Piermont waterfront, Cornetta's Seafood Restaurant boasted a sight found at no other eatery in the Hudson Valley. Mounted on the wall of the upper dining room was a seven-foot ten-inch Atlantic sturgeon. When alive, it probably weighed 250 pounds. "There isn't a person who doesn't say, 'I can't believe this is out of this river,'" proprietor Suren Kilerciyan told me. "And they all call it ugly—until they learn that sturgeon is where caviar comes from, and then they change their minds." It was by no means the largest sturgeon ever caught. *The Guinness Book of Animal Facts and Feats* reports a documented female sturgeon captured in the Volga estuary in 1827 that weighed 3,250 pounds and measured twenty-four feet long.

Its natural history would be the sturgeon's most remarkable aspect were it not for its stunning decline. Only shark and humans prey on sturgeon. Guess which has decimated the population? Overharvesting of its meat and caviar, pollution, habitat alteration, power plant intakes, the list of insults that humans have invented trump every challenge thrown in the sturgeon's path during 2 million centuries of life on Earth. Imagine those millennia as a twenty-four-hour clock; it has taken us less than one-tenth of a second to endanger all twenty-six species of this enduring prehistoric fish worldwide. Worth remembering the next time someone passes you the caviar or you think to cast off a rubber band.

We can still learn from our imprudence. Whether the planet's water or atmosphere, whether the decline of oceans or the impacts of climate change, whether in what we consume or how we dispose of our wastes, the lesson is the same: The greatest environmental threat on the planet is the collective impact of the day-to-day lives of 6.7 billion people. And most of them live near the world's estuaries.

I am asked often if I am optimistic about our environmental future. I am. The fate of the global environment hangs on the ability of humans to be a successful species. We can be. But success does not mean the same for us as it does for other species. It requires that we apply our intellectual and ethical abilities. It requires that we cross political, cultural, economic, and social boundaries. It requires that we re-examine contemporary values and contemporary environmentalism.

In his State of the Union address, on January 22, 1970, exactly three months before the first Earth Day, President Richard M. Nixon said, "We have incurred a debt to nature and now that debt is being called." He asked Congress for a decades-long program to restore air, land, and water. He called for more open space, aggressive investment in pollution control, and a new body of environmental regulation. He said that the cost of waste disposal should be incorporated into the costs of production. He added rhetorically, "It is time for those who make massive demands on society to make some minimal demands on themselves."

We can learn from the surprising prescience of the speech but also from its surprising source: a conservative Republican president with little environmental reputation who occupied office forty years ago. We have an abundance of expertise and intellect among us, often in unexpected places. We must reach out for it wherever it occurs. We must retire worn-out rivalries and biases, most especially the notion of permanent bad guys, if we are to bring out what is best in all of us. We must connect our higher values to our continued development as a species and as a global civilization.

In that same speech, President Nixon said, "The argument is often made that there is a fundamental contradiction between economic growth and the quality of life, so that to have one we must forsake the other. The answer is not to abandon growth, but to redirect it. For example, we should turn toward ending congestion and eliminating smog the same reservoir of inventive genius that created them in the first place."

We possess that "reservoir of inventive genius." It is spread across our colleges and universities, the private commercial sector, the nonprofit community, government, and our population at large. Its watershed includes the qualities of compassion and justice, discovery and collaboration that are hardwired into our species.

We can save the world's estuaries, rivers, lakes, and oceans. We can save ourselves. We need only tap that reservoir.

Reasons to Worry
About the Dead Zones
Wilma Subra

*When Erin Brockovich was still a teenager, Wilma was already
chasing down polluting companies, doing the chemistry on their
various harms, and presenting her results to lawyers, politicians,
and, most important, the communities they were affecting.
More than thirty-five years ago, she was part of a group of
Gulf State scientists who identified the causes of what we
now know as the dead zone, which grows larger each year
in the Gulf of Mexico, as do those in another 400 similarly
tarnished gulfs around the world for similar reasons.*

In 1972–1973, I was part of an initiative known as the Gulf Universities
Research Consortium (GURC), made up of representatives of universities
and research institutes from the coastal states bordering the Gulf of Mexico
(Texas, Louisiana, Mississippi, Alabama, and Florida). Our primary task
was to determine the chemical and biological impacts of drilling and production of oil and gas in the coastal area of Louisiana and the outer
continental shelf area of the Gulf of Mexico offshore of Louisiana. My
responsibility was the physical and chemical monitoring and chemical
characterization of the water column and sediment around targeted well
locations in Timbalier Bay west of Leeville and Port Fourchon and in the
outer continental shelf area south of Port Fourchon and Grand Isle.

During the offshore sampling excursions around two production
wells south of Port Fourchon and Grand Isle, the sampling of the water

column revealed a layer of water near the bottom that was milky in appearance. Using a nephelometer to measure the clarity of the water, we discovered that in the nepheloid layer just above the seafloor, there was very low to no dissolved oxygen. Afterward, in the chemical analysis I performed on the samples, the nepheloid layer was also determined to have elevated concentrations of nitrogen and phosphorus. With further research, the nepheloid layer was found to be most prevalent during the summer season and was always observed near the bottom of the water column. After sampling every quarter for two years, it is this layer that we now know as the dead zone.

After reporting the results of the consortium's investigation and through presentations at scientific meetings and in various scientific publications, interest in this nepheloid layer was expressed by a number of universities along the Gulf Coast. At that time we didn't know whether the problem in this dead zone, where nothing was growing, all life throttled, was a result of all the oil and gas drilling and production in the region or something else. During the mid to late 1970s, the Louisiana universities that were focused on the marine environment along the state's coastline created the Louisiana Universities Marine Consortium (LUMCON). Working with LUMCON investigators, we were quickly able to document that this dead zone was recurring each year and each year growing bigger.

∿∿∿

I AM AN ENVIRONMENTAL ACTIVIST focused on addressing the issues that are responsible for the dead zone. However, my environmental activist work is always grounded in science and backed up by the large database associated with the investigations of its causes and impacts.

After several years of study, it became clear that fertilizer running off into the Mississippi River from thirty-one states was creating the dead zone. It was nitrogen and phosphorus, primarily from fertilizers and animal manure, gathering in the Gulf of Mexico that was killing . . . everything. It was not a problem created in Louisiana: The United States Geological Survey (USGS) has determined that nine of those thirty-one states contribute 75 percent of the nitrogen and phosphorous pollution to our dead zone. The biggest culprits are Iowa, Illinois, Indiana, Missouri,

Arkansas, Kentucky, Tennessee, Ohio, and Mississippi. Runoff from Louisiana contributes only 2 percent of the nutrient pollution.

These nutrient-loaded waters of the Mississippi River enter the Gulf of Mexico in Louisiana from the Mississippi and Atchafalaya Rivers, which then flow westward along the coastal and offshore area of Louisiana, carried by the gulf jet stream currents. The dead zone forms in the spring of each year as the two rivers transport their nutrient-rich waters, peaking during the summer months and declining during the early fall.

All these nutrients stimulate the overgrowth of algae and plankton in the Gulf, and when the algae and plankton die off, they settle and decay in its bottom waters. The decomposing algae and plankton consume oxygen faster than the oxygen can be replenished from the surface waters, and the result is low oxygen levels near the bottom of the water column. This low-oxygen layer is known as hypoxia. In essence, this hypoxia layer suffocates aquatic organisms that cannot swim or move out of the area ahead of the dead zone formation; all bottom-dwelling organisms in the area die due to the lack of oxygen.

Large quantities of fish and crustaceans are also vulnerable to these low-oxygen waters, unable to migrate far enough out of the area to survive. Given the large size of our dead zone, many species are simply not able to get far enough out of the way to save themselves. It is estimated that more than 235,000 tons of seafood is lost to the dead zone each year, food vital to the health and survival of all marine species in the Gulf of Mexico.

$\sim\sim\sim$

LUMCON HAS BEEN MEASURING THE DEAD ZONE off the coast of Louisiana and eastern Texas every year since 1985. Today it extends from the mouth of the Mississippi River to the Bolivar Peninsula on the southeastern coast of Texas. In 1985, the dead zone was approximately 4,000 square miles in size; by 2002, it had grown to cover 8,300 square miles. In the summer of 2008, it covered 8,000 square miles of the Gulf of Mexico, equivalent to the size of New Jersey.

In 2009, the dead zone decreased, covering an area just over 3,000 square miles (1.5 times the size of the state of Delaware). Why? In July 2009, the flow of the Mississippi River fell below average, and persistent winds from the west and southwest in the weeks before the monitoring, which takes place every July, pushed the low-oxygen water mass to the east, piling its mass along the southeastern Louisiana shelf. Essentially, it was far thicker and denser than usual but covered a smaller mass of ocean floor.

We expect the Gulf Coast's dead zone to keep growing due to more and more nutrient loading of the Mississippi, thanks in part to the increase in corn production in the Midwest because of a growing demand for ethanol, which requires lots of fertilizer. Agricultural interests in the Midwest are not very concerned about the dead zone and its impacts on the aquatic resources in the Gulf of Mexico. Their focus is sharply on the production of more corn. Even measures that would reduce the quantity of fertilizer needed for the production of crops are viewed as attempts to put the brakes on their production.

Growing corn has a variety of environmental impacts. It is a very fertilizer-intense crop; corn subsidies encourage farmers to intensify its production and plant corn on environmentally sensitive lands; production on environmentally sensitive lands results in increased soil erosion and polluted runoff. The push for corn-based ethanol— a "greener" fuel—has also caused a boom in corn production, resulting in a nitrogen loading increase of 37 percent to the Gulf of Mexico from 2007 to 2008. This increase was primarily due to the boom in corn production in the Midwest, the accompanying escalation in fertilizer runoff, and an increase in flow of the Mississippi River due to heavy spring rains in the Mississippi Valley.

〜〜〜

THE DEAD ZONE IS LOCATED IN WATERS of the Gulf of Mexico that are or were prime fishing grounds, waters that previously supported successful commercial fish and shellfish species. It is having disastrous impacts on the fisheries resources in the Gulf, which are declining badly, resulting in huge economic losses in the $3 billion a year fishing industry across Louisiana. One result of the growing dead zone is that commercial and recreational fishermen must go farther out into the Gulf of Mexico to find live fish and shrimp. Those longer trips result in sizable increases in time and fuel costs and thus less profit.

In addition to the more than 235,000 tons of food in the Gulf of Mexico lost to the dead zone each year, food sources that are critical to maintaining the seafood species living and growing there, entire species are being killed off or devastated.

The impact on the Louisiana fisheries is having a direct impact on the availability of seafood for the rest of the United States. Forty percent of the seafood consumed in the United States that comes from the Lower 48 is caught in Louisiana's coastal and offshore waters. As the availability of the fish species declines due to the dead zone, the cost of fishing increases, and the seafood markets across the United States bear the rising prices. Thus, the dead zone in the Gulf of Mexico may seem like a local Louisiana–Texas problem, but in fact, it should be of concern to everyone in the United States who eats fish.

THE SOLUTION TO REDUCING the size of the dead zone is reducing the quantity of nutrients running off the land and into the Mississippi River. A 2001 agreement by states and federal agencies to reduce fertilizer runoff failed. More recently, the Interagency Gulf of Mexico/Mississippi River Watershed Nutrient Task Force established a goal of reducing the dead zone to 2,000 square miles or less by 2015. However, states do not have to provide information on how they plan to meet the target until 2013, a mere two years before the target is scheduled to be met.

In addition to establishing that goal of 2,000 square miles or less, I have been working with federal and state regulatory agencies and environmental organizations along the main stem of the Mississippi River to assist states draining into the Mississippi River Basin to develop numeric water quality standards for nitrogen and phosphorus. In addition, I am working with the Environmental Protection Agency and environmental organizations to assist in developing water quality criteria for nutrients at the federal level. Along with the environmental organizations, I am encouraging the Environmental Protection Agency to develop a federal Total Maximum Daily Load quota. Enforcement of the water quality standards and monitoring of the nutrient runoff by state and federal agencies are critical to attaining nutrient load reduction to the Mississippi River.

The worst-case scenario for the dead zone would be if the program recommended by the Gulf of Mexico/Mississippi River Watershed Nutrient Task Force fails to be implemented in the time frame set forth by 2015. The dead zone will then continue to increase in size, covering more and more of the Gulf of Mexico. Aquatic species would continue to die and be displaced from their ecosystem, marine habitats would continue to be wiped out, fisheries resources would continue to dwindle, commercial fishing would be a thing of the past, and the Gulf of Mexico would become an increasingly damaged and dying ecosystem, perhaps beyond repair.

~~~

THE GULF OF MEXICO DEAD ZONE is not alone. Currently more than four hundred similar zones are growing around the world, almost everywhere rivers and oceans meet. We have to remember that dead zones are not a natural part of the planet's evolution. Human activities, sustained by humans' continued ignorance of their impact, create them. Because the dead zone is the result of synthetic disasters, it is possible to reverse. It is not acceptable to consider the dead zone as something we now have to live with. In the 1980s, when hazardous-waste sites were being identified and evaluated, many wanted to write off the worst sites and consider them as sacrifice zones. It is unacceptable to consider the dead zone in the Gulf of Mexico—or any dead zone around the world—as a sacrifice zone and walk away from it.

For the Love of Fishes
Tierney Thys

Tierney is one of the world's experts on the Mola mola,
*the giant ocean sunfish. But her love, understanding of, and
curiosity about the importance of all fishes is boundless.*

What is it about fish?

I've revered them ever since I met my first goldfish, named Lucky.
I was six years old and a member of my community swim team. Each
year, the team hosted a crazy event to mark the end of swim season. First,
the coaches would purchase hundreds of unsuspecting goldfish from
a nearby pet supply house. Next, they'd dump the fish into our heavily
chlorinated community pool. Then they'd raise a starter's gun into the
air and yell, "Swimmers to your marks! Get set! *BANG!*" The gun would
fire, and the screaming hordes, including me, would plunge into the pool,
flailing in a mad scramble to capture as many poor fish as we could with
Ziploc baggies. After a few minutes, the novelty would wear off, and we'd
haul ourselves out, having transformed the pool into a confetti broth of
sparkling scales and belly-up bodies. It was during one of these insane
events that I found Lucky.

The community center stopped this practice years ago. Too many fish died too quickly, of course. If the chlorine didn't get them, the rough handling did. But Lucky turned out to be a rather hardy fellow. He lived for many years in a tank at home where I could watch his liquid-gold antics play out for hours. I'd daydream that I possessed his sleek talents, his seamless swimming skills, and I'd close my eyes imagining I could breathe underwater just like him.

Three decades later, bathed in blue light, I stood before the Outer Bay tank at the Monterey Bay Aquarium, gazing at massive bluefin tuna. For most visitors, tuna simply exist as oily chunks of meat stuffed into a can or neatly splayed atop a bed of sticky white rice. Catching a full-bodied glimpse of these muscle-bound living torpedoes, snapping the light, effortlessly dodging hammerhead sharks and sunfish, makes for a breathtaking experience.

Something almost sacred happens when you enter this viewing area at the Aquarium. It's dark and cozy yet still wonderfully expansive. Your back against a wall, the entire field of view in front is open to the fish. You can almost feel yourself in the water with them, buffeted by their wake, brushed by their fin tips. The place has a quiet, planetary power; surrounded by blueness, even amidst hordes of other visitors, you can have what author Spalding Gray called "a perfect moment." You can start to feel what it must be like to be a powerful aquatic creature, an element of the sea . . . what it must feel like to be a fish.

Since time immemorial, humanity has revered fish. For the Celtic peoples of the north, fish carried the sacred power of prophecy. For the ancient Egyptians, the mythological fish god, Rem, fertilized the parched land with his life-giving tears. In Arthurian legend, the crippled Fisher King was the keeper of the Holy Grail, with fishing his favored pastime. In North America, it was a fish, the North Atlantic cod, that helped fuel the discovery and exploration of this new world, leading eventually to the dismantling of the British empire. Stretching further back in time, anthropologists have suggested that the consumption of fish along ancient shorelines catalyzed the evolution of our big, metabolically expansive brains.

Today fish, high in healthful omega-3 fatty acids, are still heralded as brain food. Fish are esteemed as weather forecasters, symbols of fertility, and enhancers of creativity, luck, and longevity. They have inspired poets, novelists, and artists across the ages from Rumi to Neruda, Basho to Picasso, Heaney to Hemingway, Melville to Miro, and countless more.

Their size range alone boggles the mind, from half the size of your pinky nail (the 6.2-millimeter male deep-sea angler fish) to the size of two school buses (behemoth whale sharks, stretching sixteen meters from tip to tail). They are supreme masters of adaptation and occupy nearly every aquatic habitat on the planet. Be it scalding sulfurous vents thousands of meters deep off Galapagos, brackish tidal ponds, or icebound polar seas, if it holds water, it likely holds fish. To keep from freezing solid, some polar fish run antifreeze through their veins. Others, such as the bluefin tunas swimming in the Aquarium's Outer Bay tank, keep their brains toasty by shunting blood heated by their active swimming muscles up into their heads.

When it comes to sex, spawning, and parenting, the sheer diversity of fish habits is unmatched, from being male and female simultaneously like surfperch; to giving birth to live young like great white sharks; to releasing up to 300 million eggs like ocean sunfish; to mouthbrooding hundreds of little ones like African cichlids. Perhaps most impressive are those fish that undergo epically romantic thousand-mile migrations against Herculean obstacles to spawn in their home waters; think salmon, tunas, and European eels.

Some fish make lovely nests for their eggs and guard them with the ferocity of a crazed canine. I've swum with countless sharks and dangerous sea creatures, but one of my most harrowing experiences was encountering a ten-centimeter damselfish guarding its clutch. I swam closer for a look and well, that little aquatic Jack Russell would have nothing of it. After repeatedly grunting warnings at me—at an impressively high-decibel level I might add—the wee blighter got right up in my face, snatched up a large strand of my hair in its tiny teeth, and yanked backward. It yanked so hard, in fact, that I involuntarily yelped in pain, a cry that was immediately followed by spluttering as I flooded my mask laughing.

Needless to say, fish are not dullards. They have distinct personalities, can learn, can feel pain, and can even be taught tricks. Some species, such as yellow-eyed rockfish, live for longer than 200 years. Fish have been on this planet far longer than we humans have, with an evolutionary history extending back to the dawn of complex animal life half a billion years ago. It was at that time that the first fish wiggled its way onto the world stage. From that piscine Eve descended hundreds of thousands of species, with one distinct lineage taking a bold step onto land. This fleshy-finned group ultimately transformed through millions of years into sentient beings with the ability to scribble love notes, drag bottom trawlers, cinch up purse seines tasseled with corpses, and then watch in horror as once teeming seas become barren.

At the tank, I watch as my children press their hands and faces to the tank. They crane their necks up and down, back and forth, hoping not to miss a single tail beat. The tank thrums with activity, and if you didn't know better, you could trick yourself into thinking it a perfect proxy for the wild ocean crashing just outside the walls. Here, every inch of blue is alive with life, big healthy life. Out there, in the concertina sea, the tune is different.

We've perpetrated oceanic felonies many times over, and our seas are hemorrhaging life. Most of our technological advances have not been kind to the world of fishes. Until recently, we were able to increase our annual catch each year by perfecting our fishing gear. Not so today. The fish just aren't there. We've decimated so many of our big commercial fish stocks, such as Atlantic swordfish, bluefin tuna, and cod, that even if we stopped all fishing today, populations would still take decades to rebuild. Some will never rebuild. When these large commercial species are fished out, smaller baitfishes become our next target. And when they're fished out, the whole system unravels. With fewer fish, low-energy animals such as jellies can bloom in great numbers and gain a stronghold on the sea.

Here at the Aquarium, immediately behind the open ocean tank, is a section brimming with displays of jellies. Moon jellies, sea nettles, egg yolk jellies, nothing but jellies. It's like walking into the future seas. It's still hard to imagine that this brainless lingerie of the seas, trailing their tentacled petticoats, could really be replacing our commercial fisheries. However, report after report attests to a rising tide of jellies infiltrating our waters globally from the Bering Sea to Australia, from Japan to the coast of Africa's Namibia.

Recently a ten-ton Japanese trawler sank when fishermen attempted to haul up too many giant Nomura jellies. Weighing more than 450 pounds each, these behemoth Nomura jellies are exploding in numbers here, ruining reams of fishing gear and even clogging up and shutting down nuclear power plants. Jelly blooms have recently shut down beaches in Australia and the Mediterranean as well, costing the tourism industries there hundreds of millions of dollars. Off the coast of Ireland, jelly blooms have destroyed valuable salmon farms. In my home state of California, massive moon jelly blooms recently clogged intake pipes at the Diablo Canyon power plant, causing a temporary plant shutdown.

In my own work, I've watched my research specialty, the decidedly odd giant ocean sunfish, *Mola mola,* go from relative obscurity to center stage. One reason for this is the fact that jellies comprise a major component of the ocean sunfish's diet. So are sunfish numbers going up? It's hard to tell because hundreds of thousands of them are regularly snagged as bycatch and maimed or outright killed in the process. Hopefully, we will have time to answer this question, but we must reduce bycatch first and, most important, give the ocean a rest.

As grim as it may seem, we are making some progress. According to renowned social anthropologist Stephen Pinker, human society has grown increasingly pacifist through the centuries. We are relying less and less on violence to solve our problems. Though we've taken centuries to come around, we *are* slowly changing our ways. We no longer dump fish in overly chlorinated community swimming pools for entertainment. We now recognize that fish do indeed feel pain. We've set in place stronger protocols for conducting nonhuman animal research. Steadily and measurably, we are starting to extend our circle of compassion to the life in the sea, to those brilliant fishes that rose from the water to become you and me.

Renowned game designer and researcher Dr. Jane McGonigal recounts that no matter who we are, no matter what our nationality, gender, or social standing may be, four distinct things contribute to our happiness. They are: 1) satisfying work, 2) being good at something, 3) spending time with people we like, and 4) having the chance to be a part of something. By living consciously and taking time to think about what fish we eat or, more important, do not eat; by making sure we don't deplete wild fish from the sea; by reducing the garbage we create; and by getting involved to make our voices heard, we can find satisfying work that we are all good at doing. In saving the fishes, we can all have the chance to be part of something enormously important. And if we do it together, we will, by default, be spending time with people we like.

In my case, that means spending time with my family, including my energetic four-year-old girl and wide-eyed infant boy. Back at the Aquarium, in front of the tuna tank, my daughter turns to me. And with those big sea-green eyes of hers, she asks, "Mamma, what's it like to be a fish?" Before I can utter a word, she turns back to the tank and whispers to the glass, "I wanna be a fish. Fish live in the best place in the world."

How deeply I want that to be true—down to the very salt water in every one of my cells.

Whither Whales and Dolphins?
Naomi A. Rose

*Senior scientist with the Humane Society International
and a member of the International Whaling Commission's
Scientific Committee, Naomi has carried her concern
and passion for whales and dolphins through her
transition from fieldwork to policy making.*

Almost twenty-five years ago, as a PhD student at the University of California in Santa Cruz, I spent five summers camping on an un-inhabited island and bobbing around in a small rubber inflatable boat, following the ins and outs of the lives of a pod of killer whales, or orcas, in the waters off British Columbia. These were the northern resident orcas, which spend their summers in the Inside Passage of Vancouver Island, particularly in Johnstone Strait. I was interested in the social dynamics of the males, who stay by their mother's side for life in this population yet somehow still manage to father offspring outside of the family.

When I started studying these whales, researchers had been taking their photographs—by which these dramatic black-and-white animals are easily identified—for about fifteen years, following individuals year after year. Using actuarial techniques similar to those used by insurance companies, they had determined that the females in this population were, in the words of one scientist, "immortal."

Obviously this was a bit of an exaggeration, but the fact is that by the mid-1980s, after having followed these individuals since 1973, orca researchers had observed the loss of very few prime-age adult females. Juveniles of both sexes faced many risks, and adult males seemed prone to any number of midlife health crises. However, if a young female managed to make it into adulthood—past the age of fifteen, more or less, which is when the average female orca starts bearing calves—she was almost certain to live into her sixties, seventies, or eighties.

All of that changed in the 1990s.

The change may have simply been a matter of probability. Perhaps in such a long-lived species, fifteen years wasn't really long enough to gather enough representative data, and the seeming immortality of adult females was just what statisticians call an artifact of a small sample size (in this case, the small number of years the animals had been followed). Maybe after ten more years of data collection, the data set was giving a more accurate picture of orca lives. Maybe it was normal, after all, for a fair number of females to die in their twenties, thirties, or forties.

However, other research was showing that deaths of both sexes and all age classes of orcas increased in years with bad Chinook salmon runs. The orcas of British Columbia aren't marine mammal hunters but, rather, specialize in feasting on salmon. And not just any salmon; they are very picky and love the prized Chinook, or king, salmon. In the 1990s, due to a host of mostly human-caused factors, there had been a number of poor salmon runs. In these years, a larger number than usual of northern resident orcas were dying, including adult females who should have been in the prime of their lives.

I was shocked when I heard this news, not having been back to British Columbia in almost a decade. The orcas of Johnstone Strait had been frozen in time in my memory, hale, hearty, and thriving. It was appalling to hear that the "immortal" females of my graduate career were dying at the height of their reproductive years, sometimes with a dependent calf left behind to starve. Many of these females had been the sisters and mothers of the males I had studied for my dissertation research, animals

I knew on sight, who had names and personalities and histories. And they were dying not in the natural course of events but because human beings were causing the degradation of their habitat (and that of their salmon prey), polluting their bodies with toxins, and overexploiting the fish on which they depend.

The situation for the southern residents, cousins of "my" whales, who live mostly in the Puget Sound area of Washington State, was even worse by the 1990s. There were far fewer of them, primarily because in the 1970s an entire generation of juveniles had been captured for public display in orca shows. Their bodies were also more contaminated thanks to the more polluted waters off the Washington coast. The southern residents also had a far more urbanized environment to navigate, with more coastal development, more boats and ships, and simply more human impacts of all sorts to contend with. In 2005, the U.S. government finally recognized the dire straits of this population (not without some legal prodding by environmental groups) and designated them as endangered under the U.S. Endangered Species Act.

THE CURRENT STATE OF AFFAIRS for the world's cetaceans (whales, dolphins, and porpoises) is that some populations are doing okay, some are definitely doing poorly, but all of them face a growing number of threats that put even the most robust populations at risk. In most parts of the world, the main threat is the large-scale commercial fishing industry. Every year, the gear that big factory fishing vessels deploy or discard entangles marine mammals by the hundreds of thousands. This carnage is euphemistically called bycatch and, in some places, it is pushing some species, such as the tiny vaquita porpoise in the Gulf of California or Hector's dolphin in New Zealand, not just to the brink of extinction but right over the edge. Beyond bycatch, industrial fishing competes with cetaceans for their prey. Overfishing is a serious problem in almost every national fishery as well as on the high seas, including in Antarctica. International authorities conclude that as many as 80 percent of the world's fisheries are fully or overexploited, leaving little room for natural predators to fit in.

In all parts of the world, cetaceans are threatened by entanglement in the (mostly plastic) debris left behind by human activity; chemical and noise pollution; outbreaks of novel diseases; harmful algal blooms; collisions with ships; and even, in some cases, the loss of river-mouth habitats that shelter and foster their prey as human activities upstream, far from the dolphins' home, siphon off freshwater for agriculture and industry.

And despite what many people think, cetaceans are still being hunted around the world. Aboriginal people in several countries kill cetaceans for subsistence, but certain industrial nations are also still hunting large whales for "science" and commerce. We thought we had saved the whales from the harpoons of whalers in the 1970s, but although many battles to save wildlife are fought and sometimes won, it seems this particular war is never over. Today, thousands of large whales and small cetaceans continue to be killed deliberately, even though we now know many cetacean species are intelligent, socially complex, long-lived, and even self-aware. The cruel fact is that no matter what the technique—harpoon, gun, or spear—it is nearly impossible to kill a cetacean humanely. Even a whale hit by an exploding grenade harpoon can take many minutes, even as much as an hour or more, to die.

The worst examples of continuing cetacean hunts are the drive fisheries of Japan and the Faroe Islands (a protectorate of Denmark). Communities in these countries continue to stampede terrified dolphin pods, such as bottlenose dolphins, false killer whales, and pilot whales, into shallow coves and bays with the roar of their engines or by clanging metal pipes underwater. Once the group is trapped behind a net and milling about in stupefaction and confusion, the hunters proceed to stab and slice at them with long knives and spear-like instruments. The living attempt to escape through the blood of the dead, until they too are thrashing about in their final death throes. It is a scene from hell. Even for those who think it is sustainable and reasonable to continue to hunt dolphins just as other countries hunt other wildlife, this grotesque and cruel method of killing an intelligent, social creature cannot be justified.

Just as archaically, commercial capture operators are still pulling live dolphins from the sea for display in amusement parks and dolphinariums; indeed, some of the dolphins corralled in the Japanese drive fishery are set aside during the slaughter and sold to display facilities. Representatives of dolphinariums generally tell the public that the dolphins seen in shows either were captured long ago or were captive-born. This is at best propaganda and at worst a flat-out lie. In fact, the majority of cetaceans in display tanks and pens around the world were caught from the wild—recently. Active live captures, particularly of bottlenose dolphins, beluga whales, and false killer whales, are ongoing in places such as Cuba, the Solomon Islands (in the South Pacific, near Australia), Russia, and Japan.

∿∿

I LONG AGO HUNG UP MY RUBBER BOOTS and mothballed my camping gear, and as a biologist for the Humane Society of the United States and later its international arm, I now spend most of my days at a desk or in meetings. Still working to protect marine mammals, I travel all over the world trying to convince governments to increase their efforts to preserve at least some parts of the ocean for the benefit of wildlife.

Healthy cetacean habitat is shrinking exponentially, nowhere more evident than in Taiwan, where a critically endangered population of Indo-Pacific humpback dolphins, or *Sousa chinensis*, struggles to exist in one of the most industrialized coastal habitats in the world. The Taiwan *Sousa* faces almost all of the threats previously listed, including the loss of estuarine habitat as the Taiwan government dams rivers and diverts the water before it can reach the ocean, as it has for millennia past. These highly coastal dolphins, rarely seen far from shore, spend much of their time feeding at river mouths, prime habitat for their fish prey. Yet this vital habitat is disappearing under concrete factories, land reclamation, wind turbines, petrochemical plants, and harbors.

I visited Taiwan in 2007 to participate in a workshop convened to discuss how to keep this beleaguered dolphin population from disappearing. (The Taiwan *Sousa* was discovered and identified by scientists only in 2002!) There are other populations of *Sousa* in Asia and Africa, but the Taiwan group has unique characteristics that strongly suggest that if this population goes extinct, no other *Sousa* will come along to replace it; once gone, it will be gone forever.

Those of us attending the workshop were taken to one of the most likely spots to view the animals from shore. As our driver parked the bus, we saw signs identifying the massive pier that jutted three hundred feet into the surf as a prime viewing area for the dolphins. In any other place, this spot would have had beach or rocky shore on either side, perhaps with buildings or roads nearby, but certainly with some natural vegetation and terrain as well. In Taiwan, all we saw were factories pouring smoke into the sky and a concrete culvert pouring frothy polluted water into the sea.

We saw no dolphins.

The air in the Taiwan *Sousa*'s habitat is brown, as is the water. There are probably fewer than ninety-five dolphins left alive in this nightmare landscape. That there are *any* of them left is a testament to the survival instinct that rages in all living creatures. For anyone who insists that the marine conservation situation isn't really as bad as we might make it out to be, they probably haven't been to the west coast of Taiwan.

In one respect, I have a unique window onto the severity of the marine conservation situation because I compile, with two colleagues, an annual digest of the previous year's published research on various aspects of the marine environment for the Scientific Committee of the International Whaling Commission (IWC). It is called the "State of the Cetacean Environment Report" (SOCER) and summarizes research articles reporting on many of the threats facing cetaceans. These threats do not affect cetaceans in isolation; they interact synergistically (so that the whole may be worse than the sum of its parts) and cumulatively (piling burden after burden on species and their habitats). SOCER is an attempt to present the cetacean conservation situation in its, at times, overwhelming entirety.

As a consequence of combing the literature for the past six or seven years for key papers investigating how human activities are affecting cetacean habitat, I feel almost as if I have been watching a massive pile-up on the highway in slow motion. Each year, the many vehicles on the road—industrial fishing, commercial and "scientific" whaling, small cetacean hunting, shipping, military sonar training, seismic surveys for oil and gas deposits, industrial and agricultural effluent discharged into coastal areas, coastal development, marine trash, toxic chemicals, oil spills, climate change, even "green" renewable energy such as marine wind turbines and tidal energy generators—inch ever closer to each other. One day in the not-so-distant future, an inevitable head-on collision waits.

International treaties, such as the International Convention on the Regulation of Whaling (ICRW), the Convention on Biological Diversity, the Convention on Migratory Species, the Convention on International Trade in Endangered Species of Wild Fauna and Flora, and others, were negotiated by the nations of the world in a well-meaning effort to prevent this disastrous crash. However, some of these agreements, which might look good on paper, are problematic in execution, most notably the ICRW, which established the IWC almost sixty-five years ago. For decades, the IWC "managed" the great whales to the brink of extinction, and despite finally banning commercial whaling in the 1980s, loopholes in the treaty allow whalers in Japan, Norway, and Iceland to continue to ply their bloody trade. Flawed treaties like this, political paralysis, and other social, bureaucratic, and economic factors mean that inexorably the crash still looms ahead.

So why am I still trying to save these marine species if the situation is so grim?

Because every once in a while, I am reminded of the great beauty in the ocean; that dedicated, passionate crusaders for the marine environment still toil ceaselessly (and often thanklessly), sometimes in the most unlikely places; and, more pragmatically, that some functioning habitats still exist and are worth saving.

In 2002, I was contacted by Professor Idelisa Bonnelly de Calventi, a highly respected marine biologist in the Dominican Republic, winner of numerous scientific and conservation awards, and a co-founder of the Dominican Academy of Sciences. Nearly seventy years old then, she is still going strong today. Profesora Idelisa was seeking help with dolphin protection in her country; she was a marine invertebrate specialist herself, but an arguably illegal capture of eight bottlenose dolphins had just occurred in the waters off the tiny village of Bayahibe in the southwestern corner of the Dominican Republic, and she was determined to tackle the problem head-on. She had founded a small nonprofit research and advocacy group sometime earlier, the Fundación Dominicana de Estudios Marinos, or FUNDEMAR, and through that organization she was seeking to stop further captures and exhort her government to protect its dolphins rather than support their exploitation.

Through her tireless efforts and the cooperation of key parties, including the Dominican Republic government, municipal authorities, local tourism representatives, academics, and domestic and international advocacy groups, the Dominican Republic has established a model research program focused on Bayahibe's bottlenose dolphins. Called El Proyecto Amigos de los Delfines, this program has been, for the past seven years, accumulating data on the local dolphins, publishing papers, presenting at conferences, conducting tourist surveys, and working with local residents to develop responsible tourism activities that will promote dolphin protection. In addition, numerous workshops and educational courses have been held for fishermen, tourists, hotel operators, and others to ensure that all stakeholders coordinate and collaborate to the maximum advantage of the dolphins.

There have, of course, been setbacks. Funding is a constant struggle. The Dominican Republic has four dolphinariums and may license even more. But the future is nevertheless brighter for Bayahibe's bottlenose dolphins today than it was in 2002.

Another example: In 2005, I was invited to give a presentation at a workshop on dolphin-protection issues in Venezuela. We spent most of the four days inside a building, listening to presentations, trying to address various local conservation issues. The workshop was held in a small town in the state of Aragua, far from any major urban center, but I could have been in any hotel conference room in the world.

On one glorious day, however, the participants were taken on a boat tour of the coast, not primarily to watch cetaceans but rather to snorkel, to bird-watch, and simply to enjoy the scenery. There was, however, a good chance of encountering a local population of common dolphins. I had a new camera and optimistically had it ready to capture any distant dorsal fin we might see.

But when we finally crossed the path of a lively group of dolphins, they weren't distant or just dorsal fins; they were right next to the boat, in crystal clear water, and they chose to approach us rather than the other way around. It was the perfect encounter, with the animals not being chased against their inclination but rather choosing to ride our bow for part of the journey as we made our way to our destination, a prime snorkeling spot. The entire encounter lasted only about ten to fifteen minutes before we eventually left them behind and they broke off to continue their business. I managed to shoot several absolutely fabulous photos of the animals underwater or just breaking the surface.

This experience was a reminder to me of several important things. First, there are still remote, relatively pristine habitats left on the planet. Second, dolphins are of course among the most curious of animals, and, unlike most wildlife species that run when they encounter humans (perhaps showing more common sense but less empathy and connection), dolphins sometimes choose to interact with humans. Third, the workshop organizers were determined to protect these animals from exploitation (local entrepreneurs had recently been caught illegally capturing dolphins in Venezuela's waters) through the development of responsible dolphin watching.

So on the one hand, my job exposes me on a daily basis to the harsh reality of the status of the world's cetaceans. On the other, it occasionally grants me the privilege to see that the world can still be a marvelous place.

The biggest threat of all? Human indifference. The ocean seems a remote place to many people, but it is the life-support system of the entire planet. We ignore and abuse it at our peril. Saving the world's cetaceans may seem like a luxury to some who think they're being pragmatic. But as the cetaceans go, so go we. If we can't save them, we will not save ourselves.

Of Dolphins and Decency
Richard O'Barry

*Ric has worked both sides of the dolphin street, the first ten years
with the dolphin captivity industry (as the trainer of Flipper) and
the past thirty-eight against it. He was the motivating force behind*
The Cove, *the documentary that showed to the world the horrific
slaughter of dolphins that goes on in a quiet corner of Japan.*

*In situations of great stress in captivity, dolphins have been
known to commit suicide by starvation, battering against walls,
or drowning.*
Columbia Encyclopedia, *6th Edition, 2001–2005*

When you consider that dolphins and other whales have been on this
planet for at least 50 million years compared with much less than a single
million years for us human beings, you have to wonder how we got
control over them so quickly. They have larger brains than we have.
They're bigger and stronger, faster, sleeker, and altogether more perfectly
formed than we are. And yet, just as we have come to dominate the
30 percent of the planet that is not water, it is easy to argue that dolphins
and whales are the dominant species in the other 70 percent, in the
water world.

We are actually very much alike. We're both mammals of a high order,
both self-aware, both breathe air, and both have adapted almost perfectly
to the world we live in. We both have mothers that suckle their young in

loving family groups around which is woven a way of living that fosters social rules maintaining a balance like the golden mean of ancient Greece.

That last is at least true of dolphins and other whales.

Where did we go wrong? What happened in our world to make so many of us rush with such abandon into the exploitation of our counterparts in the watery 70 percent of the world? Why do we capture these beautiful fellow creatures and make them objects of fun? And, oddly enough, the most fun we seem to have is capturing them, penning them up, and making them pull us through the water, one after the other. Why would anyone who understood what was actually going on enjoy this? How can we, who do understand what's going on, tolerate it? And how can those who exploit dolphins and other whales do so without a ripple of conscience, as if they had a right to?

The short answer is that we have a long history of doing just this. After all, human slavery was only recently put aside as an okay thing to do (in part when it was no longer economically feasible). Indeed, where it is still feasible today, as in enforced prostitution of children, it continues. Maybe at the heart of this attitude is our sophisticated worldwide economic system whose goal is to maximize profits regardless of collateral damage. But the history of slavery in general is a clue to how we can stop this travesty. If we stop it from being profitable, it will go away.

The first so-called dolphinarium opened in 1938 at Marine Studios in St. Augustine, Florida, where captured dolphins performed tricks several times a day for paying humans. Today, there are scores of them all over the world, with more in the works. If you could collect all the abuse to dolphins—the pain, the horror, the frustration, the suicides, the cries for help—the accumulated atrocities would equal a thousand hells.

Most countries would not permit this abuse except for one reason: money. Most countries have laws against cruelty to animals, first adopted in the early nineteenth century. But these laws obviously have loopholes because, despite all our efforts, displaying dolphins publicly for money is now a multibillion-dollar industry. Many participate and profit: hunters, suppliers and shippers of dolphins, marketers, park construction workers, trainers, the list goes on. Some nations allow it because they've got bigger problems. Some nations see nothing wrong with it. The rest allow it for the wrong reason, suggesting that it's "educational." Those who suggest that dolphinariums are educational argue that many people would otherwise never get to see a dolphin. But what about all the people who will never see a snow leopard? A saber-toothed tiger? Or the dodo? Their argument is a fraud, because these dolphinariums are not educational; they're anti-educational. They show not a dolphin in his own world but a dolphin trained to act like a clown in our world. And then they have the unmitigated gall to tell us, "Look! See how they smile? They love doing tricks for us!"

Don't be fooled. Those dolphins are not smiling. If one of those same performing dolphins were to fall dead on the dock, he would still wear that look and it would still not be a smile.

Some may argue that we are not personally to blame for what is happening to dolphins and other whales around the world. And that's true. We don't personally capture them and put them in what, to them, are tiny torture chambers. We don't withhold food till they perform silly little acrobatic tricks to our liking. We're not to blame, not a single one of us, in the same way we're not personally to blame for the world's murders, arsons, and kidnappings. Over the years, we have passed laws against murder and kidnapping, not because of some abstraction about society or the rule of law but because we're sick of them. Similarly, those who capture dolphins in the wild and imprison them for the rest of their lives now revolt us. (Letting them breed in captivity and citing that as "freedom" doesn't wash either; dolphins born in captivity never learn to catch a live fish in the wild and are unequipped to live there.)

A lot of misguided talk surrounds another similarity between human beings and dolphins in captivity: committing suicide when stressed. When dolphins in captivity are greatly stressed, they sometimes obviously feel the need to escape by whatever means. This is a big problem because they don't have guns or poison as we do in such circumstances. What can they do? Some will batter themselves to death against the walls of their prison. Others refuse to eat until they waste away and die. Although humans and all the other mammals breathe automatically, dolphins don't have that automatic reflex; every breath they take is deliberate. When human beings fall into deep water, we drown because we lose consciousness and then, when the automatic reflex kicks in, we breathe water. Not so the dolphin. The dolphin will kill himself by drowning if he deliberately breathes water, but more likely he dies for lack of oxygen in his blood caused by not breathing at all. This suicide option the dolphin takes is another proof of his self-awareness, without which suicide would never even occur to him.

If words, logic, reason, facts, and history were enough to destroy this dolphin industry, it would have disappeared by now. Now we need laws to stop it. It cannot be done overnight and may take many years. But now is the time to start eliminating this evil, or it will endure through our lifetime.

Adelita: Heart of a Revolution
Wallace J. Nichols with Andy Myers

J—as he goes by—is as passionate about the entire ocean
as he is about turtles and thinks we are on the verge of a new way
of looking at ocean science. His Oceanophilia theory posits that the
next step toward understanding our water planet is linking
neuroscience with marine biology, emotion with science.
But he still gets excited tracking sea turtles.

AUGUST 10, 1996. A few miles off the coast of the dusty Baja California peninsula, the land appears as a thin ribbon on the horizon, and the wind rips across the water unimpeded by anything but a prayer. In a small boat, a handful of people is gathered around a female loggerhead turtle. She is called Adelita after a local fisherman's daughter, herself the namesake of the heroine of the Mexican Revolution. The team affixes a Bible-sized box to the turtle's brown and yellow heart-shaped shell. In the box is a satellite transmitter, one of the first ever to track the migration of a sea turtle. It will allow them to follow her wherever she might roam for the next year or so, perhaps longer if the batteries hold. After a wait for the slow-curing resin to set, the team lowers Adelita into the water and a historic journey is on.

Back in the late summer of 1996, I was still a graduate student in marine biology. Debate was then rife among scientists about the logger-heads of western North America. Specifically, where did they come from? Loggerheads love Baja California. They bide their time in Baja like so many tourists, floating around, soaking in the warm sun, feasting on the innumerable red crabs that thrive there. Hundreds, perhaps thousands, of loggerheads can be found in Baja—once there were millions—yet no one had ever located a single loggerhead nesting on any beach anywhere along the miles and miles of twisting Baja coast or on the entire Pacific coast of the Americas for that matter. Not one.

As most schoolkids will tell you, the first, and perhaps most impres-sive, thing you learn about sea turtles is that they are known to return to the very same beaches where they were hatched to nest as adults. With no known loggerhead nesting beaches in Pacific Mexico, there were many questions to be answered.

The team and I watched Adelita swim away, our *panga* bobbing in the immense ocean. We stared out across the expanse of blue before us and thought maybe, perhaps, possibly these turtles aren't born in Baja at all. Maybe they migrate here only to return from whence they came. We gazed at the horizon. Somewhere out there, across the vast Pacific, lay Japan and the nearest known loggerhead nesting beaches, a mere 7,000 miles west. Genetic evidence suggested the possibility of epic ocean-spanning migrations. But dwarfed by the vastness of the Pacific Ocean, the hypothesis was revolutionary at the time.

Each day, the small box on Adelita's back relayed her location to us via satellites linked to a base station in France. Each day, we studied the data and then uploaded it to the Internet. Tiny dots aligned on a map, surrounded by nothing but blue. Soon, other people took note. And then more. Schoolkids, scientists, and turtle lovers the world over were watching Adelita's progress.

Alone, but not *alone,* Adelita stroked on through the deepest, wildest, most humanless expanse of our planet.

People would write. "Hi J., this is Meghan and I was just wondering if you are as excited about this as we are?" At night, I couldn't sleep. I'd lie awake thinking about Adelita. Praying for her safety. Wonder-ing what was beneath her and above her. Was she hungry? How did it feel to be going home after so many years? I became obsessed with checking my email for the latest position. I'd imagine members of our loosely connected club sitting in front of glowing blue screens all over the world, plotting, imagining, hoping, and dreaming about that vast blue space.

We tracked her due west out of Baja making a steady twenty miles per day, a healthy walking gait for you or me. By January 1, she was just north of Hawaii. From there, she tracked west and ever so slightly north. Sure enough, she was headed straight for Japan.

Brie wrote, "What are you gonna do when Adelita gets to Japan? I mean are you gonna send a team to get her, J?"

"I'm not really sure," I wrote back.

MARCH 9, 1997. Barbara Garrison, a teacher who was following Adelita's progress across the Pacific with her students, receiving my regular emails and thoughts, wrote this poem during the journey as the turtle neared the international dateline:

Adelita sleeps.
Do you ever find yourself
thinking of her
in the middle of the day?

Sister of mercy
adrift in the world
her carapace around her
like a habit
following the liturgy of longitude
like the Stations of the Cross
the draw string of dream
gathering with each dive.

A sea shadow
cradled in the arms
of the great Turtle Mother.

The Virgin of Cobre guiding
through the dangerous sea
the black sand memory
of her natal beach
ringing her course
in peals of instinct.

Cartographer
explorer
world traveler
Adelita sleeps.

A Shinto priestess
leads the way
a goddess path
from Mexico
to the arribada
on a distant
Kyushu shore.

AUGUST 13, 1997. Three hundred and sixty-eight days after we lowered her into the Pacific, Adelita's signal finally went dark—her final location put her near Sendai, a port in northern Japan.

In the years since Adelita, much has changed scientifically, environmentally, and, most significantly, socially. Prior to Adelita, flipper tagging was how we tracked long-distance turtle migration. But with a metal tag, all you know is point A and point B; a turtle that was once there, then is here, now, nothing more. Satellite tracking, then a nascent technology, held great promise, but it was expensive and tricky to do in the water. Think of your cell phone in 1996: unwieldy and unreliable to say the least. How long would the glue hold? Would the battery last? Can the transmitter survive in the salty sea? And sea turtles are far from safe out there. All these questions and more were laid to rest when Adelita reached Japan.

Since Adelita, we have tracked over fifty turtles along the Baja Peninsula. Today's gear is better, smaller, and cheaper. Methods of attachment are more reliable, and analysis tools are much more powerful. The information provides a greater understanding of migration and life cycle, ecology and behavior as well as threats and potential solutions. The technology has expanded to include tiny cameras that provide a turtle-eye view and tiny transmitters that are injected to give biofeedback: body temperature, heart rate, respiration, and other valuable information. It is becoming standard procedure to track dive patterns and locations of endangered ocean wildlife, watching when, where, and how deep animals descend in search of food or to avoid predators. Such data is now used in real time to help fishermen and boat captains avoid interactions with such endangered species.

In terms of sea turtle biology, Adelita jump-started an era of tremendous growth in what we understand about where and how turtles live. Scientists now know that loggerheads born in Japan spend the first months of life adrift on the ocean, moving away from nesting beaches. The lucky ones do, anyway, those who make it to adolescence. But only a small percentage of hatchlings make it through the gauntlet that awaits them: foxes, crabs, sharks, seabirds, and fishermen's nets; even the carelessly discarded plastic bag can be lethal when mistaken for a jellyfish, a favorite food.

Many young loggerheads will then migrate east across the North Pacific, moving both with and against the predominant currents in search of food. Little is known about the beginning of this eastward trip. The youngest loggerheads are too small to be affixed with satellite tracking devices. Recently, however, a team of U.S. and Japanese researchers has tracked dozens of young loggerheads released into the Kuroshio Current. The results suggest young loggerheads feed along the meandering, invisible ocean edges where currents meet, temperature changes, and soft-bodied animals from the deep accumulate, providing plenty of good food for hungry turtles. Eventually, some make it to Baja and, once there, they hang out, often for decades, growing large and fat for the long journey back home. They become big, powerful swimmers. Adelita weighed 223 pounds—more than me—just ripe for a satellite tracking device.

At some point, an as-yet-unknown biological trigger, a hormonal surge perhaps, tells the turtles it's time to head home. And then they are gone. On the trip back, we know that turtles follow the ocean's convergence areas, picking up as much help as they can from Mother Nature—and maybe some food along the way. Ever the masters of efficiency and resourcefulness, they make a near-straight shot across the Pacific. The details of that long journey, other than location and depth, remain largely a mystery. I would love to trace Adelita's track in a boat. It is a transect through the North Pacific, crossing an area now known best for its accumulating bits of plastic waste, the product of five decades of unbridled consumption by distant civilizations. During the years since Adelita's journey, we have worked to raise awareness of plastic pollution in the ocean, a menace whose full impacts on animals and humans are only now being appreciated.

The decade since Adelita has also witnessed a transformation of scientific collaboration. Once, sea turtle conservation was a relatively homegrown endeavor, transpiring on nesting beaches, mostly at night. There was no need to partner with or seek out scientists on the other side of the world because they had their own turtles to worry about. Groups of scientists, conservationists, and activists worked together locally to protect specific beaches or to reform fishing industries of the countries where they lived and worked. Handwritten data became typewritten reports, most bound for file cabinets and dusty shelves. The critical nightly beach work continues, but the playing field has expanded to include international partnerships that sprout fresh ideas and knowledge. Our ability to collaborate at the speed of light has to be considered a revolution in itself.

As it turns out, turtles aren't local at all. We know now that the health of turtles and the ocean in Baja is closely tied to the health of turtles in Japan and all points between, and vice versa. To understand sea turtles everywhere, we must share data and collaborate globally. And it's not just geographic. It's interdisciplinary. We now work with experts on mammals, birds, fish, invertebrates, and other species as well as with chemical and physical oceanographers to understand how all these elements act together as an ecosystem.

Perhaps most significantly, however, the changes since Adelita have been social. The world has changed. People have changed. There has been a revolution in ocean conservation and in how the world views the environment in which we and all life on Earth exist.

Though I am a research scientist by training, I have long since abandoned the pure pursuit of knowledge in favor of combining my experience with advocacy and perhaps a fair share of social marketing to advance the greater cause of conservation. There just isn't enough time to wait on scientific consensus on everything before we do something about what's happening to our planet. I think, above all, Adelita showed me that a thin thread runs through each living thing on Earth—plant or animal—and binds us together. The sea turtles of Baja California are a microcosm and a metaphor, perhaps.

So while I have not abjured science altogether, I have become a vocal advocate for action. I now work with local communities to forward conservation based on the best science we have; but the best science is not always perfect, and I can live with that. We do the best we can with what knowledge we have, and we adjust when something or someone provides us with a different truth.

Nowhere is the social shift more apparent than in the fishing communities of Baja California Sur. Baja fishermen are working to find economic alternatives to sea turtle hunting, an industry that blossomed in the middle of the last century then crashed hard. Regulations came too late and turtles virtually disappeared. Still today, sea turtles are a delicacy to the people of Baja, and there is money to be made on the black market from their meat and eggs as well as their shells.

Baja is a place where a few dollars from the sale of a single turtle can be enough to feed a family for a week or more. So even modest economic incentives go a long way to stem their being hunted. Our team has been working with local fishermen to promote ecotourism and the establishment of a network of sea turtle refuges. There is a burgeoning interest in sea turtles, much of it started by, if not inspired by, Adelita. Local fishermen are skilled and knowledgeable guides, and they can earn good money leading tourists to turtle hot spots to witness loggerheads and greens and hawksbills in their native environment—graceful, gorgeous, and free. Ecotourism can offset the potential money they might make on the black market or from fishing with deadly gill nets. And new research from Australia makes it clear that when people spend time near wild turtles, whales, and dolphins, it inspires behavior change favoring conservation back home.

JANUARY 30, 1999. A few years after Adelita, I helped found Grupo Tortuguero—the "turtle-people group"—a network of individuals, communities, organizations, and institutions from Baja and around the world dedicated to sea turtle conservation. We envisioned sea turtles fulfilling their ecological roles on a healthy planet where people value and celebrate their continued survival rather than see them as a chance for a quick meal or a quick buck. We are encouraging people and their communities to conserve sea turtles by strengthening relationships within a conservation community, developing innovative programs and partici- patory research projects, and sharing knowledge and information as widely as humanly possible.

Now in its second decade, the Grupo Tortuguero works to restore sea turtles to their ecological role on Baja's reefs, sea grass beds, bays, and *esteros.* In places such as Bahia Magdalena, Cabo Pulmo, Laguna San Ignacio, and the Loreto Marine Park, these diverse habitats provide refuge for the endangered turtles.

When the Grupo Tortuguero first gathered for its annual meeting in 1999, forty-five fishermen, scientists, and conservationists showed up. We fit in a classroom. We laid out our ground rules: one member, one vote; annual meetings, more if possible; and we would be known as the Grupo Tortuguero. Each member pledged to save at least one sea turtle during the following year. Within a decade, the Grupo Tortuguero grew tenfold and filled half of Loreto's municipal auditorium. The meeting is now equal parts conference, fiesta, and family reunion. Successful con- servation efforts require good science, but music, beer, and tacos don't hurt. Countless thousands of sea turtles have been rescued, protected, and rehabilitated by members, mostly fishermen and their families.

Grupo Tortuguero's former coordinator, Rodrigo Rangel, grew up on Isla Magdalena in Baja California, one of a long line of fishermen. Sea turtle meat was common fare in his home. "At first, my family called me an *ecologista* and tempted me with sea turtle soup," he said about the time he first told his family of his new profession. "Now they get it. They respect my work, and they help me to protect sea turtles. The sea turtle revolution is happening . . . one person at a time."

ONCE I WAS ALLOWED TO WITNESS the fate of an illicit turtle. As difficult and distasteful as it was to me, I felt I had to watch it to understand the culture, people, and traditions of the communities of Baja. I waited as the green turtle was turned on its shell to "live" a few more days in anticipation of a homecoming celebration where traditional turtle soup would welcome the guest of honor. I considered the drastic "rescue" operations I might undertake and how I'd then need to leave the community, perhaps forever. In the end, I watched an efficient slaughter. I didn't speak. I was motionless, fascinated, paralyzed, curious—a visitor, a guest.

Local myth holds that a sea turtle heart, disembodied, will beat for as long as twenty minutes, pumping nonexistent blood to nonexistent organs. I now know this to be a fact.

Today, some of the fishermen with me that day lead the local sea turtle monitoring and conservation efforts. One of them, Julio Solis, is the executive director of the Waterkeeper chapter fighting unsustainable development projects, championing clean water, and restoring sea turtles. These young men are also inspiring the next generation of conservationists by speaking in the schools, holding sea turtle festivals, and bringing kids on overnight turtle monitoring expeditions. They are among my most trusted friends on this planet.

In my profession, words such as *dedication, passion,* and *love of nature* are deemed overly sentimental, kind of soft. In science, deep personal relationships interfere with goals. Some say that it's hard, if not impossible, to maintain one's status as a respectable scientist and be an effective advocate for the ocean. Some say that to restore nature is only a matter of dollars and enforcement. Then again, some say that's all bunk.

Here is what I know: If we are to repair what is broken in nature, if we are to replace its heart with one that still beats, it will take a revolution full of passionate celebration of nature and commitment to and compassion toward each other. On the Baja Peninsula, within a growing number of people who inhabit the towns along its shores, you'll find the beating heart of a revolution. The conservation leaders in Baja respect and understand nature, and they have rallied to help protect sea turtles in their own economic and cultural—maybe even spiritual—interest.

We have a long way to go. But the revolution is spreading one person at a time, and it certainly goes beyond Baja and beyond sea turtles. From efforts to stanch the flow of plastic into our oceans, to beating back climate change, to changing the things we eat, to protecting invaluable coral reefs, there is an ocean revolution raging. Adelita didn't ignite the flame, but she surely fanned it and sparked a few small fires along the way.

Without question, the world—and I—owe a great deal to Adelita. She was a sea turtle who was merely adhering to a millions-of-years-old ritual. She was going home. But she took us with her.

~~~

ADELITA'S EXACT FATE, however, remains a mystery. After she reached the coastal waters of Japan, I continued to receive tracking points from her transmitter, each set more peculiar than the next. The first coordinates fell in a scattershot pattern, inconsistent with those of a turtle making its way along a coastline, as I expected to see. Then, for a time, nothing. Then, there she was again, this time moving in a straight line on a direct path to the port of Sendai, Japan, but far faster than any turtle could possibly swim. Eventually, the signal disappeared for good.

Curious to see the place where Adelita made land, in 1999, I trekked to Sendai, GPS in hand. When I reached the coordinates I'd programmed in—the exact point of Adelita's arrival, her last known location on Earth—I found myself on the dock of a small Japanese fishing village, Isohama, a fleet of squid boats lining the harbor.

I cannot say for certain what happened to her or her transmitter. She may still be out there. Deep inside, I believe she is. One thing is certain— her heart still beats. In places like Baja and Sendai and Sydney and Santa Cruz, all across the world, the heart of an ocean revolution still beats.

The Bluefin's Uncertain Future
Richard Ellis

*One of the most prominent writers on ocean issues,
Richard is also a preeminent wildlife painter and a research
associate at New York's American Museum of Natural History.
His book,* Tuna, A Love Story, *is the definitive take on the health
of one of the world's most elegant—and endangered—fish. This
"quintessential ocean ranger, the wildest, fastest, most powerful
fish in the sea," may be gone from the oceans as soon as 2012.*

The canned substance in tuna fish sandwiches and salads is either skip-jack, a three-foot-long tuna species that is caught in prodigious quantities around the world and served as "light-meat tuna," or albacore, another small tuna that is marketed as "white-meat tuna." A couple of larger species of tuna that are also heavily fished are the yellowfin and the bigeye tuna, but neither of these makes for particularly desirable sushi, and they are usually served grilled. The bluefin tuna, a giant among fishes, is the fish of choice for sashimi; it has become the most desirable food fish in the world and, as such, has vaulted to the top of another, more insidious list: It is probably the most endangered of all large-fish species.

Reaching a maximum known weight close to three-quarters of a ton and a length of twelve feet, the bluefin is a massive hunk of superheated muscle that cleaves the water by flicking its scimitar-shaped tail. It is one of the fastest of all fishes, capable of speeds up to fifty-five miles per hour, and able to migrate across entire oceans. Whereas most of the 20,000-odd species of fishes are cold-blooded, with a body temperature the same as the water they swim in, the bluefin is one of the few hot-blooded fishes. During a dive to 3,000 feet, where the ambient water temperature can be 40 degrees Fahrenheit (4 degrees Celsius), the bluefin can maintain a body temperature of 80 degrees, close to that of a mammal. Like wolves, bluefins often hunt in packs, forming a high-speed parabola that concentrates the prey, making it easier for the hunters to close in. Tuna are metabolically adapted for high-speed chases, but as opportunistic (and, by necessity, compulsive) feeders, they will eat whatever presents itself, whether fast-swimming mackerel, bottom-dwelling flounder, or sedentary sponge. A study of the stomach contents of New England bluefins by Bradford Chase revealed that the most popular food item (by weight) was Atlantic herring, followed by sand lance, bluefish, and miscellaneous squid. (In addition to these prey items, Chase also found butterfish, silver hake, windowpanes, winter flounder, menhaden, sea horses, cod, flounder, plaice, pollock, filefish, halfbeak, sculpin, spiny dogfish, skate, octopus, shrimp, lobster, argonaut, crab, and sponges.) Tuna will eat anything they can catch, and they can catch almost anything that swims (or floats, crawls, or just sits on the bottom). By and large, they hunt by vision.

At one time, the bluefin tuna was known as horse mackerel, and its red, strong-flavored flesh was considered suitable fare only for dogs and cats. Around the turn of the last century, while still thought of as inedible, the bluefin was targeted by big-game fishermen off New Jersey, and then Nova Scotia, because these powerful fish, reaching a weight of half a ton or more, were considered worthy opponents for fishermen in quest of sport and world's records. Zane Grey was one of the most popular authors of the 1920s, with western novels such as *Last of the Plainsmen* and *Riders of the Purple Sage,* but his passion was big-game fishing, and he invested most of his not inconsiderable royalties (his books sold more than 13 million copies) on fishing gear, fishing boats, and travel to exotic locales in search of tuna, swordfish, and marlins. Other sportsmen wrote of their fishing exploits, but in *The Old Man and the Sea* (1952) and *Islands in the Stream* (published posthumously in 1970), Ernest Hemingway took up where Grey had left off, elevating his fishermen to heroes and his great game fishes to icons. Although swordfish were certainly considered edible, the other big-game fishes, such as tuna and marlins, were thought of as objects of the hunt, to be fought and conquered by brave fishermen with expensive gear and more expensive boats, plying the world's offshore waters in pursuit of records. The record bluefin tuna, caught off Nova Scotia in 1979, weighed 1,496 pounds.

At one time, it was believed that there were two separate populations of North Atlantic bluefins, one that bred in the Gulf of Mexico and stayed in the western part of the ocean and another that spawned in the Mediterranean and hung out in the European quadrant. But tagging experiments, pioneered by Frank Mather and Frank Carey and followed by Barbara Block, showed that, as with so many aspects of bluefin biology, the fish confounds the conventional wisdom. Yes, the Gulf of Mexico and the Mediterranean are the breeding grounds of bluefins, but individual fishes can (and do) migrate across the entire Atlantic Ocean, and the two populations are actually one meta-population distributed across the entire North Atlantic. The International Convention for the Conservation of Atlantic Tunas (ICCAT) consistently based its catch quotas on the two-population concept and has therefore failed utterly to set realistic limits on who could fish and where, resulting in a massive collapse of the entire Atlantic bluefin population.

If possible, things are worse in the Mediterranean. Employing ideas and technology originally developed in South Australia (with the southern bluefin, *Thunnus maccoyi*), fishermen corralled schools of half-grown tuna and towed them in floating pens to marine corrals where they were fed and fattened until they could be killed and shipped to Japan. There are catch limits on tuna fishing in the Mediterranean but none on catching immature tuna and fattening them in floating pens. Every country (except Israel) on or in the Mediterranean takes advantage of this loophole and maintains tuna ranches offshore. The fishermen of Spain, France, Italy, Greece, Turkey, Croatia, Egypt, Libya, Tunisia, Algeria, Morocco, and Malta are capturing half-grown tuna by the hundreds of thousands. If you had to design a way to guarantee the decimation of a breeding population, this would be it: Catch the fish before they are old enough to breed, and keep them penned up until they are killed. In 2006, the World Wildlife Fund called for the cessation of all tuna fishing in the Mediterranean, but in the light of all that money to be made, you can imagine how effective the WWF plea was.

Unless tuna can be raised as if they were domesticated animals, the world populations will continue to decline, eventually reaching the point of no return. In November 2006, fourteen marine biologists published a major study in the journal *Science* in which they said that unless things change dramatically, in fifty years there would be nothing left to fish from the oceans. The study, innocuously called "Impacts of Biodiversity Losses on Ocean Ecosystem Services," points out that as of 2003, 29 percent of all ocean fisheries were in a state of collapse and, as Ransom Myers and Boris Worm pointed out in 2003, 90 percent of the big fishes are already gone, and we are fishing on the remaining 10 percent. Of course, it is not only fishing that has contributed to this sorry state of affairs; worsening water quality, toxic algal blooms, dead zones, invasive exotic species, and the disappearance of animals and plants that filter pollutants from the water have all played a role. Notice that all these calamities are anthropogenic: caused by humans. Homo sapiens is by far the greatest threat to environmental stability (especially if you throw global warming into the mix) but also its only hope. Solutions to the problems of over-fishing are painfully obvious—don't fish so heavily—but very difficult to implement. If we can't keep the tuna fishermen from catching all the tuna, then it is our responsibility to somehow ensure that the tuna will survive and prosper far from the longlines and nets. We owe it to ourselves (and to the tuna, whose populations we have ravaged) to preserve this great and wonderful creature for the balance of life on Earth. If we can't protect the most celebrated of all fishes, what can we protect?

Most people see tuna in a can or on a plate. Few of us have ever had the opportunity to fish for giant tuna and, because of the decline of the tuna stocks, even if we had the opportunity, we might not see one, let alone catch one. Recently, however, I had an experience that, if possible, made me appreciate the great bluefin even more. At the Monterey Bay Aquarium in California, the Outer Bay tank has some thirty-odd bluefin and yellowfin tuna swimming majestically past the viewing windows. Occasionally, for reasons known only to the tuna, one of them accelerates, and you are forcefully reminded of the amazing speeds attainable by bluefins: fifty mph in the blink of an eye. Admittedly, tuna in tanks are not the wild ocean rangers that I've been raving about, but tuna in tanks are not going to end up as sushi, either. Some of these giants weigh four hundred pounds, and while they will probably never get the opportunity to dive to one thousand feet or migrate for thousands of miles to their breeding grounds, they can accomplish what none of their pelagic brethren can: They can show us the streamlined quintessence of the most spectacular of all blue-water corsairs.

But spectacular beauty has never been enough to protect a species, and the rolls of extinct or near-extinct creatures include many of the most gorgeous ones. Think of the tiger, in efficiency, grace, power, and beauty the terrestrial equivalent of the mighty bluefin, now endangered through-out its diminishing range by the needs of Chinese traditional medicine. If the world's tigers are being slaughtered out of existence so that aging Asian men can enhance their virility, what hope is there for a fish and, moreover, a fish that people all over the world love to eat?

The tuna populations of the world, northern, Pacific, and southern, are all in very serious trouble. Most of them are being caught at an early age and placed into pens where they are fattened for the all-but-insatiable sashimi market of Japan, but the popularity of sashimi is spreading, and restaurants serving raw tuna are popping up in an inverse ratio to the numbers of tuna being caught. Although it seems contradictory, it is a perfect example of the law of supply and demand: The fewer tuna there are, the more people want to eat them because they have become a rare and exotic delicacy. Of course, increased demand will drive up the price, which means intensified fishing, for everyone wants to cash in before the "resource" runs out. Even the Port Lincoln tuna industry, awash in money, will eventually suffer the fate of every intensive wild fishery and begin to run out of fish. Farming, which once seemed the answer to overfishing the wild stock, only exacerbates the problem by harvesting too many tuna before they can attain breeding age. If the reproduction rate drops, the population drops.

We know that certain fish species will spawn only in selected areas and only in water within very narrow temperature ranges. Scientists have observed the mating dance of yellowfins in captivity at Achotines (Panama), where they saw "pairing of individuals, chasing, rapid color flashes exhibited by individual fish, and rapid horizontal or vertical swimming." In his 2001 discussion of the reproductive biology of various tuna species, Kurt Schaefer wrote,

> There is a very limited amount of information on size and/or age at maturity in *Thunnus thynnus*. A maturity schedule based on valid histological evidence has not been established.... Regardless of these inadequate experimental designs and invalid conclusions, subsequent researchers have accepted the age of 100% ... maturity for the west Atlantic to be 10 years of age (200 cm), and 5 years of age (130 cm) for the eastern Atlantic.

He goes on to say, "Even less research has been carried out on reproductive biology of *Thunnus orientalis* in the Pacific Ocean, and size and/or age is poorly understood." Schaefer then observed that "The spawning time during 1998 and 1999 of *Thunnus orientalis* broodstock held at the Amami Station, Japan, was between 1900 and 2300 h[ours.] The observed courtship behavior is apparently similar to the captive *T. albacares,* with more than one male commonly chasing after the same female and the same body stripes and/or darker coloration displayed by the males during this period." It may be no more complicated than recognizing that at certain seasons, and under certain conditions, the presence of mature males and ripe females triggers the simultaneous release of eggs and milt, guaranteeing the production of fertilized eggs.

There may be a way to get bluefin tuna to market without catching wild juveniles and fattening them up for slaughter. News item in the *Adelaide* [South Australia] *Advertiser* for October 28, 2006:

TUNA BROODSTOCK NOW SETTLED

> Nine southern bluefin tuna, each weighing around 130 kilos [285 pounds], have been individually transferred by helicopter from a Clean Seas Tuna sea farm to the new onshore breeding facility at Arno Bay. The move took eight hours. Just a few days later the fish were obviously settled in at the hatchery. The broodstock, seven years old, are expected to spawn in February or March 2007.

They didn't in 2007 or in 2008, but they did in 2009. Earlier, Clean Seas had entered into a partnership with Japan's Kinki University, the only hatchery in the world to complete the cycle of raising bluefin tuna from eggs to maturity. Something in that collaboration must have worked, for by March 2009, the tanks at the Arno Bay facility were teeming with tuna hatchlings. Because tuna are carnivores, the question of what to feed the baby tuna was resolved when a Queensland company called Ridley Aqua-' Feed produced a new vitamin-enriched fish food that replaces the small fish that would otherwise have been required to feed the growing tuna. (The concept of catching fish to feed fish has always been considered an ecological disaster.) By September 2009, the stocky little tuna at Arno Bay were approaching one kilogram in weight and were about the size of your shoe. They are expected to double in size within their first year of life, and the yearlings will be transferred to sea cages, where they will be fattened and raised to adulthood.

It will be years before the Arno Bay tuna will achieve market size, usually around 330 pounds, but there is no question that the Clean Seas enterprise will contribute to the worldwide tuna equation. Pressure on the Mediterranean tuna fishery has been so intense that the species is expected to become extinct in ten years, and the stocks of wild southern bluefins, those fished by the Australians, are threatened, too. Clean Seas' breeding program appears at first to be a step toward the salvation of the endangered bluefin, but because it is a purely commercial enterprise, it will not save much more than the investments in the Australian hatchery. Like their wild cousins, the tuna raised at Arno Bay will be fattened, killed, and shipped to Japan. But because these fish will not reach market size for several years, the pressure will continue on the Mediterranean and Australian bluefins. And if and when the Arno Bay tuna are ready for the Japanese fish markets, the wild-caught (and pen-raised) tuna may be so scarce that the price will skyrocket. What seemed to some as a breakthrough may in fact contribute further to the precipitous decline of the bluefin.

The big-game fisherman sees the bluefin tuna as a sleek and powerful opponent; to the harpooner, it is an iridescent shadow below the surface, flicking its scythe-like tail to propel it out of range; the purse seiner sees a churning maelstrom of silver and blue bodies to be hauled on deck; the longliner sees a dead fish, hauled on deck along with other glistening marine creatures; the tuna rancher sees the bluefin as an anonymous creature to be force-fed until it is time to drive a spike into its brain; the auctioneer at Tsukiji (Tokyo's giant fish market) sees row upon row of tailless, icy, tuna-shaped blocks; Japanese consumers see it as *toro,* a slice of rich red meat, to be eaten with wasabi and soy sauce. To the biologist, the tuna is a marvel of hydrodynamic engineering, its body packed with modifications that enable it to outeat, outgrow, outswim, outdive, and outmigrate any other fish in the sea. And to those who would rescue *Thunnus thynnus* from the oblivion of extinction, it has to be seen as a domesticated animal, like a sheep or a cow. For some, such a shift is almost impossible; the bluefin tuna, the quintessential ocean ranger, the wildest, fastest, most powerful fish in the sea, cannot be—and probably *should* not be—tamed. But if it isn't, we will be able to say only that we loved the tuna not wisely but too well.

Open Ocean
Coming Fights over the Arctic
Lynne Cox

A long-distance ocean swimmer and elegiac writer,
Lynne has an obviously unique take on the ocean, having spent
hundreds of hours stroking through it across the Bering Strait,
across the English Channel, along the Antarctic peninsula.
Her concern here takes her north, to the Arctic Ocean.

Whenever I gaze across vast blue oceans, my mind wanders without limitations, and I envision the possibilities of life. I see the oceans as the dynamic connection between the countries of the world. The water circulates from one continent to the other, carrying the influences of the earth from one land to another and affecting depths of the sea and the atmosphere above. As I walk the beach and watch the tide ebb and flood, I see the gravitational pull of the moon made visible and the ocean's connection to the sea of heavens and the universe.

As a young child, I swam off Rye Beach, New Hampshire, and off Old Orchard Beach, Maine. By the time I was twelve, my family moved to California so I could train with the U.S. Olympic coach. At age fifteen, I swam across the English Channel and broke the men's and women's world records. My time was broken, so I returned the following year and broke the men's record a second time. I realized that I could spend my entire life swimming the English Channel, but there were parts of the world I had never explored, and my way to get there was to swim. I became the first person to swim around the Strait of Magellan and the Cape of Good Hope and was the first woman to swim across the Cook Strait in New Zealand. It was exciting to break world records and to become the first person to swim across great waterways, to enter the unknown and learn, but I wanted to do something more significant. My father suggested that I swim across the Bering Strait from the United States to the Soviet Union as a way to demonstrate that the United States and Soviet Union were neighbors, only 2.7 miles apart.

I grew up during the Cold War, at a time when the relations between the two superpowers, the United States and Soviet Union, were very poor. I was afraid that we might engage in a nuclear war, and that would affect all life within the oceans as well as on land, but I was also hopeful that the two nations could figure out how to become friends. For eleven years, I wrote to U.S. presidents and Soviet leaders to obtain permission and support for the swim. Ultimately, Secretary of State George Shultz and Soviet Premier Gorbachev endorsed the project; in 1987, I swam across the Bering Strait, and the U.S.–Soviet border was open for the first time in forty-eight years. Four months later, when Gorbachev and Reagan signed the INF missile treaty at the White House, they toasted the swim, and Gorbachev said that it showed how close to each other we live and how the relations between the countries were improving.

I went on to do other swims that were about bridging distances between countries, and in 2002 I swam in a bathing suit, swim cap, and goggles in 32-degree Fahrenheit water from the ship *Orlova* 1.22 miles to the shores of Antarctica to research the ability of the human body to acclimate to the cold. In 2007, while writing *South with the Sun,* a book about polar explorers past and present, I followed in the wake of Roald Amundsen through the Northwest Passage, swam in colder waters, and gained a greater understanding of the issues currently affecting the polar oceans.

AS I WALKED ON THE MALIBU BEACH, a small wave rose above the Pacific Ocean and broke like the slow exhalation of a breath, sliding across the even shores of the sand, filling the air with a rush of coolness and the salty essence of the sea. Cold water rose up along our warm legs, and Cody, my Labrador retriever, wagged his long white tail. He was excited; this would be his first swim in the Pacific Ocean. I loved this moment. For years, I had watched earthbound people of all ages from different countries around the world enter the ocean for the first time. There was always a moment when their eyes grew wide and their smiles wider as the ocean lifted them into a new world. They were suddenly buoyant, swimming, flying across the ocean, unharnessed by gravity. They were free, and now my pal was, too.

As the wave lifted Cody off his paws, he turned his big white head quickly from side to side to see what was happening. He hesitated and then paddled strongly, instinctually, over the cresting wave. He was a natural-born swimmer. His nose pointed high above the water and he breathed easily, swimming at a constant pace, his long tail stretched behind him like a rudder. He looked at me with bright golden eyes, and it seemed as if he was smiling. I think he was enjoying his first swim as much as I was. I took a breath and dove down under the water to watch his underwater pull.

He was pulling efficiently, his stroke powerful. From just beneath the sea surface, Cody's stroke reminded me of a polar bear's, and I remembered what Adam Ravtech, a wildlife filmmaker and friend, had told me about polar bears, that the sea ice where they hunt for seals was receding and that the multiyear ice was disappearing. One result was that the chunks of floating ice that the bears would climb onto and rest, as well as leapfrog from to make it to shore, were dwindling. The bears now had to swim farther, which could exhaust them. In a warming Arctic, the bears' future will rely heavily on their ability to adapt and diversify their food sources.

~~~

LIKE THE POLAR BEARS, our future as human beings will depend on our ability to adapt to the changing Arctic, our ability to recognize that everything in nature—the oceans, earth, and rest of the universe—

is interconnected, as are the relationships between all the world's great nations.

With the Arctic sea ice melting, the shipping lanes that have long been blocked by frozen seas are opening, making it cheaper and quicker to carry cargo from Europe to Asia over the top of the world through either the Northeast or Northwest Passage rather than through the Suez Canal or around the Cape of Good Hope. Minerals and energy resources that have been inaccessible for hundreds of thousands of years are becoming exploitable, and new fishing areas will open with no regulations to control either exploitation or overfishing. There will be an increase in tourism and new and growing chances for pollution.

As the Arctic Ocean opens, there needs to be an opening of minds, a way for the nations of the world to assume stewardship of the Arctic region, to manage our interests with an awareness and concern for the animals and the entire Arctic ecosystem.

This stewardship in Antarctica, in the world's most southern region, has been accomplished. On December 1, 1959, forty-nine nations signed the Antarctic Treaty, agreeing that the Antarctic would be only for peaceful purposes and for scientific research. The military is not permitted to conduct weapons testing, and the Antarctic environment is to be protected. The collaboration between scientists of the various nations, along with the humanitarian support of the U.S. military for transportation of the scientists, cargo, and support personnel, has allowed research to flourish and has given us a greater understanding of Antarctica and our connection to the universe. Antarctica has also become a great example of peace and cooperation in the world.

I believe a similar treaty is needed to protect the fragile and changing Arctic environment. In 1982, the United Nations Convention on the Law of the Sea (UNCLOS) drew up an international agreement known as the Law of the Sea Convention treaty, which defined the rights and responsibilities of individual nations in regard to how the world's oceans would be used. The treaty created guidelines for protecting the ocean environment, for managing the natural resources in the marine environment, and for running businesses.

Although the Law of the Sea Convention was negotiated to be the framework for international law for all the oceans, the Arctic nations took care to address the specific needs they foresaw in the future.

Caitlyn Antrim, the executive director of the Rule of Law Committee for the Oceans and a former deputy U.S. representative to the Law of the Sea Conference, notes,

> The LOS Convention makes three very important provisions for peace and protection of the Arctic. First, article 76 of the Convention provides clear rules based on scientific, not political, principles to establish jurisdiction over the mineral and energy resources of the Arctic shelf, ensuring that they will be managed by states with Arctic interests. Second, article 234, negotiated mainly between Canada and the United States, recognizes the right of coastal states with ice-covered exclusive economic zones to impose internationally agreed ship design standards and scientifically based rules and regulations to reduce marine pollution. The third issue, of fishing on the high seas, is likely to be addressed under the framework for regional fisheries agreements that was negotiated under the Convention in 1995. Taken together, these provisions provide for peaceful resolution of sovereignty claims and protection of the living resources and marine environment in the harsh Arctic waters. That they were negotiated three decades before they were made necessary by the melting ice is a testament to the foresight of the negotiators more than a generation ago.

One hundred fifty-eight countries plus the European Community have signed the treaty and, in the United States, the treaty has had support from Republicans and Democrats. President George W. Bush endorsed the treaty, as did Republican Senator Richard Lugar of the Foreign Relations Committee and the committee's chairman, Democrat John Kerry, who said at the time, "Acceding to the Convention is in our national security, economic and environmental interest." But still today, the treaty has not yet been ratified, which requires a two-thirds vote of the Senate. Secretary of State Hillary Clinton has urged the

United States to ratify the treaty, and Admiral Michael Mullen, head of the Joint Chiefs of Staff, and Coast Guard Commandant Thad W. Allen also support it. President Barack Obama, raised in Hawaii, an island state embraced by the oceans, should understand the tremendous importance of the changing oceans and the need for the treaty.

The United Nations Convention on the Law of the Sea would help us have a voice in what happens in the Arctic as well as gaining us some stewardship in the far north. But the real need for the treaty is simple: We are all living together on this planet, aware that the world is getting ever more complex. A straightforward way for dealing with the challenges of managing this newly opened ocean, especially in times of pending crisis, is essential.

Antarctica on the Edge
The Future of the Southern Ocean
Jon Bowermaster

My first assignment for National Geographic *introduced
me to Antarctica twenty years ago; since then, I have been
back many times, both to its high, cold interior and to the coast
of its one-thousand-mile-long peninsula. You cannot talk about
the future of the world's ocean without talking about Antarctica's
impact on it. As Antarctica changes—and it is changing, and
fast, thanks to temperature rises along the peninsula greater
than anywhere else on the planet—it affects all of us.*

If in the final equation the surface of Earth is a single, complex system, then Antarctica is its heart, the slowly beating pump that drives the whole world. Each austral winter, a 7-million-square-mile halo of sea ice forms around the continent, and each spring, trillions of tons of freshwater are released into the ocean as it thaws. This is the planet's great annual climate cycle, the thermodynamic engine that drives the circulation of ocean currents, redistributing the sun's heat, regulating climate, forcing the upwelling of deep ocean nutrients, setting the tempo of the planet's weather. The Antarctic affects all our lives but through forces so deep and elemental that we're not even aware of them.

Conversely, the Antarctic is where global change is most clearly seen. The effects of ozone depletion and global warming are strongest in polar regions, where they are reinforced by atmospheric and meteorological conditions. Because Antarctica is essentially uninhabited and without industry, there is virtually no local pollution; any ecological and climate disturbances on the continent are certainly caused by global forces. The continent is not owned and, by international treaty, has been set aside for the pursuit of scientific discovery. From outposts spread across the frozen continent, scientists from around the world monitor Antarctica's climate, ice, and animals, assembling a picture of a planet in flux.

Global warming models from the early 1970s predicted that climatic effects of human-generated greenhouse gas emissions would be felt first and most strongly at the poles. More than two decades ago, scientists prophesied that one of the first signs of human-caused climate change would be the collapse of the Antarctic Peninsula's ice sheets. Which is exactly what is happening.

In March 2002, scientists watched the 500-billion-ton Larsen-B ice shelf shatter into thousands of icebergs before their eyes. Its breakup was an early warning sign; the collapse of the peninsular ice shelves is considered among the first indicators of global warming. What happened so dramatically to the Larsen Ice Shelf suggests the rest of the peninsula's ice may one day calve off or deteriorate. No one knows how quickly that will happen. Best-guess projections are that the melting on the peninsula will raise the world's sea levels by twenty inches to three-and-a-half feet in the next century. All this warming and shifting is also having a clear and extremely troubling impact on life around its shores.

Spurred by warming coastal air and waters, many of Antarctica's glaciers and ice shelves have accelerated their melting, suggesting that ocean levels might be irreversibly on the rise for centuries to come. The changes are detected each year by separate satellite and aircraft surveys of small glaciers along the east side of the Antarctic Peninsula, the rugged, sharply warming arm reaching toward South America, and along the giant ice sheets feeding into the Amundsen Sea.

The potential rise in seas in this century already constitutes a slow-motion catastrophe for places such as Bangladesh, New Orleans, and low-lying island nations such as the Maldives. But the findings add weight to the idea that rising seas could be a fact of life for centuries to come, requiring serious reassessment of the human penchant for living along coasts. Many of the clues to that evolution lie in Antarctica's changing ice.

THE VERY BEST WAY TO ASSESS THE STATUS of Antarctica's ice and the ocean that surrounds it is to go have a look. I have done this frequently and can report that every year the place, especially the ice along the length of its peninsula, changes. Visit one of the peninsula's science bases, Palmer (U.S.), Vernadsky (Ukrainian), or Rothera (U.K.), and invariably one longtime scientist or several will take you outside and point to this glacier or that and remark how in his or her experience—usually ten consecutive seasons or more—they've seen it recede by thirty, forty, fifty feet, exposing new land below, even new islands no one knew existed.

At the height of the austral summer of 2007–2008, I led an expedition by sea kayak, sailboat, foot, and small plane along the peninsula. The goal was to take a truly sea-level look at how that part of the continent is changing and changing fast. One caution regarding Antarctica: It is a very big place and thus hard to generalize about. (The United States could easily fit inside its continental boundaries.) Parts of Antarctica's interior, much of it covered by up to two miles of ice, are currently recording colder temperatures. But it is its long, skinny peninsula that deserves most observation. Air temperatures along its one-thousand-mile length have warmed by 5 to 9 degrees Fahrenheit (3 to 5 degrees Celsius) during the past fifty years, the greatest warming on the planet, which is having great impact on its ice, its wildlife, and its surrounding ocean.

For the previous decade, I'd been circling the world by kayak, one continent at a time, looking at both the health of the world's ocean and the lives of people who depend on it. I long knew we would complete the ten-year-long project—dubbed OCEANS 8 because it took us to seven continents plus Oceana—in Antarctica. Once we arrived, our plan was straightforward: Get as far south as possible until stopped by the ice.

THE SKY IS DARK AND CLOUD-FILLED when we lift off from King George Island in a Chilean Navy Twin Otter headed for the tip of the Antarctic Peninsula. Over Sunday morning tea, we struck a deal with the *commandante* to make a three-hour round-trip flight over the Weddell Sea. Our objective is to see just how much pack ice still surrounds Vega and James Ross islands, which we hoped to circumnavigate by kayak. The flight would be the closest look anyone would have had that season of exactly how much ice still lingered in its bays.

In Antarctica, it's all about the ice. Each year, the continent doubles in size as the sea ice freezes around it at a rate of two miles a day. Each spring, much of that frozen sea breaks away from the continent, drifts out to sea, and melts. Thanks to variations in winds, currents, and temperatures, that breakup differs each year. Sometimes the edges of the peninsula are chocked with icebergs ranging in size from small cars to sizable battleships; increasingly, its coastal waters are clear of ice. Where we are flying today is not far from where Ernest Shackleton lost his *Endurance* to the crush of the ice pack; interestingly, if he sailed down here today, the place where his ship lost its fight with the ice would now be nearly absent of ice, just black, open water.

This constantly evolving pack ice is not what the world should worry about in regard to rising sea levels. Pack ice is frozen sea, so when it melts, like the ice in a cocktail, it doesn't increase the ocean's volume. But for tens, hundreds of thousands of years, this frozen sea has protected the continent's glaciers, which run in long tongues down to ocean's edge. Today, with less pack ice and thus less protection, these freshwater glaciers are moving faster, deteriorating, calving with increased frequency, dropping more and more new ice into the sea. It is the loss of this *land* ice that has scientists around the world worried because it is happening faster than anyone predicted.

Our access to the Weddell Sea is through the Antarctic Sound, a narrow channel between the continent and northern islands. As we skim five hundred feet above the Southern Ocean, we are at first surprised by how little ice is in the channel. The big bergs I'd seen blocking the entrance to the sound for the past month, via satellite images on the Internet, had apparently been blown out.

But as we banked around to the backside of Vega Island, any optimism was dashed. Extremely thick pack ice, some of it more than a year old, choked the waters between it and James Ross Island, negating any possible route between them. Not even a major windstorm would clear these channels in time for us to paddle here. Although we could barely hear each other over the roar of the props, shared looks made it clear that the route we'd been planning for more than a year would be impossible even to attempt.

Although we were disappointed, the ice conditions below reminded me that one thing you can count on in Antarctica is that you can't count on anything. Now the adventure would begin. As we circled the islands for another look, I spread maps out on the metal floorboard and, from five hundred feet above the ice, began assessing our options.

～～～

WE TOOK OUR FIRST PADDLE STROKES on a gray day, about 150 miles down the west coast of the peninsula, circumnavigating Enterprise Island. We would spend the next several weeks nudging our way southward down the glacier-lined and iceberg-strewn western coastline of the coast as far as the ice would allow.

It was a relief to be off the sailboat, sausaged into dry suits, and snugged up in the carbon-fiber-Kevlar-and-fiberglass kayaks. The sea was calm as we pulled around the first corner to find the channel leading out to the Gerlache Strait choked with icebergs. Near shore, we thudded the specially designed kayaks through thick brash ice, like paddling through a field of bucket-sized ice cubes. Big, spectacularly blue icebergs temporarily grounded studded the heart of the channel. Although the sky above was clear and windless, the far horizon was dark and foreboding, a snowstorm on its way.

We spend our days over the next few weeks coming and going from our support boat, camping, climbing, exploring by paddle and foot. Ten days into our exploration, we pull our kayaks onto the rocks at Peter-mann Island, where we'd spied from the sea a trio of yellow tents, unusual in a region that only a few dozen scientists call home for three months each year.

Calling out, I hear rustling from inside one of the tents, and Melissa Rider crawls out under a light snowfall. Pulling up the hood of her red parka, she introduces herself and motions to follow her alongside a penguin trail, deep-etched into the snow, for one of her thrice-daily countings of the Adélie and Gentoo penguins and blue-eyed cormorants that nest here. This is the fifth summer in a row she's camped on Petermann, along with another two penguin counters, on behalf of the Washington DC–based environmental group Oceanites, which has been monitoring wildlife in Antarctica for nearly two decades. On Petermann, the results are clear: The Adélie penguins are disappearing.

"French explorer Jean-Baptiste Charcot was here one hundred years ago," says Rider as we walk, "and photographed the island covered with penguins, so we know exactly how much things have changed. In the past five years, the Adélie population is down dramatically."

"Dying?" I ask.

"Perhaps but not necessarily," she says. "They may just be moving further south. They are a cold-loving bird and are having a hard time 'making a living' here, which means building nests, having chicks, and feeding them. It's simply gotten too warm for them, which I can't believe I'm saying since it's Antarctica. What we don't know is where they are going. . . . There aren't many scientists working further south of here to monitor them.

"I was surprised when I started coming here four years ago; I had worked previously in other, colder parts of Antarctica. One hour after the first time I arrived, it started to rain and didn't stop for fourteen days. I was shocked. All this warming means that just since last year, we've lost 20 percent of the Adélie population on Petermann. If you do the numbers, that means the island will be devoid of them by 2020."

∿∿∿

RICK ATKINSON CAME TO ANTARCTICA as a sled dog driver for the British Antarctic Survey when he was twenty years old. Thirty-five years later, he's still coming back, though his job has changed. He now oversees a World Heritage site on the tiny island known as Port Lockroy, Antarctica's only retail shop, which was visited last season by nearly 17,000 cruise ship tourists and sold them eight tons of T-shirts and fleece. He sometimes sees two and three ships a day and welcomes as many as 300 visitors a day. "It's a draining, full-time job," he says, "but I keep coming back for the beauty of Antarctica. No two days, no two seasons, are ever alike."

Like the penguin counters, Atkinson is very worried about the warming temperatures along the peninsula and the accompanying rains. What used to be snowstorms that lasted for days are now drenching rains. For me, the rain and its impact on Antarctica's ice is the clearest sign I've seen of how warming conditions are affecting Antarctica's ice and threatening the world's sea levels. The penguin chicks that cover Port Lockroy are Antarctica's canaries in the coal mine.

"The penguin chicks are suffering and dying because of all the rain," he says. "Their nice, fluffy downy coats, which keep them protected from the dry and cold, are soaking wet. The only thing that's keeping them alive is that they have full bellies. If the rain suddenly stops and the temperatures drop, thousands will die.

"Last year, it was a different problem. We had hot, sunny weather, which the chicks don't deal with well either. They couldn't cool down, and the skuas chased them until they were dropping from heat exhaustion.

"But this rain is the worst thing that can possibly happen to Antarctica. It's a triple whammy: It falls into the crevasses, lubricates the base of the glaciers so they move even faster, and eliminates the insulating layer that keeps the snow solid. The result is that each year, there is less and less ice."

I counter that from our kayaks, it still looks like there's a hell of a lot of ice, that the peninsula resembles one Alaska piled on another Alaska piled on yet another.

"True, but ice has a horrible habit of disappearing very fast when you get to a critical point," he says, "and I think we are at that point now."

～～～

THE ANTARCTIC TREATY, signed by forty-nine nations in 1959 and amended most recently in 1991, specifies that Antarctica is to be home solely to international science and cooperation, not to nationalistic claims or military. Neither environmental concerns nor the impact of tourism was mentioned in the original document. At that time, no one ever thought either could reach this remote corner.

The treaty did ban resource exploitation from the continent and, in 1991, it extended that protection, primarily against oil and minerals prospecting, until 2041. But today, those seemingly ironclad dictates are being tested. Just as we are witnessing in the Arctic as its ice disappears, as Antarctica's ice changes, nations are starting to negotiate anew over who owns what. Since man first stepped onto Antarctica, its ice has protected it from drilling for oil and mining the diamonds buried under it. Offshore oil rigs are impractical here, threatened by the miles-long icebergs that prowl the Southern Ocean. But as technology improves and the ice along the peninsula continues to disappear, there are renewed fights on the horizon over ownership.

Most brazenly, in November 2007, the U.K. announced a new claim to nearly one-quarter of the continent, overlapping claims made decades ago by Chile and Argentina. Its rationale? To reclaim a pre-treaty claim just as ownership of Antarctica's coastal shelf was being argued over by the United Nations. During our exploration, we would see evidence at a few of the bases of far more military men than scientists, representing nations that don't want to give up their claims on Antarctica but are not willing to put money into real science programs. (Fights for "ownership" have been going on for years; on King George Island, where there are nine science stations and a runway long enough to land big cargo planes, Chile has flown in a pregnant woman to give birth in Antarctica so it can say it has Antarctica's only "native peoples." Road maps in both Argentina and Chile still include their pie slices of Antarctica claims, which were supposed to be rendered moot by the treaty more than fifty years ago.)

$\sim\sim\sim$

VERY REAL SCIENCE IS STILL DONE at the Ukrainian base of Vernadsky. Once a British base called Faraday, ten years ago the U.K. opted to give it to the Ukrainians rather than tear it down when it decided to give it up. We pull into the base on a sunny day, knowing it will be the last contact we'll have with humans for the next two hundred miles. South from here, Antarctica grows more exposed, windier, and wilder, even less forgiving.

Fourteen Ukrainian men live, sleep, and work at Vernadsky for twelve continuous months. Strangers when they begin their yearlong assignment, most from Kiev, they continue what may be the best meteorological record on the continent, started by the Brits and going back more than fifty years, the best record of just how much temperatures here are warming. It was at this metal-and-cement block station that the ozone hole growing above Antarctica was discovered twenty years before.

A rudimentary wooden ladder leads up to a tiny bedroom where, five times a day, Dennis, a geophysicist from Kiev known here simply as Ozone Man, slides back a small square panel in the roof and pushes the scope of his oblong measuring machine out into the sky. Every day for more than twenty years, someone has been doing exactly the same from this same small room, and it is the reason the world knows about the ozone hole, which was created by manufactured chlorofluorocarbons (CFCs) in the atmosphere.

Black ponytail hanging down his back, light-blue overalls over a heavy wool sweater, Ozone Man shows us graphs pinned to the wall, charting the monthly variations in ozone coverage going back two decades. It was at its thinnest in 1993–1994, and he explains how proud he is to be the sole monitor of the hole for the world, which has rethickened during the past decade, in part due to the worldwide ban on new CFCs.

When I suggest amazement that such a seemingly simple machine jammed up through a small hole in the roof is responsible for such an important discovery, he jumps at me, smiling. "It is not a simple machine! There are very complicated opticals inside! There is nothing automatic about it; it is all manual. It is the very best!" When the Brits first discovered the ozone hole, they replaced the machine, thinking it might have been askew. When the new machine returned the same results, they reinstalled the original. The discovery of the ozone hole, and its mitigation, is an international environmental success story, one that gives some small hope that the problem of Antarctica's disappearing ice may be solved, too.

~~~

A WEEK AFTER PADDLING AWAY FROM VERNADSKY, on a sunshine-filled January day, we reach nearly 68 degrees south, at the southernmost point of Crystal Sound. Two degrees south of the Antarctic Circle, the temperatures reach into the 40s, and sunburn is our biggest concern.

Our map shows a pair of narrow channels leading farther south to Marguerite Bay. Our goal is to sneak through one, but as we attempt to thread our way by kayak through the two-foot-thick pancake ice, we run into solid ice running several miles to shore. Through powerful binoculars, we can see that both channels we'd hoped to navigate are frozen solid. Clambering onto an ice floe, we pull our kayaks up and consider our options. One is to drag the kayaks twenty-five to thirty miles over the ice to Marguerite Bay, which might allow us to keep paddling south. The downside is we would most likely have to drag them back again, requiring a weeklong journey we simply can't afford. Sadly, like every visitor to Antarctica, we've reached our turnaround point.

To celebrate our southernmost point, we dig a red cabbage out of the hold, jump up onto a big sheet of floating ice, strip to a solitary layer of fleece, and, under a hot Antarctic sun, play a short game of cabbage rugby before turning around and heading for a long, slow, beautiful ride back north, away from the ice.

Every season I come to Antarctica, I leave with a mix of joy and regret. The former because I know I will continue coming back to this spectacular corner of our ocean world. The regret because, each year, the place changes and not for the better. One note of optimism is that, thanks to the unique treaty that governs Antarctica, it remains an example of how countries around the world have banded together not for riches but for the common good. Suggesting that if there are solutions to solving the risks facing Antarctica and its surrounding ocean that can be found by international agreement, there just might be solutions nations could work on together to address other, seemingly daunting challenges facing Planet Ocean.

PART III

SAVING IT

Water Planet
Leonardo DiCaprio

*For ten years, the Leonardo DiCaprio Foundation has funded
social action, education, and short films on environmental issues,
including the feature documentary* The 11th Hour.

Consider this.

We live on a water planet.

Through the millennia, the water cycle has supported all life.

Water shapes the weather, the seasons, and the climate and provides habitats for most of the world's living things; most of them, including us, are almost entirely made up of water.

Now consider this. Water is a finite resource. A limited resource. Only a tiny fraction of the earth's water is fresh.

It supports everything from agriculture and sanitation to aquatic ecosystems such as rivers and streams. Water falls unevenly across the planet, and much of it is locked up in glaciers, permanent snow cover, ice, and permafrost. Water is also stuck underground, deep in the earth and hard to reach.

To make matters worse, water is threatened by pollution, overpopulation, climate change, mismanagement, and war.

Pollution is so severe that diseases are increasing in both humans and animals, and habitats are being destroyed. Rain is turning into acid. So many chemicals flow into rivers and lakes that the actual composition of water in some places has been fundamentally changed.

Human encroachment is also drying out aquifers, diverting the natural flow of rivers, and straining water supplies. Hidden in everyday consumption is the careless and unnecessary waste of water.

Dams displace millions of people and destroy whole ecosystems.

Global warming is altering the water cycle, causing more severe and unpredictable flooding and droughts, ultimately shifting where water flows. Unregulated corporate privatization threatens access to water for the poor. Some governments fail to deliver water where it is needed most. These stresses have created military and political conflicts that will only get worse.

Ultimately, humanity is poisoning, squandering, and overburdening water resources. The result is that billions of people lack access to clean water. Millions of children die every year from preventable waterborne diseases. Lack of clean water and basic sanitation cracks people in poverty. People are fighting and dying for it.

We are at a crisis point, but we still have time to turn this around. We can conserve water, not waste it. Invest in smart water infrastructure and technologies. Increase environmental regulations for polluting industries. Tell government leaders to fulfill financial pledges for clean water. Ensure that water is not treated like a commodity.

But most important, we must recognize that access to clean water is a basic human right, and the United Nations should adopt a global treaty for the right to water.

Water equals life; there is no separation. By protecting water, we can protect ourselves and this blue planet for future generations.

Stories from a Blue Planet

Alexandra Cousteau

In 2009, Alexandra's Expedition: Blue Planet took her and a small crew to five continents in one hundred days, to tell the stories of our water planet and the interconnectivity of our water resources. From the depths of the ocean to the peaks of mountains, she found herself constantly seeing the link between the ocean, our freshwater resources, and the sustainability of human societies.

The ancients told of water. Carved deeply in stone and crafted carefully in story and song, their superstitions and histories and wisdoms cascade across centuries and flow through our lives today: "From the heights of a mountain . . . ," "By the banks of a river . . . ," "Upon the shores of a homeland . . . ," and so the stories go. And so we tell them still. For history has always been written in water.

And yet, for all the wonder and worship, throughout most of human history the mysteries of this water planet were out of sight and beyond understanding. The oceans were vast unknowable surfaces across which ships sailed bravely in search of wealth or distant lands and adventure. Beneath this plane lay a mysterious void filled by the wild creatures of myth, an inexhaustible supply of fish, or some combination of both. Rivers cradled civilizations, nurturing the evolution of societies while carrying away the waste and transgressions of communities. And the rains came as they would for reasons most everyone could explain but seldom in the same way or for the same purpose. So man spoke of water as one who sees without knowing, hoping somehow to explain the wonders beyond and beneath the water planet he called home.

But as time passed, the siren call of exploration tempted the hearts of both pilgrims and wanderers to pierce the dark night of ignorance and see the planets spinning, to step beyond the binding traditions of mortality and think the thoughts of gods. And they too told of water. Some throwing sheets into the wind would rush to the edge of the world to drown echoes of scorn beneath a bending horizon. Some would chart water's course through our veins and some would harness its steam to build a bigger and better life. So story follows story as man wielded reason and exploration to unravel the mysteries of his world.

But in spite of centuries of charting the expanses of Earth's boundaries, no one had yet searched out the depths of her oceans, and this frustrated my grandfather, Jacques-Yves Cousteau. Tethered to shallow, short dives by the aching in his lungs, he longed to see more, to know more, and so, as centuries of explorers before him had done, he sat down with a friend to rewrite the boundaries. The invention they would call the Aqua-Lung in 1943 allowed humans to explore the underwater world for the first time, opening new fields of study and changing how we understand much of our natural surroundings.

The thrill of what he saw—of what he discovered—was more than he could contain, and soon he was back at the drawing board to design gear for my grandmother Simone and, eventually, even for my father, Philippe.

Just four years old when his father taught him to dive, my father was so exuberant about all he saw beneath the calm surface of the water— a darting school of fish here, a brightly colored coral there, a waving forest of life just beyond—that he repeatedly tried to call out to my grandfather. He was blissfully unaware that each exclamation caused the regulator to fall out of his mouth, which my grandfather deftly and repeatedly replaced to keep his small, excited son from drowning.

When they finally got back aboard the ship, my grandfather scolded my father for his reckless enthusiasm, saying, "You must be quiet underwater because it is a silent world." My grandfather's description of the new world to which he had introduced my father that day later became the title of his best-selling book and Oscar-winning documentary, *The Silent World*. And so we Cousteaus have joined the generations of those who tell the stories of water.

Twenty-six years and a host of inventions, discoveries, and awards would follow from that day. President John F. Kennedy would bestow the National Geographic's Gold Medal on my grandfather at a White House ceremony honoring his work. The award-winning series he developed, *The Undersea World of Jacques Cousteau,* would be welcomed into living rooms around the world. His storytelling would launch a new generation of environmentalists and forever change how we see the oceans. And then Neil Armstrong walked on the moon.

I remember my grandfather telling me that the day he saw the headlines, "Two Men Walk on the Moon" (knowing my grandfather, probably not without some healthy envy), was the day he knew our perception of the world would forever change. For the first time, we saw ourselves from outer space and realized unmistakably that our planet is in fact blue. Finally, people would see what he saw every day from the deck of the *Calypso*: We live on a water planet.

By the time I would arrive on the scene, joining the family for an expedition to Easter Island at just four months old, the role of humans in the story of water had changed dramatically, moving from awestruck witness to actor and from actor somehow to author.

When I took my grandfather's hand as my father had done, to slip beneath the same waves off the southern coast of France for my first dive at the age of seven, the giant grouper my father had observed, weighing as much as 400 pounds, had been wiped out. Today, the red tuna that I watched on my first dive are quickly disappearing, and by the time I have children old enough to dive, this species of tuna will likely be extinct.

With each new generation, reason replaces wonder, and soon reason is lost to resource. Across the ages, water has been god and goddess to the ancients—source of life and death and savior of souls. She has played the muse for the awakening spirit and laid down a highway for the restless. But having seemingly exhausted her store of "new" places, we've returned to carve up the old, liquidating her bounty as though our ability to extract and carry to market were a license to sell what those before us intended for our children.

For the first time in history, humans have the ability to reach far beyond the environs of the local to consume and affect water in places their eyes will never rest upon and upon which their feet will never fall. Our technologies for extraction and global exchange are not limited by the hours of the sun. We have expanded our consumption to the farthest points of the earth and plumbed the depths of our oceans. Carefully crafted, that reach can end the ancient scourges of hunger, thirst, and abject poverty as resources and technology from one region provide sustenance for another and exchange generates opportunity for progress. But out of balance, our nearly insatiable quest for profit drains ancient stores to irrigate industrial crops, often of marginal or subsidized value. It scrapes the oceans bare to gather a few marketable species, leaving the rest to rot and none to restore. And it propagates a willful ignorance of the impacts of our waste as if science ends at the exhaust pipe or does not reach into the watershed or past the boundaries of property lines or arbitrary jurisdictions. Out of balance, our thirst exhausts our ability to reason. Out of balance, our reach exhausts our resources. Out of balance, the gifts of our fathers bring a curse to our children. And we are out of balance.

Nearly every system that shapes the availability and quality of water on our planet is dramatically and historically out of balance. From the nitrogen and phosphorus cycles to the carbon cycle, local ecosystems, and more, our century of progress has largely ignored the simple principles of basic grade-school science: We share a single interconnected hydrosphere, one that puts us each quite literally downstream from one another.

The view my grandfather commanded from the deck of the *Calypso* for a good deal of the past century and the images Armstrong brought us from space both set the stage for putting our water planet into perspective. Indeed, 71 percent of Earth is covered by water. But only a tiny percentage of that water is fit for human consumption. In fact, if you could fit all the water in the world into a gallon jug, less than a teaspoon of that would be available for our use. Our actions throughout the full water cycle dramatically affect that tiny teaspoon. And with climate change escalating the impacts of cycles out of balance, that teaspoon is shrinking.

But that isn't all. The quality of the water in the teaspoon is declining as well. Runoff and pollution have led to dead zones throughout our oceans. In India, hundreds of tanneries dump chemicals into the sacred Ganges. Aquifers are falling in the Middle East, in the United States, and around the world. A simple look at water consumption in the great and growing cities of the world makes it clear that we are racing down a collision course with history, doomed to be remembered by the same epitaph that marks the ghostly ruins of the once great Khmer Empire, builders of Cambodia's Angkor Wat: Unsustainable consumption of resources, mismanagement of critical infrastructure, and destruction of water-shaping ecosystems during a period of climate change leads to collapse.

The rulers of Angkor may not have understood what they were risking, but we do. Water is the mark of sustainability in a society and the canvas on which the pendulum of our struggle to maintain balance traces shaky arcs that ripple throughout our systems. It is within these telling ripples—the shrinking surfaces of our ice stores, the erratic running of our rivers, the shifting patterns of precipitation, and the rising of our seas—that we have already begun to feel the effects of climate change. In the face of such a challenge, in just such a moment, we can't afford to continue dealing with water issues in sterile little silos. We cannot continue to make the focus of our conversation on "water" just about the fragility of coral reefs, the scarcity of free-flowing river habitat, or the depletion of fish stocks. We can't continue to divide over protecting fresh-water of a single region or focusing on the world's oceans.

So it could be said that the challenge for my generation is largely about establishing a new water perspective and ethos, one recognizing that it is this regionalized and compartmentalized understanding of water that has led to many of the poor management practices that we have as a society. It is our insistence on confining water policies and water rights to the autonomous circles of "agriculture," "energy," "industrial use," "human consumption," "rivers and streams," "oceans," and so on that has led to wholly independent and often entirely incongruent systems of standards, measurements, and practices. Confined to neat bubbles of discussion and management, we've failed to build and maintain intelligent infrastructure and, too often, in our pursuit of progress, we've completely destroyed the water-shaping ecosystems that could have provided sustainable solutions. It truly is time for us to redefine what it means to live sustainably on a water planet.

With this in mind, my work took a decidedly global scope when Blue Legacy, the nonprofit I founded in 2008, secured funding to launch our first expedition in February 2009. Traveling from the oceans that in so many ways have defined much of my family's history, I made my way to the roof of the world, to the Himalayas, where the tallest mountains on Earth rise and seven great rivers begin. Fed by the snow and ice blanketing these stunning peaks, the Ganges, Mekong, Yangtze, and their four sister rivers support a stunning 2 billion people—nearly one out of every three people in the world.

My expedition team and I pushed high into the mountains, tracing our way to the glaciers that feed those rivers. We stopped at the mountaintop temple of Kunjari, where tiger statues guard the gates and pilgrims ring bells for entrance. Pilgrims of a different sort, we climbed what felt like a million steps, pausing often to catch our breath in the thin mountain air. And at the top, we stood still for a moment, lifted our eyes, and gazed out at the landscape.

As stunning as it was, we had not traveled all these miles and climbed these steps to see its beauty. We were there to tell the story of water. And in the shadow of the mighty mountains, we witnessed fragility. The Himalayas are the largest storehouse of freshwater outside the polar ice caps. And like so many others, the Himalayan glaciers are melting as a result of global climate change. They are retreating ten to fifteen meters every year, with science predicting that they could disappear altogether within twenty-five years, perhaps even sooner.

As Professor Veer Bhadra Mishra, the Mahant of Varanasi's second-largest Hindu temple and an ardent environmentalist, would share with us so poignantly, the "waters of Mother Ganga (the Ganges) would someday flow in the Hudson," would fall on the plains of Africa, would make a cup of tea. And yet, for the nearly 1 billion Hindus of the world, 900 million of whom live in India, the seasonality brought to the Ganges by climate change would spell the end of the most enduring symbol of the world's oldest living religion. We strolled the streets and villages with that inescapable thought in mind. The sacred promise for so many was quickly being laid low by a century's quest for progress; the pollution clouding its pools was stealing health while failing sources were robbing hope.

The impact on the rivers and everything that depends upon them— from rainfall patterns to wildlife to agriculture—will be disastrous. Ecosystems will collapse. Hundreds of millions of people will be displaced. And the steady rivers that once shaped the course of society and the soul of cultures will shift seasonally, delivering floods and landslides to some and unimaginable drought to others. This is not theory. It's not opinion. It's a fact. Unless we do something, all of this will come to pass within our own generation.

So this is the water story my generation is left to tell, for we must each tell the stories of our own time. And while I still love to steal away to experience anew the nearly sacred silence of the underwater world my grandfather showed me as a small child, I remain convinced that it takes bearing the weight of the known to claim progress in discovering the new. The solutions for the challenges of our day will be born of restoring balance in how we understand and interact with water in our daily lives, for history has always been written in water. And as it falls to me to bridge the days between the stories I've been told and the ones I will tell my own children, I'm determined to live this moment so they will someday speak not of what was but of what can be.

Why We Need a National Ocean Policy

Christopher Mann

The Pew Charitable Trusts has long been a leader in promoting ocean conservation and education, twinning scientific research with advocacy. Its Pew Ocean Commission reports, published in 2003, helped set a national agenda for ocean issues. Chris is a senior officer with the Pew Environment Group, its environmental emissary to both Congress and the executive branch. He firmly believes the current administration will make the ocean a priority where others have not.

OCEANS IN CRISIS

The oceans are the cradles of life on this planet. The ancient progenitors of land animals first slithered out of the seas some 350 million years ago, but human beings return to that primordial nursery time and time again for sustenance and nurture. We are drawn to it by its rich bounty of life and minerals, to be sure, and because since prehistoric times it has provided a vital means of transportation. But there is something more that draws us to the sea. Something about the sights, sounds, and smells of that briny stew of all things living and not living on the planet that compels us to seek out its power, majesty, and mystery.

And what a mystery it is for most of us. It is amazing how little most people know about a natural system that covers 71 percent of the planet's surface and has played such a huge role in shaping our history and culture.

Human beings are, after all, terrestrial animals, so perhaps we can be forgiven for failing to understand something so seemingly alien. For all but a few decades of our history, we were able to do little more than tow nets in the deep and examine what came up. Imagine how primitive our understanding of forest or desert ecology would be if the scientists studying those ecosystems were forced to fly over them at several thousand feet, scooping up animals and plants and trying to reconstruct how the whole thing works together. Although advances in technology in the second half of the twentieth century have enabled us to begin to get a much more detailed—and nuanced—understanding of how marine ecosystems work, this understanding is still relatively primitive but is evolving rapidly.

The very technologies that have allowed us at long last to begin to understand the environment that most life on the planet calls home have also unlocked the door to the unprecedented exploitation of that life. We have now reached a point at which our technology, combined with our sheer numbers, is leading to widespread degradation of the oceans. In the late nineteenth century, ocean fisheries were considered by leading marine scientists of the day to be virtually inexhaustible. By the end of the twentieth century, we would prove those scientists wrong.

Marine mammals were the first to go. Large and relatively slow moving, and vulnerable because of their need to surface for air, the great whales were decimated even with nineteenth-century technology. Seals, sea lions, sea otters, and manatees could be shot or harpooned from shore or small boats. They were quickly reduced to a fraction of their former abundance. A number of species vanished and others teeter on the brink of extinction. Diesel engines, and mechanically propelled harpoons with exploding heads, brought many whale species to the brink of extinction in the second half of the twentieth century.

Fish fared better for a while because they were more numerous and harder to get to. But with the powerful diesel engines and sonar developed during World War II, fishing vessels could fish in deeper water, travel faster and farther from shore, and pull huge trawl and purse seine nets to snare ever larger numbers of fish. Deployment of these technologies was subsidized by governments eager to take advantage of the seemingly endless bounty of the seas and to supply a burgeoning postwar population with relatively inexpensive protein. After all, it was free for the taking. The fact that marine resources are seemingly free goods turns out to be the root of the problem, but we'll return to that later.

Scientific research shows that more than 90 percent of large fish are now gone from the oceans. The giant bluefin tuna, whose image graced ancient Greek urns, is in danger of commercial extinction from over-fishing. Sharks are slow growing and slow to reproduce, yet they are being harvested by the tens of millions each year, often only for their fins. After a shark is finned, it is often thrown overboard to spiral down to its death, bleeding out and unable to swim or breathe. Although we both fear and admire these awesome predators, the marine predator we should be most concerned with is ourselves.

The unparalleled fishing grounds of Georges Bank off Cape Cod, which for five hundred years supplied cod and other fish for food and trade, have been brought to their knees by industrial overfishing. Stocks of cod are at a few percent of their historical level, and fishermen are now limited to a few days a year of fishing effort. Despite a near-cessation of targeted fishing for cod on Georges Bank, the stocks have failed to recover, and some scientists believe that the ecosystem might have been pushed so far that the cod may not come back, even if left unfished. Unfortunately, these grim patterns are being repeated all around the globe as too many boats pursue too few fish with lethal modern technology. Despite their amazing capacity to produce protein, we have found—and exceeded—the ability of marine ecosystems to replenish the life that we are extracting.

What we take out of the oceans is only half the problem. Although overfishing is probably the greatest single threat to the structure and functioning of marine ecosystems, the water pollution and marine debris we put into the oceans is fouling the very waters we rely on to produce the fish that we—and the marine mammals and seabirds that have nowhere else to go for dinner—eat. Many industrial chemicals and other residues of modern society are toxic to marine life, and whether they go on the lawn, to the landfill, or down the drain, they all end up in the sea eventually. In developed nations, people consume so many drugs, such as pain relievers and antibiotics, that these chemicals are being found in fish and other aquatic organisms, with poorly understood effects on the organisms themselves and the ecosystems they inhabit.

Plastics are ubiquitous nowadays, and the vast majority is not recycled. Much of it ends up washing down storm drains into rivers and eventually to the sea. Researchers have documented an area twice the size of Texas in the central Pacific where ocean currents concentrate plastic and marine debris. This ocean trash heap has approximately doubled in size since the early 1990s, and researchers suspect ocean currents are piling up trash in similar ways in the Sea of Japan and the Sargasso Sea. Sea turtles and seabirds frequently mistake floating plastic for jellyfish and other natural food sources. Many of these creatures are found dead, starved of real food, their guts stuffed with plastic. This is of particular concern for some species of birds and turtles, which are already endangered by a variety of factors, including habitat loss and accidental ensnarement by fishing gear.

Used in the right amounts, fertilizers have been a great boon to humanity. By increasing and helping maintain crop yield, they have contributed substantially to the "green revolution" in agriculture. But too much of a good thing can be bad, and these fertilizers, particularly nitrogen, are often applied incorrectly or in too large an amount. When excess fertilizer runs off of cropland, lawns, or golf courses, it can cause excess algae growth in our estuaries and coastal waters. Although algae are the base of the marine food chain, too much of it clouds the water, blocking light for sea grasses, an important habitat for fish and crustaceans. When these algal blooms die off, the natural processes through which bacteria decompose this excess organic matter can consume all the oxygen in the water, resulting in dead zones where fish and other marine life cannot live. Although fluctuations in oxygen level are a natural part of the seasonal cycle in many estuaries and coastal waters, the massive addition of nitrogen and other nutrients by human beings has spun up this cycle to many times its natural level, so much so that huge areas of oxygen-starved water are now annual occurrences in the Gulf of Mexico, off the Oregon coast, in the Chesapeake Bay, and in other areas.

One of the greatest threats to the health of marine ecosystems is one that has only recently been recognized: the effects of global climate change on the oceans. It is easy to appreciate that rising sea level will affect marine as well as human life. Although sea levels fluctuate naturally over geological time, the rise in sea level due to the thermal expansion of water and the addition of freshwater from the melting of glaciers and the polar ice caps may occur too rapidly for wetlands, coral reefs, and other important habitats to adapt. Water can naturally absorb a lot of heat, but an increase of just a degree or two in sea temperature can affect the survival and reproduction of corals, fish, and a wide variety of marine species. Changes in salinity and water temperature affect ocean circulation, with large-scale implications for the structure and functioning of marine ecosystems.

The increase in greenhouse gases affects the chemistry of the oceans as well as the atmosphere. As the concentration of carbon dioxide increases in the atmosphere, more of it is absorbed by the oceans as well. When carbon dioxide dissolves in water, it produces acid. The increased acidity of seawater resulting from global climate change threatens the base of the marine food chain. Shellfish and many kinds of plankton make their protective shells out of calcium carbonate—chalk. At a certain level of acidity, it becomes impossible for these creatures to produce and maintain their shells, and they die. This threat is particularly acute in the Arctic and Antarctica because the colder, less saline water near the poles absorbs more carbon dioxide than warmer water.

In fact, all of this is a lot to absorb, but the take-home message is this: Our society has reached the point at which what it puts into and takes out of our oceans is profoundly degrading marine ecosystems. We obviously depend on the oceans for economic goods, but we also depend on them for ecological services, like air and water purification, which cannot be replaced at any price. We like to think of the oceans as a wild place, and in some ways, they still are. But in more ways than not, our oceans, like the rest of the planet, are now dominated by the activities and the pressures of more than 6 billion human beings.

If we don't find some balance, some equilibrium, between the demands we place on the oceans and their capacity to renew themselves, they will suffer irrevocable harm. And because we so depend on the oceans, economically, culturally, and spiritually, the harm we inflict on the oceans we ultimately inflict on ourselves. The question is no longer whether we need to do something about this. The question is what we will do and whether it is in time to save our seas.

THE TRAGEDY OF THE COMMONS

In 1968, Garrett Hardin published a seminal paper in *Science*, titled "The Tragedy of the Commons," in which he explains why any resource open to common use almost inevitably will become overexploited. In simple terms, overuse occurs because nearly all the benefit from using a resource (such as catching a fish or disposal of waste) inures to the individual, whereas the cost of degradation of the resource is spread among all the users.

There is no better example of the tragedy of the commons than our oceans. With no overarching framework for their management and no entity responsible for their well-being, the world's oceans bear the cumulative effect of a growing list of ad hoc resource-use decisions. Most of these decisions are rational from the standpoint of the individuals who make them, but the cost to society is cumulative and growing. Making matters worse, most ocean activities are managed under laws and pro-grams narrowly designed to address specific management needs as they arise, such as ocean fisheries, offshore oil and gas development, and water pollution. According to the U.S. Commission on Ocean Policy, in the United States there are some twenty federal agencies that administer more than 140 laws affecting the oceans. Under these many laws, agencies often have overlapping or conflicting mandates. This is a recipe for chaos, confusion, and—ultimately—degradation of our ocean resources.

Given the large and growing number of ocean uses and ocean users, single-sector management approaches are simply not up to the task of addressing the complex interactions and effects of multiple stressors on the oceans. After all, you can drill for oil, float wind turbines, or ship cargo over a warm, dead ocean, but you can't fish in it, and you wouldn't want to swim in it. To address these shortcomings, two ocean commissions in the United States recommended that narrow single-sector resource management give way to a more integrated ecosystem-based approach implemented at the regional level and supported at the national level. The changes in ocean governance recommended by the Pew Oceans Commis-sion and the congressionally chartered U.S. Commission on Ocean Policy would be a transformative and much-needed change both in the way society views the oceans and in the way we manage our ocean resources.

This does not suggest that we will no longer need laws and policies governing individual activities such as fishing. Management of specific activities requires specific expertise and conservation measures. But unless and until we insist that our government take responsibility for the overall health of the oceans, the seas will continue to be degraded by the tyranny of small decisions.

Since the ocean commissions released their findings in 2003, progress has been mixed. A number of states have adopted a more comprehensive approach to ocean planning and management in their own waters and are working with adjacent states on regional efforts. Yet these state-based efforts to improve ocean management are limited to the narrow band of coastal waters over which they have jurisdiction and are frustrated by the lack of coordination among federal activities.

Congress has enacted important reforms putting fisheries management on a more sustainable course. But marine ecosystems are about much more than fish. Although science-based fisheries management is a critical element of sound ocean management, fisheries management cannot by itself safeguard the health of marine ecosystems. And it is the overall health of marine ecosystems on which fisheries ultimately depend. Legislation to put in place the broader ocean governance reforms recommended by the ocean commissions has been introduced in Congress but has never moved beyond the subcommittee level.

As we struggle to transform our energy economy, there is renewed interest in offshore oil and gas extraction as well as in emerging opportunities for ocean renewable-energy development. At the same time, the environmental damage that our dependence on fossil fuels is causing to marine and terrestrial ecosystems alike has become more apparent. These new challenges are perhaps nowhere more evident than in the Arctic, where a poorly understood ecosystem already under stress from rapid environmental change is at the same time being exposed by reduction in ice cover to increased resource extraction and maritime traffic.

A NATIONAL OCEAN POLICY FOR THE UNITED STATES

President Obama took an important step to address needed changes in ocean governance when he established an interagency ocean policy task force in June 2009 to recommend a national policy to protect, maintain, and restore the health of marine ecosystems. The president directed the task force to formulate a national ocean policy, a strategy for its implementation, and the institutional and planning framework to carry it out. This effort engages the broad suite of government agencies with activities that take place in or significantly affect the oceans. It is chaired by the White House Council on Environmental Quality, which is responsible for coordinating environmental policy among the many federal agencies. That is exactly what is needed here: an entity with the president's ear and the authority to coordinate among the many agencies and departments whose combined activities have a profound effect on ocean health.

The broad outlines of that plan have already been transmitted to the White House, and a final report from the task force is expected to be delivered to the president early in 2010. With luck, by the time you read this, the president will have codified in an executive order a national ocean policy and the structural and procedural means for its implementation in the water.

Having the federal government, on behalf of the people, actively and explicitly take responsibility for protecting, maintaining, and restoring the health of marine ecosystems is a critical first step in averting the tragedy of the commons for our oceans. Legal jurisdiction over the oceans is divided between the states and the federal government, with coastal states generally controlling marine resources out three miles from the shore and the federal government controlling resources in the exclusive economic zone, or EEZ, which extends from three miles to two hundred miles offshore. The problem is that the marine ecosystems that provide the goods and services we want from the oceans do not coincide neatly with our arbitrary legal jurisdictions. To address the mismatch between ecosystem and jurisdictional boundaries, the federal government should plan and manage ocean uses on an ecosystem basis within its geographic purview; provide incentives for states, Indian tribes, and local govern- ments to take an ecosystem approach; and coordinate regional planning and management with these entities.

The process that the president has set in motion is critical, but it is only the first step. Formal establishment of a national ocean policy must be followed by robust implementation in the water. The president will need to provide ongoing leadership to ensure that the often fractious federal agencies continue to work together toward a common set of goals. The initial progress is encouraging, but damage done over many decades will not heal overnight, and the new linkages across jurisdictional lines will need to be nurtured and reinforced.

After establishing a national ocean policy, the Obama administration needs to take some important steps over the next two years to give that policy life beyond the shelf. First, the federal government needs to develop and carry out detailed action plans to make sure that the lofty rhetoric of a national ocean policy has impact on and in the water. The president's task force has embraced the need to plan and manage the wide and growing variety of ocean uses on an ecosystem basis, ensure that decisions are based on science, and identify gaps in information and support research to fill those gaps. These priorities need to be incorporated into specific projects designed to improve ecosystem resiliency, restore fisheries and marine habitat, curb toxic and nutrient pollution of coastal waters, and provide comprehensive regional plans so that ecosystems and coastal communities, in the Arctic and elsewhere, are better able to adapt to global climate change.

Second, the president should request, and Congress should provide, substantial funding to implement the national ocean policy action plans. Protecting marine life may seem like a low priority in these tough economic times, until you realize that commercial and recreational activities that depend on living marine resources provide more than 2 million jobs and are responsible for more than $120 billion in annual economic activity. Although numerous programs and agencies receive funding for activities related to ocean conservation, having a coherent national policy in place will make it much easier to set budget priorities, justify their funding by Congress, and measure return on the public investment by results in the water.

In addition, the president should work with Congress to establish a permanent source of funding for ocean conservation and management. The United States receives more than $10 billion each year in royalties from the development of offshore oil and natural gas. Setting aside just 10 percent of that amount every year would dramatically increase our ability to conserve and manage marine resources. There is an inherent logic in reinvesting some of the revenue derived from development of nonrenewable marine resources into the conservation of renewable marine resources.

Last, Congress should codify the national ocean policy and the process for its implementation into federal law. In an executive order, the president can direct agencies to take action only within their discretion under existing law. There is ample discretion within the many laws governing federal ocean activities to do a much better job at ocean conservation and management. But as the agencies begin to carry out an ocean policy, they will no doubt encounter conflicts in their various mandates and gaps in their authority to achieve the spirit of that policy. Moreover, an executive order may not endure from one presidential administration to another. For both these reasons, Congress should enact the national ocean policy and the process for its implementation into law.

In the long term, a more holistic approach will provide significant benefits to marine ecosystem health and productivity. But those of us who love the oceans need to seek a deeper change—a change in society's attitude toward the ocean. Rather than a resource there for the taking, a commons for the exploiting, we need to think of it more as a water garden in need of tending. The great American naturalist Aldo Leopold wrote in *A Sand County Almanac* of the need for a land ethic—a personal and societal ethic of stewardship toward the land. To turn the corner fully from mere exploitation to stewardship of the oceans, we need an ocean ethic. The great power of democracy is that the authority of the government derives from, and only from, the people. A national ocean policy will succeed only if Americans themselves embrace, and demand that their government reflect, an ocean ethic.

A Holistic Approach to Healing the Ocean

An Interview with NOAA Administrator Jane Lubchenco

Environmental scientist, marine ecologist, and biologist, Jane was named administrator of the National Oceanic and Atmospheric Administration (NOAA) in early 2009, the top political job in the country on ocean issues. She is using everything she has learned from her many days on the sea as a scientist and activist to shape a national ocean policy. Can politics really make a difference?

Jon Bowermaster: Is it easy for you to name a highest priority?
Jane Lubchenco: There are multiple. One is definitely oceans, another is climate and, obviously, they intersect with one another. Those are the focus of NOAA's responsibilities and are just so incredibly timely right now because of the importance of oceans and the importance of addressing climate change, both on the mitigation side as well as the adaptation side.

JB: Which is easier, mitigation or adaptation?
JL: Well it's not an either/or; both are central to our future health, prosperity, and well-being. I think that one way to think about them is: Mitigation is really about avoiding the unmanageable and adaptation is about managing the unavoidable.

JB: Are you having good success selling that theory?

JL: I think that there is still a lot of educating to be done. For far too long climate change has seemed, to many Americans, like something that is so far down the road and so nebulous that it was difficult for people to understand why it mattered, or how it might affect them, or what they could do about it.

JB: And really hard to illustrate to people.

JL: It is hard, but we're making good progress. NOAA was the lead agency in a report from the federal government released in June (2009), focusing on the impact of global climate change on the United States by region and by sector. It describes changes that have already happened and that are well documented. The report is an example of the kind of information that is beginning to make a difference. Its main message is that climate change is actually happening right now, in our own backyards, and that it affects the things that people care about. From significant increases in heavy precipitation, more droughts and more floods, more extreme heat days, and sea level rise, climate change is beginning to transform the United States, affecting health, food production systems, roads, and coastal cities. Not included in the report, but important for Americans to understand, are the economic and social opportunities associated with reducing greenhouse gas pollution and growing clean energy.

JB: Is a national ocean policy a priority, something you feel strongly about accomplishing while you're in this job?

JL: A very high priority, both for the administration as well as for NOAA. Fifty percent of Americans live in coastal areas, and the other half of the country goes there to play. Increasing numbers of Americans eat seafood. Oceans help regulate our climate, provide our oxygen, and are a source of jobs as well as fun and inspiration. So what happens to the ocean impacts everybody.

It is high time that the country declared clearly what it wants from and for oceans. The task force that President Obama set up, called the Interagency Ocean Policy Task Force, recognizes that we have a responsibility to protect our oceans and coasts and Great Lakes, for both current generations and future generations. The president made it very clear in his memorandum setting up the task force that one of its charges is to recommend a national ocean policy. In September, the task force delivered an interim report to the president that describes what a national ocean policy might look like. The report sends a very clear signal that as far as the administration is concerned, healthy oceans matter, and they matter because they are vital to our health, to our prosperity, to our security, and also to our ability to adapt to climate change. They matter because they affect the quality of our life. From that policy should flow a new way of thinking about the variety of practices and policies on land and in the ocean that affect the health of the ocean. As administrator of NOAA, I find it greatly encouraging that the president and his top leadership are focusing on the oceans, why healthy oceans matter and how we can protect and restore them so that they can provide the wealth of benefits that we want and need.

JB: Do you think we'll actually see legislation titled "National Ocean Policy" during this administration, during your term?
JL: There has been interest on the Hill in doing just that, going back to the work of the Pew Oceans Commission and the U.S. Commission on Ocean Policy issued in 2003 and 2004. Clearly, Congress has a lot on its plate right now, but I truly believe it's a matter of when, not if. The decision for the members of Congress now is more about strategy. Should it focus on one holistic law or start writing legislation piece by piece? There are currently different opinions about that, all quite legitimate.

JB: Is there a nation or a region in the world that has done a good job policing their ocean coastline?
JL: I think there are a lot of lessons to be learned from a number of efforts, including some by individual states. California, for example, has some very progressive legislation; a number of states, particularly Massachusetts and New Jersey, have been creating marine spatial planning frameworks that are beginning to enable more holistic approaches to consider the combination of activities that can coexist in an area with the idea of minimizing conflict across different uses and minimizing impacts on the environment. Marine spatial planning is, in fact, one of the charges that the president gave to his Ocean Policy Task Force, to create a

framework for doing coastal and marine spatial planning. The framework will coordinate across the federal agencies and help us work in partnership with the states.

JB: Do you see a future where the U.S. coastline is dotted with marine reserves, off-limits to all fishing?
JL: The science of marine reserves is clear: No-take areas are powerful tools to protect habitats, biodiversity, and the large individuals in fish or invertebrate populations that are so critical for the future health of the population. In many cases, reserves can also help recover depleted fisheries, acting as natural hatcheries to provide a source of fish or other species to repopulate adjacent areas. They are definitely one of the tools in our tool-box, and a very important one, but not the only one. Reserves need to be considered as part of a broader strategy that considers what kinds of activities, what kinds of use, and what kinds of protection are needed in different areas of the ocean, and on different parts of the coastline.

JB: Historically around the world, marine reserves—putting sections of the ocean off-limits to fishing—have often been established only after the fish are already gone. It's a tough sell to try to get people to set the sea aside in advance of it being depleted.
JL: True, that is often the case. There are a number of exceptions to that, but even areas that have been significantly degraded and have been set aside can often recover at least to some degree. But I think the real message from a lot of the scientific studies is that the healthier they are when you protect them, the more benefit there is. So that should be our goal.

JB: From a policy maker's perspective, that's got to be a tough sell, convincing people to stop fishing a place they've always fished while there are still fish. I saw a documentary a few years ago about Scotland, where the coast had been so depleted that they'd actually held a lottery to decide which boats could continue to fish and which needed to be taken immediately to a yard and cut up. That was the only way they could come up with a way to lessen the pressure on their coastline.
JL: In many countries, there is significant overcapitalization of the commercial fishing fleet resulting in too many boats chasing fewer and fewer

fish. Transitioning fisheries into a sustainable enterprise is not an easy task, but it is vitally important around the world, and doing so will require more than just addressing fleet overcapitalization.

Traditional fisheries management regulates fishing by controlling effort: You can fish so many days a year, you can catch so many fish on a single day, etc. Despite the best of intentions, this effort control often does not result in the desired outcome of achieving sustainable fisheries. In traditionally managed commercial fisheries, there is an incentive to fish intensively, often under unsafe conditions or even at times when market prices are low.

The approach that we are taking at NOAA is a different and innovative one. Consistent with the president's commitment to base policy on sound science, we at NOAA have paid special attention to recent scientific analyses of what kinds of fishery management are most likely to result in sustainable fisheries and healthy ocean ecosystems. Recognizing that oftentimes the economics of commercial fishing drives unsustainable practices, and based on scientific analyses, we are encouraging a different economic approach called catch shares. Catch shares take a particular fishery and allocate portions (a share of the catch) to shareholders who might be individuals or local communities. For example, a community or an individual might have 10 percent of the total annual catch, and another might have 15 percent. The total catch is set based on scientific information; each shareholder has his/her set fraction of that total. If the total increases, each share increases, so the healthier a fishery, the more valuable the share. A good analogy might be a pizza. Each shareholder has, let's say, one sixth of the pie. If the pie gets bigger, the size of a one-sixth slice is larger, too. Shareholders are responsible for stopping fishing when they have reached their limit. Catch shares thus align economic and conservation incentives by enabling fishermen to have a stake in the future.

Instead of the intense competition we have right now to catch the very last fish, this system enables fishermen to be more conservation minded and to think long term because they have a stake in the future. They stand to benefit if the value of their portfolio grows through time.

JB: There are several very specific threats endangering the ocean, ranging from acidification to pollution to overfishing and the impacts of climate change. Do you see any one of those as being a worst concern, or are they all kind of equal?

JL: Well, at the global scale, overfishing and use of destructive fishing gear are currently the greatest drivers of depletion and disruption of ocean ecosystems, with nutrient pollution, habitat destruction (especially in coastal areas), and invasive species all serious problems that vary in intensity from one place to another. But, of course, climate change and ocean acidification interact with and exacerbate all of those problems. So we really do need to address all of them. This more holistic approach is encapsulated in our proposed national ocean policy and the use of ecosystem-based marine spatial planning. Business as usual is leading to serious degradation of oceans, as pointed out in the Pew Oceans Commission and U.S. Commission on Ocean Policy reports. There is great urgency in recovering the lost bounty and health of oceans—what I call a mutiny *for* the bounty. In lieu of a piecemeal, sector-by-sector, issue-by-issue, agency-by-agency approach, a more holistic approach with the goal of ensuring sustainable use of oceans is in order.

JB: Simply taking the ocean for granted has traditionally been our biggest problem, thinking of it as an infinite resource.

JL: Which continues to plague attempts to fix all of the problems. We have for so long thought of oceans as inexhaustible and impervious and endlessly resilient, and that kind of thinking is at the root of all the ocean's problems.

JB: Congress has said it would like to see overfishing in U.S. waters ended by 2010. That's a big job; is it going to happen?

JL: The Magnuson-Stevens Act, when it was reauthorized in 2007, requires us to end overfishing for most fisheries by 2010, i.e., this year. We are not on track to do that.

JB: How off track are we?

JL: Well, 33 percent of the 199 stock or stock complexes that NOAA oversees are overfished. We have a good track record of rebuilding some stocks, having rebuilt 14 stocks since 2001, but we still have a long way to go to end overfishing. Around the world, estimates are that 70 percent of global fish stocks are overexploited or depleted. Innovative approaches nationally and internationally will be required. This is one of the reasons why NOAA is encouraging the regional fishery management councils to consider catch shares as a better management tool for some commercial fisheries. We believe that the goal of ending overfishing is achievable and are actively pursuing doing just that.

Most of our discussions have focused on commercial fishing, but I wish to emphasize that recreational fishing is equally important in the United States. Recreational angling is both big business and a source of great enjoyment and special family experiences for many Americans. It is as important that recreational fishing be sustainable as it is that commercial fishing be sustainable. In recognition of the importance of saltwater angling, NOAA is working actively with the recreational fishing and boating communities to identify ways to ensure healthy oceans, healthy fisheries, and good fishing opportunities.

JB: You've been in this job since March 2009. You've now worked at all levels of the marine world, as a scientist, as an activist, and as a policy shaper. Where exactly does policy fit in? Is it the most important piece of the puzzle right now? More than science, more than environmental activism?
JL: Policies and regulations are incredibly important, but so too is the understanding that people have and the ethics that we bring to our actions. So educating the public about both the problems and solutions, providing both a sense of urgency and of hope, are all important. Science needs to inform and be informed by policy, opinion, and attitudes. They are intimately interconnected.

JB: When you're out on the road, or on the sea, and you meet people who ask about the health of the world's ocean, what do you advise people to do on an individual basis?
JL: There are a few really simple things. People can choose to eat or buy only sustainably caught or sustainably farmed seafood. They can become more knowledgeable about oceans and active in organizations that promote wise use of oceans or local protection or restoration efforts.

Individuals can let their elected representatives know how important healthy oceans are to them personally. And they can reduce their use of energy, be more energy efficient, minimize use of plastic bags, and reduce packaging that often ends up in oceans.

JB: Which all seem very straightforward and simple. But getting people to first hear and then to practice it in their daily lives is a big job.
JL: It is.

JB: To that end, are you mostly optimistic or pessimistic about the future of the ocean?
JL: I see the urgency of many of these issues, and it seems like a pretty heavy lift. At the same time, I know that social attitudes are often changed very, very rapidly when they reach a tipping point. And much of what we do at NOAA in terms of education and promoting good tools and good practices is designed to help us get to those tipping points, where there is greater awareness and greater willingness to be good stewards. I also am hopeful because I've seen many young people engaged in these issues. I've seen many members of the business community stepping up to the plate and saying, "We have a corporate responsibility to be part of the solution, not just part of the problem." And I see more and more faith-based groups being interested and engaged in climate change and ocean issues. So for all those reasons—the tipping point, the young people, the business community, the faith-based communities—I think that there is reason to be hopeful, but there is a lot yet to be done.

JB: On what percentage of days would you rather be out on the sea versus headed toward another Washington meeting?
JL: On any given day if given a choice, I would rather be out on the water or in the water. But that's not my job right now; my job is to provide leadership for the scientific agency that has primary responsibility for oceans and atmosphere—a scientific agency that has great credibility, great people, and great capacity. This is a special time for NOAA. The opportunity for meaningful progress on all of the issues we've discussed is unparalleled. We intend to partner with other relevant

federal agencies, Congress, states, business and industry, and civil society to tackle head-on many of the big issues of our time. It's a job I'm actually enjoying a lot. I think there are great opportunities at such a critical time, and I think it's important to be part of what's happening and help shape it.

The Future of Fish
Callum Roberts

Professor and author Callum has written exhaustively and eloquently about the rapacious history of man when it comes to the world's ocean. In the final chapter of his critically acclaimed book, The Unnatural History of the Sea, *the British writer suggests there are ways to change the future for fishes, that catching the last one in the sea does not have to be an inevitability.*

Our seas and oceans are not devoid of life. Children still find wonders in rock pools; anglers still catch fish from breakwaters; the diminutive scuttling lives of countless invertebrates continue across the gritty basement of the sea. But fishing has spread poverty where once there was plenty. We have overwhelmed the mighty armies of herring, capelin, and sardines along with their ravening consorts of whale, dolphin, shark, and tuna. The oceans of today are filled with ghost habitats, stripped of their larger inhabitants, our dismantling of marine ecosystems having destructive and unpredictable consequences.

With species loss and food web collapse comes dangerous instability. The seas are undergoing ecological meltdown. Fishing is undermining itself by purging the oceans of species on which it depends. But its influence is far more menacing than simply the regrettable self-destruction of an industry. The wholesale removal of marine life and obliteration of its habitats is stripping resilience from ocean ecosystems. Moreover, it is undermining the ability of the oceans to support human needs. Nature's power to bounce back after catastrophes or absorb the battery of stresses humanity is subjecting it to is being eroded, collapsed fishery after collapsed fishery, species by species, place by place. It is easy to point fingers and say this is the fault of greedy corporations with their factory ships, or faint-hearted politicians overeager to please the fishing industry, or the great masses of poor people reduced to bombing and poisoning their seas to extract the last few fish. But blaming others is unhelpful. Every fish and meat eater shares the responsibility for the losses, and only by working together can we restore the seas' bounty.

The face of the ocean has changed completely since the first commercial fishermen cast their nets and hooks over a thousand years ago. The twentieth century heralded an escalation in fishing intensity that is unprecedented in the history of the oceans, and modern fishing technologies leave fish no place to hide. Today, the only refuges from fishing are those we deliberately create. Unhappily, the sea trails far behind the land in terms of area and quality of protection given.

For centuries, as fishing and commerce have expanded, we have held on to the notion that the sea is different from land. We still view it as a place where people and nations should be free to come and go at will, as well as somewhere that should be free for us to exploit. Perhaps this is why we have been so reluctant to protect the sea. On land, protected areas have proliferated as human populations have grown. Here, compared to the sea, we have made greater headway in our struggle to maintain the richness and variety of wildlife and landscape. Twelve percent of the world's land is now contained in protected areas, whereas the corresponding figure for the sea is but three-fifths of 1 percent. Worse still, most marine protected areas allow fishing to continue. Areas off-limits to all exploitation cover something like one five-thousandth of the total area of the world's seas.

Today we are belatedly coming to realize that natural refuges from fishing have played a critical role in sustaining fisheries and maintaining healthy and diverse marine ecosystems. This does not mean that marine reserves can rebuild fisheries on their own; other management measures are also required for that. Places that are off-limits to fishing constitute the last and most important part of our package of reform for fisheries management. They underpin and enhance all our other efforts. There are limits to protection, though. Reserves cannot bring back what has died out. We can never resurrect globally extinct species, and restoring locally extinct animals may require reintroductions from elsewhere if natural dispersal from remaining populations is insufficient. We are also seeing, in cases such as northern cod in Canada, that fishing can shift marine ecosystems to different states where different mixes of species prevail. In many cases, these are less desirable because the prime fishing targets have gone or are much reduced in numbers, and changes may be difficult to reverse, even with a complete moratorium on fishing. The Mediterranean sailed by Ulysses supported abundant monk seals, loggerhead turtles, and porpoises. Their disappearance through hunting and overfishing has totally restructured food webs, and recovery is likely to be much more difficult. This means that the sooner we act to protect marine life, the more certain will be our success.

To some people, creating marine reserves is an admission of failure. According to their logic, reserves should not be necessary if we have done our work properly in managing the uses we make of the sea. Many fisheries managers are still wedded to the idea that one day their models will work and politicians will listen to their advice. Just give the approach time, and success will be theirs. How much time have we got? This approach has been tried and refined for the past fifty years. There have been few successes with which to feather the managers' caps but a growing litany of failure. The Common Fisheries Policy in Europe exemplifies the worst pitfalls, with flawed models, flawed advice, watered-down recommendations from government bureaucrats, and then the disregard of much of this advice by politicians. When it all went wrong, as it inevitably had to, Europe sent its boats to developing countries to ransack other people's fish for far less than those fish are worth.

We are squandering the wealth of oceans. If we don't break out of this cycle of failure, humanity will lose a key source of protein and much more besides. Disrupting ecosystem processes, such as water purification, nutrient cycling, and carbon storage, could have ramifications for human life itself. We can go a long way toward avoiding this catastrophic mistake with simple commonsense management. Marine reserves lie at the heart of the reform and can benefit fisheries in many ways. But they will not be sufficient if they are implemented here and there to shore up the crumbling edifice of "rational fisheries management" envisioned by scientists in the 1940s and 1950s. They have to be placed center stage as a fundamental underpinning for everything we do in the oceans. Reserves are a first resort, not a final resort when all else fails.

A pervasive effect of fishing is to compress the life histories of exploited animals. Species that once lived long lives in which they reproduced many times are forced to live fast and die young. Often they have time to produce only one or two broods before falling victim to hook, net, or trawl. Species that cannot adapt disappear while those that can adapt end up growing more slowly and maturing at smaller sizes because fishing favors animals that remain small and reproduce early in life. They avoid capture for longer and so produce some young before being killed. The small-bodied fish that dominate today's depleted fish populations produce few eggs, undermining their ability to renew themselves. Compared to populations with plenty of big, old egg producers, they lack resilience to fluctuating environmental conditions and the long-term shifts expected with climate change. By providing refuges from fishing, reserves raise baseline population sizes and allow the development of more natural age structures. Egg production is increased and can be sustained through periods of unfavorable conditions for the survival of young. This restores resilience. Without marine reserves, the runs of bad years that inevitably strike industries dependent on the environment could cause population and fishery collapse, as indeed they have done. It is because the way we fish today destroys resilience that depleted populations find it so hard to struggle back, even after fishing is reduced or stopped altogether.

Fishery regulations can be wiped out by the stroke of an official's pen, whereas marine reserves are more enduring because permanence is a cornerstone of the idea of protection, making it much harder to remove them on a legislative whim. They should provide inviolable asylums for marine life. If management goes wrong outside reserves, and populations are overfished, there will still be protected animals left to kick-start recovery. Reserves provide insurance against management failure.

Reserves do not just promote resilience of the species we catch to eat but will also restore it in their habitats. Putting areas off-limits to fishing allows recovery of species such as corals, sponges, sea squirts, and mollusks that create complex bottom structures that bind the seabed and perform countless other vital roles such as filtering the water. Protecting these species is important because the mechanical destruction caused by fishing has depleted populations of these animals, too. With time, after reserves have become established, such "bioengineers" will also begin to experience higher and more stable reproduction. In turn, the recovery of habitats that have been damaged by fishing will aid the productivity of commercially valuable species.

Further, by integrating marine reserves into fishery management, we can overcome an enduring dilemma that arises in managing multispecies fisheries. Fish species differ in how much fishing they can sustain. If many species are caught by using the same gear, a compromise must be struck between the needs of vulnerable and resilient species. Should you fish at a level that sustains the most vulnerable species and so maintains populations of all, or should you fish harder to catch more of the resilient species at the expense of vulnerable species? In nearly all cases up to now, the dilemma has been resolved, either consciously or by default, by sacrificing larger, more vulnerable species. These species are the weakest link in fisheries, and marine reserves provide protection while fishing grounds are exploited more intensively for bigger catches.

How much of the sea do we need to protect in marine reserves to restore what has been lost, head off extinctions, and achieve the sustainability that flits through fishery managers' dreams but evades them in daily life? Small reserves, like the networks in St. Lucia, can provide benefits to local fisheries. With a few exceptions such as Australia's Great Barrier Reef and the Northwest Hawaiian Islands National Monument in the United States, present-day reserves are small and scattered. To have any significant impact at national and global levels, our existing marine reserves would need to be scaled up by adding networks of new reserves.

Some insight into the coverage needed can be gained from the population models used by fisheries managers. Managers today aim to avoid recruitment overfishing—that is, the reduction of a population to such low levels that it cannot replace itself. According to fishery models, recruitment overfishing can be averted for most species by sustaining populations above one third of their unexploited size. For many species, much rehabilitation is necessary before they approach these levels of abundance, especially given new historical perspectives that suggest populations are often below 10 percent of unexploited population sizes and sometimes much lower. Success in recovering populations will likely be far greater if marine reserves are part of the rebuilding package. Georges Bank fisheries have shown promising recovery of scallops and groundfish because those managers complemented reduced fishing effort with areas closed to trawling and dredging. Within six years, there were five times more haddock, fourteen times more scallops, and 50 percent more cod, and benefits are spilling into surrounding fisheries. Those closures would have been even more effective if they had been real marine reserves that prohibited all forms of fishing.

You can do a back-of-the-envelope calculation about how much protection is needed to boost reproduction by depleted fish populations to sustainable levels. Populations of many fish species have been depressed to less than 10 percent of natural abundance; we've seen this in bluefin tuna, Nassau grouper, cod, Atlantic turbot, and halibut, among others. Let's assume for simplicity that the figure is 10 percent. Marine reserves, for the sake of this exercise, raise reproductive output to ten times the level, area for area, of that in fishing grounds. To lift overall population reproductive output to sustainable levels, summed across reserves and fishing grounds, roughly 30 percent of the sea would need to be covered with reserves. This calculation assumes business as usual outside reserves. If other management measures were put in place to reduce the impact of fishing in nonreserve areas, double reproduction might be expected by animals in fishing grounds. In this case, we would need about 20 percent coverage of marine reserves to meet the sustainability target.

Other scientists have used more sophisticated approaches to estimate how much of the sea we should protect. Their answers have a great deal of consistency despite the variety of methods used to make the calculations. They suggest we need to protect between 20 percent and 40 percent of the sea from all fishing. Doing this will maximize returns to the fishing industry, provide adequate refuges for vulnerable species, sustain genetic variability in populations, and afford protection to the full spectrum of biodiversity. If you have 100 percent coverage, there will be maximum conservation benefit but no fisheries. Some of the best-performing marine reserves and partially protected areas support these predictions. Reserve zones in St. Lucia's Soufriere Marine Management Area cover 35 percent of coral reef habitat. Merritt Island National Wildlife Refuge includes 22 percent of the area of northern Florida's lagoons. The trawl closures on Georges Bank cover around 25 percent of groundfish habitat and about 40 percent of scallop habitat. These are not trivial numbers; they represent the degree of protection necessary to achieve a turnaround in world fisheries.

Because all species are different, not all will benefit to the same degree from reserves. Certainly, highly mobile species will gain less protection from marine reserves than species such as rockfish, or striped bass, that spend most of their lives rooted to some reef or rock pile. But strategically placed reserves can benefit mobile species, too. The Caribbean Nassau groupers that migrated tens of kilometers to reach mass spawning sites would not be in such trouble today had those aggregations been protected in reserves. Belatedly, such protection is being extended to other species that reproduce at spawning aggregations. In the U.S. Virgin Islands, another grouper, the red hind, has shown a swift increase in average fish size on the heels of protection of their spawning aggregations. There has also been a rise in the number of large males in this hermaphroditic fish, which should promote greater spawning success. Tunas on their ocean passages use seamounts and convergence zones as way stations and refueling stops. At present, we target them in these vulnerable places where they concentrate to feed, so protecting some of these places in particular could significantly increase tuna survival. Juveniles of migratory species such as cod survive better in complex, biologically rich bottom habitats that have not been hit by trawls, so these animals too will benefit from reserves. However, migratory species, like all exploited marine life, also need some protection outside of reserves. There is no point in having a network of protected areas but scorched-earth fishing everywhere else. This is why other measures such as I have set out are also essential.

We have much to do to realize a vision of the world in which the seas are spangled with mosaics of marine reserves. With just three fifths of 1 percent of the ocean currently protected, we need fifty times more reserve areas to do the job well, spread across the waters of coastal nations and the high seas. This is far more than many politicians, fishery managers, and even some people in conservation agencies are willing to countenance. I have spoken to hundreds of them in my career. Even in unguarded moments, the most that many are willing to concede is that a few percent of the sea should be protected as reserves. The rest would either continue to be used as it is now or would be zoned to exclude certain kinds of activities such as dredging for aggregate or drilling for oil.

If we stick to that management paradigm, I am convinced that marine life will continue its long slide toward jellyfish and slime. A handful of special places protected by reserves might remind tourists of what has been lost, but these scattered reserves could sustain only a fraction of the species that live in the sea because, in the long term, they will not be sufficient to maintain viable populations of the largest, most vulnerable, and most mobile species. Diving in them would be like looking at a Roman fresco where great pieces of plaster have crumbled away. Do we really want to have to imagine what has been lost?

I believe that we need to flip this paradigm on its head. Rather than thinking that marine reserves protection should be afforded to only a few species or in only out-of-the-way places, we need to view reserves as the foundation and underpinning for all other management. According to this view, reserves would cover some 30 percent of the sea, perhaps more in some places. They would be complemented by other kinds of marine protected areas that allow a range of low-impact activities such as only certain kinds of fishing. Added to this would be areas zoned for other uses such as bottom trawling. The aim would be to contain the impacts of more invasive activities and keep them away from sensitive areas. Places given no protection would make up a small minority of the sea, not the large majority that they constitute now.

Opinion surveys show that the public is ready for such a change in thinking. For example, when Americans were polled on their attitudes toward the oceans a few years ago, they were surprised to find so little protection given to the sea. On average, they thought that 22 percent of the sea was already fully protected from all fishing in marine reserves and were upset and angry to discover that most national marine sanctuaries allowed fishing. The name *sanctuary* was a sham. At a conference in 2003,

I picked up a leaflet put out by the U.S. Fish and Wildlife Service that proclaimed "Discover Nature's Best Hunting and Fishing: The National Wildlife Refuge System." Clearly, even some conservationists have trouble with the concept of *refuge*. One of my students has also polled public opinion in Britain. On average, people thought that 16 percent of Britain's seas were already protected in marine reserves (at the time of the survey, the correct answer was 0.0004 percent). When asked how much of Britain's seas they thought should be protected this way, the average answer given was 54 percent. Ninety-five percent of people thought more than 20 percent should be marine reserves.

People love the sea. Some of our most cherished early memories are of trips to the seaside, gathering shells, paddling, fencing with seaweeds, and gazing into rock pools. The sea inspires and soothes us; it can rouse us to rapture and terror. It is in constant motion but never seems to change. The radiant blue of the Mediterranean dazzles in the same way as it did when Hannibal set forth with his fleet to conquer Rome. But many of the animals that sported around their ships are rare today or already in deep trouble and need our help to make a comeback.

A starting gun has been fired to change all of this. In 2000, President Bill Clinton issued an executive order, later endorsed by the Bush administration, charging government agencies to create a national network of marine protected areas. At the World Summit on Sustainable Development in 2002, coastal nations of the world pledged to create national networks of marine protected areas by 2012. Meanwhile, European nations had already committed to creating a Europe-wide network by 2010. However, these pledges remain vague on targets for numbers or size of protected areas and on how they should be managed. Marine protected areas must offer genuine refuges. The World Conservation Union's World Parks Congress of 2003 recommended that at least 20 to 30 percent of every marine habitat should be protected from all fishing and that marine protected area networks should straddle the high seas as well as national waters. Moves are afoot at the United Nations to develop a mechanism that would allow the establishment of marine reserves in this global commons, for which there appears to be widespread support.

Several countries have made good progress. South Africa has committed to protecting 20 percent of its waters. Eighteen percent of its territorial waters are already reserves, and the network is being expanded offshore. In Australia, a third of the Great Barrier Reef Marine Park, more than 100,000 square kilometers (40,000 square miles) of reef, sea grass, and swamp, was protected from fishing in 2004. This network of reserve zones is representative of all the different habitats in the park and sets a shining example for others to follow. Britain's Royal Commission on Environmental Pollution recommended in 2004 that 30 percent of the country's waters should become marine reserves. We are on the path to a global network of marine reserves that could restore the oceans to much of their former glory, but we have to be bold and move rapidly if we are to achieve success.

Can the world afford to protect the oceans? One estimate, made in 2004, put the cost at $12 to $14 billion per year to run a worldwide net-work of marine reserves covering 30 percent of all oceans and seas. Initial one-time setup costs would be about five times this amount. These sums seem like a lot but are put into perspective when we consider they are less than the $15 to $30 billion we currently spend on harmful subsidies that encourage excess fishing capacity and prop up overexploitation. Most countries offer fishermen tax breaks on fuel, for example, or free nets, and many countries pay for access to fish in another country's waters. Compared to global defense spending, estimated at $900 billion in 2004, the sums needed to keep our oceans healthy are trivial. The costs are also less than the $31 billion Europeans and Americans collectively spend on ice cream each year and roughly equate to the $15 billion we spend on perfumes or $14 billion more than a million permanent jobs would cost for managers, wardens, and administrators. Much of the costs of administering coastal reserves could be recouped from visitors. Some reserves, such as the Saba and Bonaire marine parks in the Caribbean, are already self-funding based on modest payments made by visitors. The world can certainly afford marine reserves. What it can't afford is to be without them any longer.

〜〜〜

IN SOUTHERN BELIZE, 50 kilometers (30 miles) offshore, is a place called Gladden Spit where an elbow in the barrier reef forms a sheer under-water promontory. Here the reef plunges to a depth of more than

1,000 meters (3,300 feet) as it falls away into the Cayman Trench. The sun has dipped below the horizon, staining the sky red and purple. A stiff breeze has kicked up the waves and rattles cables on the boat. I roll into the water with three companions, pausing briefly to check my equipment before my descent. It is a relief to leave the violently heaving boat and enter this tranquil world. I peer downward looking for the reef, but the bottom is too far below to see. Shafts of light pick out flecks of plankton like dust motes suspended in deep indigo. In this water cathedral, I feel very small. Dropping deeper, I see vague movements and a flash of silver flank, then another and another as fish wheel and turn below. When I get close, I realize they are sleep dog snappers; there must be hundreds of them. As I descend into their midst, the group parts and engulfs me in a moving wall of bodies. Countless eyes watch impassively as the fish swirl past, every cheek marked with a pale teardrop shape. Glowing silver bodies tinged with pink press in upon me in the revolving mass as the dog snappers abandon themselves to the primal urge that drew them here. I revise my estimate upward. There must be five thousand of them, maybe more. They lull me into a reverie that is broken only when the fish start to thin and then leave. But it is the current that has moved me. The fish remain in the same place as if held by an invisible force.

From a distance, I can see the whole group. They form a spinning column that rises above the reef. Where the column contacts the reef, fish fan out, giving the appearance of a plinth. Fish spiral up from this base and into the column while animals near the top turn and head downward in a continuous renewal. Many appear fat, their swollen bellies heavy with eggs. They have gathered here to spawn, many having traveled long distances, and the time has arrived. In the gathering gloom, a small group of fish makes an excited upward rush, their bodies pressed together in shivering embrace. A few meters below the surface, they release a white cloud of eggs and sperm in an explosive burst before turning to dash to the bottom. Other groups break off in similar rushes like spurting jets from a fountain. Then the fountain itself thrusts upward as a further great mass of fish follows, saturating the water with their seed before spilling down into the depths.

I drift suspended amid billowing clouds of eggs and sperm, surrounded by a frenzied but unseen struggle as new lives are forged. Out of the corner of one eye, I see a dark, moving shadow in the gloom. At first it seems small and formless, but as it approaches, I make out the rhythmic sickle tail beat that signals the approach of a shark. A gaping black grin fills the width of its broad flat head. Huge pectoral fins spread like hydroplanes from the sides of a giant body painted with a constellation of white spots. It is a whale shark, the largest fish in the sea. The leviathan ploughs into the egg cloud and toward me, opening its mouth in a giant gape to sieve eggs from the water. It barely registers my presence, betraying no flicker of alarm or recognition. Muscled flanks glide by like a submarine as I back paddle to avoid being bowled over. Then another shark appears from behind me, this one even bigger than the first. For the next half hour the sharks crisscross the area, feasting on the dispersing caviar cloud as darkness falls. With perfect timing, as if called by some aquatic dinner gong, whale sharks come to Gladden Spit when the fish congregate to spawn and then leave when the spawning is over.

There are still places in the world like Gladden Spit, where it is possible to find something of the miraculous in nature. In Alaskan estuaries, salmon still gather in impenetrable throngs as they prepare for their spawning ascents upriver. They attract packs of toothy salmon sharks, seals, otters, and killer whales to feed on them. Great shoals of hammerhead sharks still circle Galapagos seamounts. Mighty boils of tuna still erupt from the Humboldt Current, thrashing their way into dense balls of anchovies. Great white sharks still thrill as they burst clear of South African seas, twisting in midair with seals grasped in their jaws. Such scenes are remnants of the seas of long ago. They offer us windows to past worlds, letting us see the oceans as they must have looked to travelers and fishermen of centuries past. They also give us hope that today's oceans can yet recover. But even these places are critically threatened, and we are running out of time to save them. I am an optimist. We can restore the life and habitats of the sea because it is in everyone's interest to do so. The same large-scale networks of marine reserves, complemented by other measures of fish and habitat protection, best serve the interests of both commerce and conservation. You can have exploitation with protection because reserves help sustain catches in surrounding fishing grounds. But you cannot have exploitation without protection, not in the long term.

The Whale Hunter's Hunter
An Interview with Captain Paul Watson

No one ocean person is more ready to fight on its behalf than Paul.
Each season for the past several, he has sailed his ship, the Steve
Irwin, *to the icy waters off Antarctica to harass Japanese whalers,*
who insist on continuing their hunt despite international protest
and pressure, using "science" as their lone defense. The popular
Animal Planet *series,* Whale Wars, *filmed aboard the ship*
during its efforts to stop the whalers—efforts including
ramming and boarding the "enemy" ships—has brought
Paul and his Sea Shepherds to an international audience.

Jon Bowermaster: *Has your current campaign in the Southern Ocean been successful?*

Captain Paul Watson: I believe it has been successful. Our strategy is an economic one. I don't believe the Japanese whalers will back off on moral, ethical, or scientific grounds, but they will quit if they lose the one thing that is of most value to them—their profits. Our objective is to sink the Japanese whaling fleet economically, to bankrupt them, and we are doing that.

We have slashed their kill quotas in half over the past three years and negated their profits. They are tens of millions of dollars in debt on their repayment schedule for Japanese government subsidies. The newly elected Japanese government has pledged to cut their subsidies.

I am actually confident that we can shut them down this year. They are on the ropes financially.

JB: How do you measure success? Fewer whales taken by Japanese? Other signs?
CPW: Of their quota of 935 Minke whales last year, they fell short by 304. Of their quota of 50 fin whales, they took only 1. The year before, they took only half their quota and, in the past three years, did not kill enough whales to break even so have been operating at a loss. We have also exposed their illegal whaling activities to the world and initiated a controversy and a discussion on whaling in the Japanese media.

JB: How do the Japanese continue to get away with the whale hunt when so many things say they shouldn't, such as the Antarctica Treaty forbidding commerce below 60 degrees south latitude and the International Whaling Commission's ban on all whaling?
CPW: There is a lack of economic and political motivation on the part of governments to enforce international conservation law. The Japanese whalers are targeting endangered and protected whales inside the boundaries of the Southern Ocean Whale Sanctuary in violation of a global moratorium on commercial whaling, in violation of the Antarctic Treaty that prohibits commercial activity south of 60 degrees, and in contempt of the Australian Federal Court for continuing to kill whales in the Australian Antarctic Economic Exclusion Zone. There is no difference between Japanese whale poachers in Antarctica and elephant poachers in East Africa except that the Africans are black and impoverished.

JB: Do you know what the reaction among Japanese people—not scientists, not government—is toward the continued whale hunts?
CPW: I'm not actually concerned. I'm Canadian, and the majority of Canadians are opposed to the commercial slaughter of seals, but the Canadian government subsidizes it nonetheless. I believe it is a myth that once the people of a nation oppose something, things will change. First, most people are apathetic and could not care one way or another. Second, the pro-whalers have an economic motivation to lobby for continued whaling; and third, in Japan, it is considered inappropriate to oppose government or corporate policy. I've always felt that educating the Japanese public was a waste of time and smacks of cultural

chauvinism. The fact is that whaling is illegal, and we intervene for that reason, and the key to ending it is the negation of profits.

JB: They are showing The Cove *in Japan now, and most Japanese interviewed said they had no idea these dolphin hunts were happening. Are the Japanese aware of* Whale Wars?

CPW: I am not sure, nor do I care. I know that the Japanese government and the whalers are aware of it. I know that the people of Taiji are aware of the dolphin slaughters. I think the controversy over the film is allowing many Japanese people to become aware of it, despite that the killing of dolphins continues. *The Cove* has been most valuable in raising awareness outside of Japan, which motivates outside pressure on Japan.

JB: How are whale populations doing around the world? Are they growing? Shrinking?

CPW: The oceans are dying. Every single commercial fishery is in a state of economic collapse. We have destroyed some 90 percent of the populations of the large fishes. All life in the ocean is threatened. And if the oceans die, we die. This is a simple fact that humans choose to ignore. If you eat a fish, you are part of the problem. If you eat pork or chicken raised on fishmeal, you are part of the problem. If you throw plastic garbage into the ocean, you are part of the problem. All whales are endangered, although some populations are slowly recovering, but this may not save them from an overall marine ecological collapse.

JB: Are you optimistic or pessimistic in regard to how humans are treating the ocean and its marine life? The World Wildlife Fund, for example, predicts all bluefin tuna will be gone by 2012 and that every species of fish we currently know will be gone by 2050.

CPW: The World Wildlife Fund is part of the problem. I wish they would use their vast resources actually to do something instead of constantly warning us how dire the situation is. Critics call conservationists doom-and-gloom Cassandras, forgetting the fact that Cassandra may have predicted doom and gloom, but she was right, and Troy could have been saved if King Priam had simply listened to his daughter. We are the Cassandras, and no one is listening.

We are about to launch a major campaign to defend bluefin tuna in the Mediterranean, but it may be too late. Companies like Mitsubishi are literally investing in diminishment and extinction to raise the price of the tuna they have stored in vast refrigerated warehouses in Japan. The answer to this question is that the solutions are all impossible, *but* sometimes the impossible is the answer; in other words, the impossible solution is simply a solution no one has conceived yet.

JB: How do you counter critics who suggest Sea Shepherd's methods are too extreme?
CPW: Criticisms from people don't concern me. My clients are whales, dolphins, seals, sharks, fish, and seabirds. We have never injured a single person, and we have never been convicted of a single felony; therefore, there is nothing extreme about what we do. There is nothing extreme about intervening to uphold international conservation law, and there is nothing extreme about defending the lives of endangered species and defending the integrity of endangered habitats.

In today's socially challenged world, it does not matter if you are running for president of the United States or saving whales; the accusation of the times is "terrorist." In a world in which the Chinese government can label the Dalai Lama a terrorist, I have no problem with the Japanese whalers calling me the same.

JB: Lots of "green" issues are being talked about, but I wonder how many people truly operate with a green consciousness. Define an environmentalist in 2009.
CPW: First of all, we need to recognize that we are all hypocrites, and we are all guilty. If you have a birth certificate, you're guilty. The problem is that this is beyond personal choice. Changing lightbulbs and changing your diet will not stop the juggernaut of hominid destruction. The number one threat to survival on this planet for us is diminishment of biodiversity, and the number one cause of this is out-of-control human population growth. As our numbers rise, we literally steal the carrying capacity of other species. They have to disappear for the needs of more and more humans every year. I was born into a world with 3 billion people, and sixty years later, there are nearly 7 billion people. The party

will end, and it will not be pleasant. As a species, we are ecologically ignorant, and no species can survive by living outside of the three basic laws of ecology: (1) the law of diversity that the strength of an ecosystem depends upon the diversity of species within it; (2) the law of interdependence that these species are essential for the survival of each other; and (3) the law of finite resources that there is a limit to growth because there is a limit to carrying capacity.

Natural history has demonstrated that when any species steps outside the boundaries of these three basic laws, it will not survive. We will not be an exception.

The steps we need to take will be radical and will involve more than changing your lightbulbs and driving a Prius. We will need to reduce human populations voluntarily before nature does it for us, and we need to live an organic and truly sustainable lifestyle in small communities surrounded by belts of natural wilderness. We need to encourage diversity and not diminish it. We need to stop burning fossil fuels, and we need to revolutionize agriculture so that we do not depend upon just a few bioengineered select species. We need to have at least a century of banning commercial fishing to allow the oceans to recover. We need to stop polluting the world with chemicals. We need to destroy the political stranglehold of this planet by the oil companies. And we all need to be ecologists.

JB: During your life, you have spent weeks and years on the ocean. What is it that inspires you about the ocean? Are you ever scared on the ocean?
CPW: I have never been afraid of the ocean, but I do respect it. In a strange way, I feel protected when I am at sea, don't ask me how or why; I don't know, but the ocean gives me peace of mind, and I love the sea with all of her moods, from calm to storm, from the tropics to the ice fields. The ocean is the face of our planet; it really is the planet Ocean, not the planet Earth for me. It is the source of all life, and it sustains all life, and if the ocean dies, then we all die.

JB: What is it about whales you most admire?
CPW: I believe that whales and dolphins are the most intelligent, sentient, self-aware beings on the planet. Unfortunately, we humans measure

intelligence by the ability to use tools and to manipulate and control our environment. A sentient, intelligent species that has adapted to the environment without the need to manipulate it is alien to us, but it does not make them less intelligent. The whale has the largest brain ever to have evolved upon the planet and the most complex. The whale is the mind of the sea, which has so much to teach us. We spend billions searching through the universe in a quest for intelligent life, yet we spend next to nothing researching the intelligence of other species upon our own planet.

JB: A whale and a human are in trouble and you're nearby. You can save only one. Instinctively, which would you choose to save?
CPW: A Japanese fisherman asked me this question. He said if a Japanese fisherman and a dolphin were caught in a net, and you could save only one, which one would you save? I answered that I did not come all the way to Japan to save fishermen; I came to save dolphins.

In general, however, this is a complex question. It depends on who the person is, if I know them, if they are friend or foe. Would I save a whaler over a whale, the answer is no. Would I save a hunter or a poacher over an elephant, the answer is no. Would I save my daughter or my wife, my best friend, or a colleague over an animal, the answer is yes. Would I save one human, any human, including my own life, if it meant the extinction of a species, any species, the answer is no. The survival of a species must take precedence over the interests of an individual of any other species.

JB: Environmental groups have grown exponentially since you helped start Greenpeace. Are there any groups out there now other than Sea Shepherd doing a good job on ocean issues? Which environmental groups or individuals do you admire?
CPW: There is no group doing what Sea Shepherd does, but there are many groups and many individuals working to defend our oceans. Most of them are small. The one exception for a large organization is the Natural Resources Defense Council (NRDC) in the U.S. that is battling the U.S. Navy over the issue of the deployment of low-frequency sonar killing whales and dolphins. The other groups I support are Earth Island

Institute and WildAid, and we are working with the Galapagos Park Marine Reserve rangers. But the real strength of the conservation movement is individuals, filmmakers like Jacques Perrin, oceanographers like Sylvia Earle, dolphin defenders like Ric O'Barry, marine biologists like Dr. Boris Worm, scientists like E. O. Wilson, and so on.

JB: Some have suggested that if you were to relent or back off, the Japanese might quit whaling, that they just don't want to look like they're being forced to quit by Sea Shepherd. Do you believe they would stop if you stayed home for a season or two?

CPW: Twenty-two years of diplomatic efforts on the part of Australia, France, the United States, and other nations did not do a single thing to reduce the Japanese kill quotas. Greenpeace did not save a single whale with their banner hanging. We are the only organization to cut those quotas and actually save the lives of whales.

If I were to back off for a season, hundreds of whales would die, and the whalers would make a profit, and that would prolong their activities. We cannot relent, and we must keep the pressure on to ensure that we negate their profits, year after year, until we bankrupt them. We have them on the ropes economically now, and we will pummel them senseless until we achieve an economic knockout.

We are speaking the one language they understand: profit and loss. We will continue to negate their profits and increase their losses until we bankrupt them.

JB: Other than whaling, what other ocean issues most concern you? Where else has Sea Shepherds mounted campaigns?

CPW: Our next major campaign is to take on the bluefin tuna poachers in the Mediterranean, beginning in May 2010. We have an ongoing partnership with the rangers and the federal police of Ecuador to patrol and intervene against poachers in the Galapagos. We are taking fishing companies to court in Brazil and winning. We are championing sharks worldwide, working to stop the dolphin slaughter in Japan, the commercial seal slaughter in Canada, the poaching of turtles in the Caribbean. We intervene where we can afford to intervene and where we feel our interventions can make a difference.

JB: Whale Wars *has greatly expanded Sea Shepherd's audience. How has the television series helped your Southern Ocean campaign?*

CPW: Whale Wars has made us a household name in the United States and, worldwide, it has quadrupled our support base. We now return to the southern oceans with more resources than ever before. *Whale Wars* has exposed illegal Japanese whaling activities to the world, and that has put enormous additional pressure on Japan to end whaling.

JB: How has it been, having a film crew on board your ship?

CPW: The camera is the most powerful weapon ever invented, and we now go to sea as eco-pirates armed with cameras instead of cannons. As for the film crew, after a few days, the ship's crew seems to be oblivious to the presence of the cameras, which, by the way, is not always a good thing.

My policy, however, is to let the cameras roll. We have no editorial control over *Whale Wars,* nor would we want to. They are free to pursue the truth, and we are free to do what we need to do without their interference.

Saving the Whales Again!
Jeff Pantukhoff with Pierce Brosnan
and Hayden Panettiere

*Jeff has used his filmmaking skills to help alter a variety
of ocean and marine-animal fights, most notably over a Mexican
gray whale nursery and Japan's notorious dolphin killing cove.
He has also unabashedly relied on the media and committed
celebrity spokespeople to draw attention to his causes,
which he insists has made all the difference.*

I was born far from the ocean, in St. Louis, Missouri, but I can remember my first experience with the ocean and dolphins and whales like it was yesterday. When I was six years old, my parents took me to vacation in Laguna Beach, California. It was the first time I had seen the ocean, and my dad took me on a boat trip to Catalina Island. On the way out to the island, the captain hailed, "Dolphins on the bow!" I ran to the front of the boat, peered over its bow, and there they were, the most beautiful and graceful creatures I had ever seen, playing on the bow wave. I was so excited I wanted to jump in and swim with them!

Not long after that, I saw Jacques Cousteau on television and, to this day, I still remember how amazed and awed I was by his films, how I dreamed of how great it would be to live a life like his, traveling the world's oceans, diving into and exploring them, and filming their wondrous creatures while unraveling the mysteries that lay just below the surface.

But no one, not even Jacques Cousteau, had a more profound impact on my life than award-winning filmmakers and photographers Howard and Michele Hall.

I was thirty-five years old, living in San Diego, still desiring to be like Jacques Cousteau, even though I knew nothing about photography or filmmaking. I knew of the Halls because of their beautiful films and decided to seek them out, cold.

Fortunately for me, at a local dive club meeting, I discovered that Howard Hall also lived in San Diego, so I went straight to the white pages, found his number, and called. He answered and I dove straight into my story, telling him—a complete stranger who might have assumed I was nuts—all about my dreams and aspirations of being like Jacques Cousteau and asked if he might have time to meet.

After a long pause, Howard told me he was too busy to go to lunch (I thought, "Oh no, here it comes, the big blow-off"), but if I could come by his house tomorrow afternoon, he and Michele would give me some time. Not only did Howard and Michele take the time to listen to my dreams and aspirations, they gave me sound, honest, and direct advice, telling me what camera, lens, and film to use and how to use them and told me to just go start shooting. I remember Howard telling me that I really could be like Jacques Cousteau, but it would really help if I learned how to use a camera underwater. I asked whether there was any opportunity to volunteer to do any kind of work with them on one of their underwater shoots. Howard replied that he only worked with dive instructors. The next day, I enrolled in dive instructor training.

~~~

TAKING HOWARD AND MICHELE'S ADVICE, I also cashed in my life insurance policy and gave myself a Christmas present, the Nikonos V camera, 15mm lens, and Kodachrome 64 film they had recommended. On New Year's Day, I headed out hopefully to find dolphins to photograph and, within a couple of hours, found myself in the water surrounded by a pod of white-sided dolphins, the very same kind I had seen when I was six. Excitedly, I shot my first two rolls of film underwater.

The next day, I called Howard and asked whether I could show him my dolphin photos.

"What kind of dolphins?" he asked.

"White-sided," I replied.

"Are you sure?"

"Yes," I replied.

"How close did they get?"

"Close enough to touch," I replied.

"Bring them right over!"

I was nervous about showing Howard my pictures, but when I saw his reaction, my nervousness turned to excitement. He explained that white-sided dolphins are usually shy of divers; that in his twenty years of underwater filming, he had never been near them; and that many of my photos were good enough to publish. With his encouragement, I submitted them and went from novice to published in one afternoon's dive.

A couple of months later, I contacted Howard to let him know that I was now a certified dive instructor and asked if he had any volunteer work. He chuckled and told me that they didn't take on volunteers but that if I wanted a paying job, I could work with him and Michele as a member of their camera team on their IMAX 3D film, *Into the Deep*. I couldn't believe it. Here I was, getting to work with and learn filmmaking from one of the greatest underwater filmmaking teams in the world. I later discovered while working on that shoot that out of our eight-member dive team, the only other dive instructor on the team was Howard!

While filming *Into the Deep*, I asked Howard which of the gray whale breeding grounds he thought would be the best one to visit to film. He replied, "For a whale hugger like you, that's easy; go to Mexico's San Ignacio Lagoon because that's where all the 'friendly whales' are."

In March 1995, I drove down to San Ignacio Lagoon, where I happened upon a small eco-camp called *Kuyima,* which means "light in darkness." I spent five magical days there among the friendly gray whales and the local people who make this place where mountains and desert meet the sea their home. It was a life-changing trip on many levels, from being eye to eye and getting to touch these magnificent gentle giants and their newborn calves to experiencing one of the most beautiful and virtually untouched places I had ever been.

But on my last night there, I was told by one of the locals running the camp that the Mitsubishi Corporation and the Mexican government were planning to build the world's largest salt plant right in the heart of San Ignacio Lagoon. I had an epiphany there and then and remember saying to myself, "Over my dead body!" That night is when my nonprofit Whaleman Foundation was born, among the friendly gray whales of San Ignacio Lagoon.

Returning to San Diego, I immediately asked for a leave of absence from my telecommunications job, which was turned down, so I resigned on the spot and dove into the nonprofit world, never looking back. Its mission is to forever protect and preserve dolphins, whales, and their ocean habitats.

In thinking of what it was that I could actually do to make the most impact, the thing I remembered most about Jacques Cousteau was how passionate he was about raising awareness of the plight of our oceans and marine life and how he used his films as the vehicle to get that message out. So in March 1996, I began production of my first film with the intent of helping save San Ignacio Lagoon, which was both a whale sanctuary and a United Nations World Heritage site.

Not long after that, I was introduced to Pierce Brosnan and his wife, Keely. I told them about my film and what I hoped to accomplish with it and asked whether they would help. They said yes and, in 1997, Pierce and his son Sean traveled to San Ignacio Lagoon to join us in a meeting that included several environmental organizations working on its protection, including the International Fund for Animal Welfare (IFAW), the Natural Resources Defense Council (NRDC), and Mexico's Group of 100.

In summer 1998, I sent my completed film, *Gray Magic: The Plight of San Ignacio Lagoon,* to Dr. Mechtild Rossler, Director of the United Nations World Heritage sites. She shared the film with her colleagues at the UN and the World Conservation Union (IUCN) and, later that year, presented and distributed it to a meeting of the UN in Kyoto, Japan. As a direct result, in 1999, the UN sent an investigative team to San Ignacio and Scammon's lagoons and met with then Mexican president, Ernesto Zedillo. The following year, President Zedillo and his family traveled to the lagoon and, nearly five years to the day after I first found out about the proposed salt plant, the president of Mexico announced that his government was withdrawing its support for the salt plant and signed an executive order to protect San Ignacio Lagoon forever.

AT THE TIME, Pierce Brosnan was quite vocal about why he got involved. Here's what he said at our press conference announcing the withdrawal:

> There's one thing I do like and that's a good fight, and this is a good fight and I don't like to lose. And I believe in my heart we are not going to lose this fight against Mitsubishi because they know they are in the wrong, and any man or woman who has seen this lagoon would know that they are in the wrong for what they are trying to do down there.
>
> This part of the world is magical; it is sheer magic to see these great creatures out there in this lagoon and to see the trust and to see the love of these creatures to us, you know, mankind, and I was there with my son, and I saw the magic in his face and I saw the magic in every man and woman in these tiny boats when we went out every day, and I saw the trust and the love of these great creatures as they brought their calves up to the surface for us to stroke, to touch, and just the sheer joy of it has never left me, and I know it has never left my son.

SINCE GRAY MAGIC, I have written, directed, and produced four other short films on issues affecting dolphins, whales, and their habitats. My second film, on the illegal Makah Indian gray whale hunt, was presented to the delegates attending the 2000 meeting of the International Whaling Commission (IWC) and was used as evidence in a domestic lawsuit. As a result, the Makah gray whale hunt has been halted.

In 2001, *Deadly Sounds in the Silent World,* which also featured Pierce and Keely, was presented and distributed to the U.S. Congress and, in 2002, was also presented as evidence in a domestic lawsuit against the worldwide use of a deadly and dangerous new low-frequency active sonar technology called LFAS. As a result, the deployment of LFAS has been stalled, and *Deadly Sounds* won Best Short Film at the 2003 Jackson Hole Wildlife Film Festival.

In 2002, *Orcas in Crisis* was presented to the U.S. National Marine Fisheries Service (NMFS) and the Canadian Department of Fisheries (DFO) in an effort to get the U.S. and Canadian governments to place the southern resident orcas on the endangered species list. Canada did so in 2003, followed by the United States in 2007.

In 2006, *Deadly Sounds in the Silent World II,* again featuring Pierce and Keely, was presented and distributed to the delegates attending the United Nations Law of the Sea meeting, asking the UN to take the lead in regulating manufactured underwater noise pollution. As a result, the UN has made the further study of artificial underwater noise pollution a priority.

Currently, my main focus is on the Save the Whales Again! campaign, a global media conservation campaign, officially launched in Hollywood in February 2007 by campaign spokesperson Hayden Panettiere along with several of her *Heroes* cast mates. Joining Hayden as our campaign spokespersons are Pierce and Keely Brosnan, Isabel Lucas, Leonor Varela, Alexandra Paul, Dave Rastovich, and others.

The campaign's mission is to end all commercial and scientific whaling as well as the barbaric dolphin drive hunts and the offshore porpoise harpoon hunts while raising public awareness of all the threats dolphins and whales face, including toxic pollution, noise pollution, over-fishing, entanglement in nets, global warming, loss of habitat, and increasing whaling.

I believe one of the best ways to get a message out to the public and to influence decision makers is to use the power of celebrity and the media to deliver the message. My experience is that you can put the brightest scientist or the world's greatest expert on any given subject in front of people and more often than not, the audience will get glassy-eyed and lose attention. But put a passionate celebrity in front of them delivering exactly the same message, someone the listeners believe they know and relate to, and they will pay attention.

But it can't be just any celebrity. Merely lending their name to a cause, which many celebrities do, doesn't often make a difference because they are only doing so to help improve their own image. To be truly effective, your spokesperson has to be passionate, to believe truly in your cause, and to be self-motivated and committed to the point of taking direct action to help raise awareness, whether through press conferences, television appearances, protests, or more.

I believe one of the main reasons we were ultimately successful in stopping Mitsubishi from building the world's largest salt plant in San Ignacio Lagoon was because Pierce went to the lagoon with us, witnessed its beauty, and experienced firsthand the amazing encounters with the friendly gray whales there. As a result, he was deeply moved and motivated to do whatever he could to help us take on and beat one of the world's largest corporations.

When I first met Hayden Panettiere on the set of a friend's film, she was only fifteen years old. But I was immediately impressed not only by how talented she was but by how she handled herself on the set and the relationship she had with Lesley, her mother. As we talked, I soon discovered that both were animal lovers. At the time, I was looking for someone to spearhead our Save the Whales Again! campaign. After showing them some of our public service announcements and previous films, I asked daughter and mother if they would be interested in getting involved, and they immediately agreed.

The first place I took Hayden and Lesley was San Ignacio Lagoon to experience the gray whales and share our success story. The trip had a huge impact on them both. Later, when I showed them the footage of the dolphin slaughter in Taiji, Japan's notorious dolphin killing cove, and asked whether they wanted to go there and take part in an action that was being planned by my friend and fellow activist Dave Rastovich, they did not hesitate.

In October 2007, we traveled together to Taiji. Images from our visit were shown around the world, bringing international awareness to the issue later heightened with the release of the documentary film *The Cove*, which also included scenes from our visit.

Hayden Panettiere: The brutal practice in Japan of herding dolphins and small whales into coves and killing them is ongoing. The hunters blind and frighten the helpless animals by hammering on metal poles in the water, driving them into small coves where they are trapped in nets and then killed.

I experienced this slaughter firsthand when Jeff invited me to join him on that 2007 trip to Taiji. Along with actress Isabel Lucas, our Australian spokesperson, and four other activists, we took part in a peaceful paddle-out ceremony. Following Dave's lead, we paddled our surfboards out into the bloodred waters where over thirty pilot whales had already been slaughtered, and we honored all the beautiful animals that had lost their lives there. During our peaceful ceremony, the Japanese fishermen, unprovoked, became violent and physically aggressive toward us. Though being hit with large poles and threatened with spinning boat propellers, which came inches from us, we held our ground. The resulting international media attention generated by the incident was massive, and the support from people around the world has been incredible.

The irony is that most of the Japanese public is unaware that these hunts even happen, that over 20,000 dolphins and porpoises are being slaughtered by Japanese fishermen every year.

~~~

THE REASON I CHOOSE TO FOCUS MY EFFORTS on saving the dolphins and whales is twofold. First, dolphins and whales are charismatic creatures, both intelligent and beautiful. Second, dolphins and whales are also the barometer of the overall health of our oceans. I truly believe that as go the dolphins and whales, so go our oceans, and as go the oceans, so goes all life on Earth. If we can save the dolphins and whales, we will save our oceans and, ultimately, our planet and ourselves.

Fish Without a Doubt
Chef Rick Moonen

*Once the king of New York City seafood restaurants, Chef Rick's
eponymous restaurant in Las Vegas is one of the leading examples
of a cook committing to sustainable seafood. A founding member
of the Seafood Choices Alliances, which named him "Seafood
Champion" in 2006, he is an active member of Seafood Watch
and SeaWeb, practicing what he preaches—choosing
fish wisely—at home and in his restaurant.*

I was first introduced to the world of ocean-friendly seafood when I was
executive chef at Oceana in New York City in the 1990s. I was approached
by a nonprofit conservation organization, SeaWeb, which had done its
research and knew I had been highly involved in the Pure Foods campaign. I became quite outspoken that consumers, including chefs, have
the right to know what's in their food. SeaWeb was concerned about
a different issue, the North Atlantic swordfish, and wanted me to sign
on to their Give Swordfish a Break campaign. They were asking chefs
to take swordfish off their menu as a means of raising awareness that
Atlantic swordfish populations needed protection.

I had been going to the Fulton Fish Market in Lower Manhattan for
years and had seen a lot of changes in both the size and quality of fish.
In 1988, swordfish often weighed two hundred pounds; today they are

often half that size. I admit that I was quite nervous about taking such a popular seafood item off my menu, that it might not be a smart business decision. But I began to feel very passionate about the issue and signed on. I became the campaign's spokesperson; the campaign ended up being historic in that it actually motivated the government to take action.

Since then, I've enjoyed being on the front lines for other species campaigns such as Take a Pass on Chilean Sea Bass and Caviar Emptor. In 2001, I worked with SeaWeb to launch the Seafood Choices Alliance, an association of conservation organizations and seafood professionals that brings ocean conservation to the table by promoting seafood that is good to eat and good for the ocean. As a Seafood Champion for the alliance, I was often called upon to testify at management council meetings or government hearings and to participate in media functions related to seafood and ocean conservation and in development of local events to raise awareness of better seafood choices, like Seafood Watch.

But let's get one thing straight: I love fish and cooking fish. For me it's an issue of choosing the right fish. And cooking fish at home can be a very satisfying experience. We can all tick off the reasons, from fish being rich in healthy fats and quick to cook to the most primal: Fish just tastes good. No, better than that, well-prepared fish will knock your dinner guests' socks off.

But face it, for many home cooks, buying a piece of fish raises issues they don't have to face when they're on the more familiar turf of beef, pork, and poultry. There are understandable fears. "I can't get the fish this recipe calls for; what do I do?" "How do I know if it's fresh?" "What if all I can get is frozen fish?" "I don't have problems when I broil chicken, but when I try to broil fish, it sticks to the pan." "I don't know if it's done."

Let's start with the most basic reason home cooks balk. I can't tell you how many people tell me they're afraid of their kitchen smelling fishy. (Why have I never heard anyone say they're afraid of cooking steak because they don't want their kitchen to smell "beefy"?) The truth? Fish shouldn't smell fishy. If it does, it's not as fresh as it should be, and that smell is just going to get stronger when you cook it.

What should you look for, both in your fish market and in the fish and shellfish you buy? I can give you plenty of tips, easily identified cues that I've learned over years of shopping for fish, but one of the best ways

Our Overfished Oceans

The populations of the following fish are compromised, and you should avoid them, whether you're shopping for dinner or eating in a restaurant.

Bluefin tuna

Chilean sea bass

Cod (Atlantic)

Corvina (Gulf of California)

Flounder/Sole (Atlantic)

Grenadier

Grouper (Atlantic, Gulf of Mexico, and Hawaii)

Halibut (Atlantic)

Monkfish

Orange roughy

Pompano

Queen Conch

Shark/Dogfish (except dogfish from British Columbia

Skate

Snapper (red, ruby)

Sturgeon and Caviar(imported)

Tilefish (golden, from the Gulf of Mexico and our southern Atlantic)

Totoaba

to get good fish is to find a source you can trust and make friends with the guy behind the counter. Talk to him, ask his advice, and let him know your preferences and uncertainties.

Not all of us are fortunate enough to have a great fish market in our town, though. I certainly don't. My restaurant is in Las Vegas, not exactly a seaport, so I rely on some great suppliers on the East and West Coasts to ship fish and shellfish to me. The Internet opens up a world of possibilities, and you can find similar suppliers of high-quality sustainable seafood online. For those of you who wonder about the wisdom of having fish shipped to you, trust me: When you order from a reputable source, your fish arrive in pristine condition.

Despite the fact that many of the fish in the sea are overfished and many fish farms create environmental impacts of their own, that doesn't mean you should avoid eating fish. The Environmental Protection Agency says, "A well-balanced diet that includes a variety of fish and shellfish can contribute to heart health and children's proper growth and development," and it further notes that for most people, the risk from mercury by eating fish and shellfish is an overinflated health scare. However, higher levels of mercury can have a real impact on the unborn and young children. Women who are pregnant, likely to become pregnant, or nursing should watch the amount and kind of fish they eat, and parents need to take equal care in the fish and shellfish they serve young children.

Dragging the ocean bottom with tires and chain-mesh nets, a practice known as trawling, may be an effective way of catching fish, but some scientists believe that this harms the ocean more than any other activity. Bycatch, unwanted or unmarketable marine life that is accidentally caught in nets and then discarded, damages the ocean population as well. Fish too small to be sold are thrown back, dead or dying; these young fish would otherwise rebuild depleted species such as snapper or provide food for larger fish. Catching fish by longline, hook and line, and traps are all much less detrimental to the ocean environment. You should look for fish caught this way.

The oceans cannot provide an endless supply of fish. Technology and more effective fishing methods have led to fish populations being caught faster than they can reproduce. Cod have been depleted as much because of overfishing as from damage to the ocean floors. So fishermen turned to monkfish, a "trash fish" once discarded as bycatch. Now monkfish are depleted. A savvy marketing campaign renamed the Patagonian toothfish "Chilean sea bass." These are slow-growing fish, living forty years. A fish that takes that long to mature is particularly susceptible to overfishing, something that is clear when you find out how few of these fish are left in the world.

Aquaculture, or fish farming, sounds like a good idea, and often it is. Many inland farms, for omnivorous fish like catfish and tilapia, do little to damage the ecosystem. The same goes for oyster, clam, and mussel farms. In fact, because these shellfish filter seawater for their food like powerful little vacuum cleaners, farmers raising oysters, clams, and mussels are often in the fore in keeping coastal waters clean.

Net-pen farming, on the other hand, poses major issues for the environment. Here large pens, reminiscent of cattle feedlots, are built in the ocean, and the fish are often raised in crowded conditions. The farming of salmon is a prime example of the problems. These farmed fish generate a large amount of waste, which is released, untreated, into the ocean. The crowding leads to diseases and parasites, which are treated, with varying degrees of success, with antibiotics. And farmed fish can escape from the pens, spreading any disease and interbreeding with wild populations, weakening them. The escaped fish also compete with wild fish for food.

Seafood conservation has become the focus of my career. As a seafood chef, I feel I have the utmost responsibility to ensure a lasting and diverse supply of seafood. My customers have begun to know me as a conservationist and expect that everything on my menu has been caught or farmed in a way that has had minimal impact on the environment. But for the consumers who don't know me or are going to other restaurants, they should ask questions of their server or chef and educate themselves as well as possible about what makes fish sustainable.

- Where is the fish from? Be a smart shopper!
- Is the fish farmed or wild caught?
- If the seafood is wild caught, how was it caught?
- Eat smaller fish; they are lower on the food chain and better for the environment and your health.

If a server, manager, or chef of a restaurant can't provide you with this information, they do not hold the passion and commitment about serving only sustainable seafood. As a consumer, you are entitled to know what you are buying and how to choose it. If nothing's done to change the way we are purchasing, consuming, and removing biomass from the ocean, all commercially available fish will be extinct in the next thirty-five to forty years. That was reported by biologist Boris Worm in *Science* in 2006 and scares the hell out of me.

You've Got to Get Wet
Christopher Swain

A resident of Massachusetts, Christopher is in the midst of his most ambitious adventure yet: swimming down America's eastern seaboard. Previous record-setting swims have taken him the entire length of the Hudson, Columbia, and Charles rivers, as well as Lake Champlain. Using adventure to draw attention to environmental concerns can be a tricky but effective lure.

When I was a boy, I snorkeled in Buzzards Bay, a fat thumb of the Atlantic Ocean that presses into the coast of Massachusetts. I remember squinting down through my mask at acres of rippled sand, hunting for the telltale bulges of treasure chests. As an eight-year-old, I didn't know the sea was warming and turning acidic. I had no idea there was mercury in the bottom sediments or pesticides in the waves. I was just a kid who loved the ocean.

As an adult, I swam through thousands of miles of water laced with everything from motor oil to raw sewage in an effort to make more friends for our waterways. When I gave speeches about my adventures, folks would sidle up to me afterward and ask, "What can I do to help?"

Well, I don't know about you, but I've got an inbox full of spam telling me what I could be doing to help the ocean, about how I could clean up plastic trash in the Pacific or stop whale hunting in the Southern Ocean. And I have to admit it bugs me every time someone tells me what I should be doing. But when people are looking into my eyes, asking for ideas, I feel like I need to say something.

I believe we protect what we love.

When we walk the beach, play in the surf, or go for a swim in our favorite slice of the sea, we get in touch with what's going on there. We begin to care about that place. We become invested. And once we are invested, protection and restoration take care of themselves.

You know what I see when I look at pictures of our planet? Massive swaths of blue water. Continents floating like islands. And living on those islands? One people sharing one ocean.

Your ocean.

You want to protect it?

You've got to get wet.

CONTRIBUTORS

Abigail Alling has studied coral reefs and cetaceans worldwide. She is president of Biosphere Foundation, an organization that manages expeditions at sea as well as several community conservation projects in Southeast Asia. She participated in the Biosphere 2 project, a laboratory for global ecology, and created its 1-million-gallon coral reef.

Writer and filmmaker **Jon Bowermaster**, a six-time grantee of the National Geographic Expeditions Council, is author of eleven books and producer of fifteen documentary films. For the past twenty years, his storytelling focus has been the relationship between man and the sea, and he has traveled around the globe one continent at a time looking at both the health of the world's ocean and the lives of people who depend on it.

Recognized internationally as one of the most dashing and skilled dramatic actors in Hollywood, **Pierce Brosnan** is best known worldwide for his role as James Bond. In addition to his acting career, Pierce, together with his wife, Keely Brosnan, has been drawn into a passionate leadership role in environmental issues.

Susan Casey is the editor of *O: The Oprah Magazine* and former magazine development director at Time Inc. Author of *The Devil's Teeth: A True Story of Obsession and Survival Among America's Great White Sharks*, her new book, *The Wave: A Journey into the Heart of the Ocean*, will be published in 2010.

Liz Clark grew up in San Diego aboard family sailboats. She discovered surfing at age fifteen and, after earning a BA in Environmental Studies from University of California–Santa Barbara, spent three years preparing to sail off into her dream of a surfing circumnavigation. More than 15,000 nautical miles later, she is still sailing aboard her forty-foot sailboat, *Swell*.

Alexandra Cousteau, a globally recognized advocate of water quality and policy, continues the work of her renowned grandfather, Jacques-Yves Cousteau, and her father, Philippe Cousteau Sr. Dedicated to advocating the importance of conservation and sustainable management of water resources to preserve a healthy planet, her global initiatives seek to inspire and empower individuals to protect not only the ocean and its inhabitants but also the human communities that rely on freshwater resources.

Céline Cousteau explores and documents social, cultural, and environmental challenges. With a background in psychology and an MA in intercultural relations, she uses the human story to communicate the significance of these challenges. Granddaughter of Jacques-Yves Cousteau, daughter of Jean-Michel Cousteau, she is spokesperson for SeaWeb's *Too Precious to Wear* campaign, international spokeswoman for the La Prairie cosmetic company, ambassador to the Clean Up the World campaign, and a collaborator with the World Resources Institute on a public outreach campaign.

Lynne Cox is an international best-selling writer and speaker and a celebrated open-water swimmer who has set records all over the world. She is author of *Swimming to Antarctica* and *Grayson;* her work appears in the *New Yorker* and other publications.

John Cronin is director of the Beacon Institute for Rivers and Estuaries and senior fellow at Pace University. He started his environmental career in 1974, under the influence of folksinger Pete Seeger. He is an author, former commercial fisherman, former Hudson Riverkeeper, and a *Time* magazine Hero for the Planet.

Founder of Adventure Ecology, an organization that harnesses the power of dreams, adventures, and stories, **David de Rothschild** is one of only forty-two people, and the youngest British person, to reach both geographic poles. Author of *The Global Warming Survival Handbook*, he is host of the Sundance Channel's series *Eco-Trip*, a United Nations Environmental Programme Climate Hero, and a National Geographic Emerging Explorer.

Actor and environmental activist **Leonardo DiCaprio** is on the board of trustees of the Natural Resources Defense Council (NRDC) and a board member of both Global Green USA and the International Fund for Animal Welfare. His Leonardo DiCaprio Foundation promotes environmental campaigns, such as a worldwide movement to eliminate plastic bags, and is running an ongoing series of challenges to inspire positive environmental action beginning in 2010. The foundation has produced several short films, including *Water Planet*, and spearheaded production of the feature-length *11th Hour*.

Oceanographer **Sylvia Earle** is a National Geographic Explorer in Residence, founder of the Deep Search Foundation, and former chief scientist of NOAA. Called "Her Deepness" by the *New Yorker*, a living legend by the Library of Congress, and *Time* magazine's first Hero for the Planet, she has led more than 100 expeditions and been awarded more than 100 national and international honors, including the 2009 TED Prize for her wish "to explore and protect the ocean, blue heart of the planet."

Richard Ellis is one of America's leading marine conservationists and is generally recognized as the foremost painter of marine natural history subjects in the world. A research associate at the American Museum of Natural History in New York, he is the author of more than twenty books and 100 magazine articles.

Jane Lubchenco, undersecretary of commerce for oceans and atmosphere, NOAA administrator, is a marine ecologist and environmental scientist. She has studied marine ecosystems around the world and has championed the importance of science and its relevance to policy making and human well-being as a scientist and professor. One of the most highly cited ecologists in the world, she is an elected member of the U.S. National Academy of Sciences and has received numerous awards, including a MacArthur Fellowship "Genius Award"; the 2002 Heinz Award in the Environment; the 2005 AAAS Award for Public Understanding of Science and Technology; and the 2008 Zayed International Prize for the Environment.

Christopher Mann is a senior officer with the Pew Environment Group in Washington DC, where he directs projects on ocean governance, aquaculture, and fisheries management. He joined the trust with more than twenty years of experience in marine policy and science, including positions with nonprofit organizations, the Department of State, and Congress.

Brad Matsen has been writing about wonders of the sea for forty years. He is the author most recently of *Jacques Cousteau: The Sea King; Descent: The Heroic Discovery of the Abyss* (a finalist for the *Los Angeles Times* Book Prize in 2006); the *New York Times* best-seller, *Titanic's Last Secrets; Planet Ocean: A Story of Life, the Sea, and Dancing to the Fossil Record* with artist Ray Troll; the award-winning *Incredible Ocean Adventure* series for children; and many other books. He was creative producer for the *Shape of Life*, an eight-hour National Geographic television series on evolutionary biology, and has written on marine science and the environment for *Mother Jones, Audubon, Natural History*, and many other magazines.

An advocate for sustainable fishing and seafood, **Chef Rick Moonen** has a passion for conservation that has led him to national acclaim. His restaurant career has taken him from the kitchens of some of the best restaurants in New York City (Le Cirque, Le Relais, Century Café, the Water Club, and executive chef and partner at Oceana) to relocation in Las Vegas, where he opened Rick Moonen's rm Seafood at Mandalay Bay. He is a founding member of the Seafood Choices Alliance, which named him Seafood Champion in 2006, as well as an active member of the Wildlife Conservation Society and of SeaWeb and a chef's advisory board member of Ecofish.

President Mohamed Nasheed is the first democratically elected president in the history of the Maldives. Since winning a historic election in October 2008 after leading a nonviolence campaign for democracy, he has introduced legislation to improve human rights safeguards in the Maldives and has campaigned internationally for tougher action to combat climate change.

The pioneering efforts of **Wallace J. Nichols** to study sea turtles, educate coastal communities, and provide alternatives to poaching have inspired millions. He shares his experiences worldwide, building conservation networks in Latin America, Asia, and Africa with OceanRevolution.org. He co-founded SEEtheWILD.org, an innovative conservation tourism project.

Richard O'Barry, a marine mammal specialist with the Earth Island Institute, has worked both sides of the dolphin street, the first ten years with the dolphin captivity industry and the past thirty-eight against it. On the first Earth Day, in 1970, he founded the Dolphin Project, dedicated to freeing captive dolphins that were viable candidates and educating people throughout the world to the plight of dolphins in captivity. He was the primary force behind and star of the critically acclaimed documentary *The Cove*, about the fight to stop dolphin slaughters in Japan.

Appearing in more than twenty feature films since debuting in a Playskool commercial at eleven months of age, twenty-year-old actress **Hayden Panettiere** is internationally known for portraying Claire Bennet on *Heroes* but is perhaps even better known for her real-life exploits as spokesperson for the Whaleman Foundation and its Save the Whales Again! campaign.

Jeff Pantukhoff is an award-winning marine life photographer, filmmaker, and conservationist who, in 1995, founded the Whaleman Foundation, a public nonprofit research, conservation, and environmental production organization dedicated to preserving and protecting dolphins, whales, and our oceans. Spokespersons in his campaigns and films include Hayden Panettiere, Isabel Lucas, Pierce and Keely Brosnan, and more.

French film actor, director, and producer **Jacques Perrin** has worked both in front of and behind the camera. He acted in and produced *Z*, directed by Costa-Gavras, which won the Academy Award for best foreign film in 1969. More recently, he's best known around the world for his big-budget, high-concept nature films, *Microcosmos* and *Winged Migration*. His Galatee Films spent eight years on the groundbreaking new film, *Oceans*.

Callum Roberts is professor of marine conservation at the University of York in England. A prolific author and researcher, he has advised the U.S., British, and Caribbean governments on the creation of marine reserves. He authored *The Unnatural History of the Sea* for Island Press in 2007.

Naomi A. Rose is senior scientist for Humane Society International (HSI), overseeing campaigns to protect wild and captive marine mammals, and is a member of the International Whaling Commission's Scientific Committee. She has published popular and scientific articles and authored book chapters and lectures annually at several universities.

Carl Safina, recipient of a MacArthur Fellowship "Genius Award," was named by *Audubon* magazine among the leading one hundred conservationists of the twentieth century. He's been profiled by the *New York Times* and interviewed on *Nightline* and by Bill Moyers, and his books and articles have also won him a Pew Fellowship, Lannan Literary Award, and John Burroughs Medal, among others.

He is an adjunct professor at Stony Brook University and founder of Blue Ocean Institute. His books include *Voyage of the Turtle*, *Eye of the Albatross*, and *Song for the Blue Ocean*. His latest book, *The View from Lazy Point*, will be published in 2010.

Roz Savage, British ocean rower and environmental campaigner, spent eleven years as a management consultant before becoming an eco-adventurer. In 2005, she rowed solo across the Atlantic and is now attempting to become the first woman to row solo across the Pacific. She is a UN Climate Hero, ambassador for 350.org, and author of *Rowing the Atlantic*.

Lisa Suatoni is a senior scientist in the oceans program at the Natural Resources Defense Council, working on a variety of topics, including fisheries, marine ecosystem–based management, climate change impacts on marine ecosystems, and ocean acidification. She has a PhD in ecology and evolutionary biology from Yale University and an MA in environmental studies from the Yale School of Forestry and Environmental Studies. Her scientific research focuses on speciation and the evolution of reproductive isolation.

Committed to protecting the environment and the health and safety of citizens, **Wilma Subra** founded an environmental consulting firm, Subra Company, in New Iberia, LA, in 1981. A chemist, she has provided technical assistance to citizens and communities concerned about their local environments across the United States and some foreign countries by combining technical research and evaluation and developing strategies with community members. She received the MacArthur Fellowship "Genius Award" for helping ordinary citizens understand, cope with, and address environmental issues in their communities.

Christopher Swain is the first person in history to have swum the entire lengths of the Columbia, Charles, and Hudson rivers. He has survived collisions with boats, twelve-foot waves, lightning storms, class IV+ rapids, toxic blue-green algae, sea lamprey eel attacks, and water contaminated with everything from human waste to nuclear waste. Along the way he has worked with more than 60,000 schoolchildren. In 2009, he began a thousand-mile-plus swim down the U.S. coastline of the Atlantic Ocean to measure and map the effects of climate change.

Tierney Thys is a National Geographic Emerging Explorer, biologist, and filmmaker. Her award-winning documentaries have chronicled the rise of the animal kingdom and global environmental change and inspired citizen action. A world expert on giant ocean sunfish, *Mola mola*, Thys leads expeditions worldwide and delivers lectures to all ages.

Captain Paul Watson was a co-founder of Greenpeace in 1969; his official membership number is 007. He left the group in 1977 after several successful and controversial campaigns against whale and seal hunting, when the group moved away from "direct actions." That same year, he established the Sea Shepherd Conservation Society and has been fighting to protect whales and other marine animals since. The *Animal Planet* television show *Whale Wars* has taken Sea Shepherd's efforts to an international audience. He was awarded the George H. W. Bush Daily Points of Light Award in 1999 for his volunteer efforts toward conservation activism and was chosen by *Time* magazine as one of the environmental heroes of the twentieth century.

Edith A. Widder is a deep-sea biologist, a specialist in bioluminescence and technology development, and president, senior scientist, and co-founder of the Ocean Research & Conservation Association, an organization dedicated to the study and protection of marine ecosystems and the species they sustain, through development of innovative technologies and science-based conservation action.

WHAT YOU CAN DO

BLUE OCEAN INSTITUTE

Inspiration, Information, Action

www.blueocean.org

Seafood FAQs

How can I tell where the seafood at the store came from and how it was caught?

We have found that American West Coast markets label fish more precisely and extensively than markets do on the East Coast, so we know it can be done. Still, many markets and restaurants give only the common name for kinds of seafood and do not specify which ocean the species came from or how it was caught. Some seafood counters and menus use labels selectively to promote popular kinds of seafood such as "Alaska salmon" or "New Zealand mussels," but that is the exception. Furthermore, some farmed salmon is being sold as Atlantic salmon even if it was an Atlantic species raised in the Pacific. This certainly leaves many questions. The conservation community is working together with members of the seafood industry to find ways to ensure that every fish has a label indicating its species name and place of origin. Until there is more information, don't be dismayed when you select seafood. Instead, just ask where the seafood has come from, and if the waitperson or the person at the counter does not know, explain why you care! It may take time, but the market will follow.

Where can I go to find the best choices of seafood?

Some restaurants and grocery stores are catching on quickly to consumers' widespread use of various seafood lists. They are realizing the public has a real interest in having more sustainable seafood choices. Check your local stores to find out whether they offer the choices you're seeking. Good alternatives are online seafood retailers, such as EcoFish.com, who feature the most sustainable species and will deliver to your home or will supply restaurants, caterers, and grocery stores.

Will the waitstaff at my favorite restaurant be able to answer my questions when I ask where a certain fish came from or how it was caught?

Remember the expression "Rome was not built in a day"? Well, awareness about seafood issues will not grow overnight. We are at the beginning of a movement to promote best practices in the seafood industry. Although some waiters and waitresses may understand your concerns and be ready to answer your questions, for others, your questions might be the first they have ever received. Have patience and feel good about your role not only as a responsible consumer but as a leader.

If there are tons of shrimp out there, what's wrong with eating shrimp?

For some types of seafood—and shrimp is one of them—the problem is not how many are caught but how they're caught. Shrimp boats use large nets called *trawls,* which shrimpers drag along the bottom to catch shrimp. Unfortunately, shrimp are not the only species they catch. For each pound of shrimp caught, they also catch four to ten pounds of unwanted marine life—bycatch—most of which are discarded and die. Although U.S. shrimp fishermen have been successful in reducing the number of sea turtles that are caught in their nets, bycatch reduction efforts are still inadequate in some regions. And in addition to bycatch problems, shrimp trawls can cause serious impacts on bottom habitat as the nets drag along the bottom. Shrimp farming is not an acceptable alternative because many farms destroy natural habitat and create pollution or disease problems. The good news is that alternative ways exist to catch shrimp that are less damaging than trawl-caught or farmed shrimp. These less damaging shrimp traps are being used in Alaska, California, and Maine.

I am just one person. How can my seafood choices really help?

By choosing your seafood wisely, you can help shift demand away from fish and shellfish that are overfished or poorly managed toward those that are in better shape. Remember that the seafood selections you see in the supermarket and on restaurant menus are there because people are demanding them. You can contribute to the movement that encourages better fisheries management and abundance in the seas by letting your local markets and restaurants know what you'd like to see and why. Restaurant and market owners are most successful when they listen to their customers' requests. If enough people ask for a particular kind of seafood, the demand will become great enough to make it profitable to sell it. Remind your local seafood sellers that you are not part of a boycott but, rather, that you are simply asking them to offer more sustainable choices. When you tell all the seafood lovers you know to choose their seafood wisely, you are no longer one person—you are helping create the movement.

Is farmed seafood better for the environment than seafood from the wild?

As frustrating as it may seem when you are looking for a yes-or-no answer, the real answer is that it depends. Aquaculture, or the farming of fish, is a booming industry and can take the pressure off some depleted wild fish, but not all. For example, farmed catfish and tilapia are increasingly popular with seafood lovers and can be a smart alternative when the fish are raised in closed systems in which wastes are controlled and there is little chance of the fish escaping. These fish are also fed a vegetable-based diet such as corn- and soy-based feed. Other farmed species such as Atlantic salmon can be more problematic. In places such as the Pacific, they can escape and threaten native species with diseases, and when some farmed species such as salmon are fed large quantities of wild caught fish, we're not really conserving fish. By following the advice of organizations that have transparent methods of rating seafood, you can ensure that you are making choices that help solve the problem.

Is seafood the perfect food?

It's hard to imagine that eating anything that tastes so good—and can be good for you—could cause a major problem. More people than ever before are choosing to eat seafood; to meet this growing demand, more fish and shellfish are being caught and farmed than ever before. However, depending on how many fish are caught, the way they're caught, how well fishing operations are managed, and how long they must live before they're able to reproduce, some fish and shellfish are doing distinctly better than others. For example, the delicious mahimahi grows fast and matures early and therefore is less vulnerable to overfishing than a fish such as orange roughy, which takes longer to mature and reproduce. The ready availability of species in the marketplace can create a false impression that if a species is available, it must be abundant or well managed. Fortunately, when you choose seafood that is more abundant and better managed, you are making a difference for ocean life.

CENSUS
OF MARINE LIFE

www.coml.org

A Global Database

The Census of Marine Life is a global network of more than two thousand scientists from more than eighty nations conducting the first comprehensive assessment of the diversity, distribution, and abundance of marine life. The first Census of Marine Life will be released in October 2010.

Established in 2000 by about a dozen leading marine biologists concerned with gaps in knowledge of marine biodiversity, the Census of Marine Life has grown into the largest and most ambitious program in the history of marine biology. The Census encompasses fourteen field projects organized around habitats such as coral reefs or groups of species such as top predators like sharks and tuna. Thirteen national and regional implementation committees, ranging from Australia and Japan to the Indian Ocean and Caribbean, support the program. The Census has conducted more than four hundred cruises as well as hundreds of shore-based expeditions.

Overfishing, destruction of habitat, and possible changes in the temperature and chemistry of the oceans caused by human activities give urgency to the Census. Most fished stocks and near-shore marine animal populations already experience tremendous pressures, and the likely prospect is that human activities will reach farther and deeper into the oceans. Urgency—and excitement—also come from the fact that most of the deep ocean remains unexplored biologically.

The Census of Marine Life provides a way for scientists to ally to produce a global picture from near shore to mid-ocean, seafloor to sea surface, Equator to poles, and microbes to mammals. A key attractor of the Census is its geographic information system, the Ocean Biogeographical Information System (OBIS), which already integrates data on more than 108,000 marine species. The Census partners with the online Encyclopedia of Life, which provides biographies for all species, marine and terrestrial. The vision of the Census is a continuously updated database on the status of marine life, linked with counterpart projects and accessible through portals such as Google Earth.

The Census of Marine Life scheduled for October 2010 will report on all known forms of marine life, expected to number at least 230,000. The Census will offer the first complete compilation of already discovered marine biodiversity and will estimate the forms of marine life that remain to be discovered, which may total more than 1 million multicellular forms and 20 million microbial forms. For many known species, the Census will also offer maps of their likely range and estimates of abundance. Accurate estimates of abundance are difficult because of the vastness of the oceans and are the source of much conflict, especially about fished species such as cod and salmon.

The Census aims to spur a sequel, Census 2020, that would maintain a fast pace of exploration and discovery while also providing timely documentation of changes in diversity, distribution, and abundance from the 2010 baseline. The motto of the Census, "Making ocean life count," expresses its commitment to accurate information and increased public appreciation of marine biodiversity.

The Census of Marine Life helps experts concerned with marine biodiversity do their work more effectively and efficiently. It builds the global social capital of expertise in marine biodiversity. United under the pennant of the Census of Marine Life, marine biologists also have a much better chance to share with a wide public their startling, beautiful, and sometimes heartbreaking discoveries.

Although the Census of Marine Life is itself an independent nongovernmental organization, its secretariat and projects receive support from governments, private foundations, and private industries. Members of its leadership serve in their individual capacities on the basis of their expertise.

The Census of Marine Life has come to be recognized as an authoritative voice on the scientific dimensions of marine biodiversity. National governments and international organizations have used its findings and reports to nominate and define marine protected areas, for example, along the mid-Atlantic ridge and in polar seas. The intergovernmental Convention on Biodiversity (CBD) is relying on the Census to demarcate environmentally and biologically sensitive areas for CBD negotiations.

Although many of the Census of Marine Life projects require advanced professional training for participation, some of its projects lend themselves to "citizen science." For example, its near-shore project (NaGISA) has benefited greatly from regular collection of samples by high school students in Florida, Japan, and Kenya. To access raw Census of Marine Life data, visit www.iobis.org. To explore Census of Marine Life discoveries in the ocean of Google Earth, visit the Census of Marine Life and Animal Tracking layers. To learn more about the Census in general and to enjoy photo galleries of its discoveries, please visit www.coml.org.

GREENPEACE

www.greenpeace.org/international/campaigns/oceans

Dead Oceans, Dead Planet

We need to defend the oceans now more than ever because the oceans need all the resilience they can muster in the face of climate change and the potentially disastrous impacts this is already beginning to produce in the marine world.

The Greenpeace Defending Our Oceans campaign sets out to protect and preserve our oceans now and for the future by setting aside swaths of the global oceans from exploitation and controllable human pressures, allowing these areas the respite they so desperately need for recovery and renewal.

Building on a protection and recovery system established to manage land-based overexploitation, Marine Reserves are the ocean equivalent of national parks. Marine Reserves are a scientifically developed and endorsed approach to redressing the crisis in our oceans, which work alongside a range of other measures designed to ensure that the demands we make of our oceans are managed sustainably.

Beyond Marine Reserves, we need to tackle a great many threats to the oceans' viability and find better ways of managing their resources. To this end, while Greenpeace campaigns for Marine Reserves, we also campaign against the acts that have brought the oceans to this point; we expose the countless pressures, reveal the threats, confront the villains, and point to the solutions and measures necessary to create sustainable oceans. The following are key threats.

Industrial fishing

Giant ships, using state-of-the-art equipment, can pinpoint schools of fish quickly and accurately. These industrial fishing fleets have exceeded the ocean's ecological limits. As larger fish are wiped out, the next smaller fish species are targeted and so on. (Canadian fisheries expert Dr. Daniel Pauly warns that if this continues, our children will be eating jellyfish.) Simply put, more and more people are competing for fewer and fewer fish and worsening the existing oceans crisis.

Bycatch

Modern fishing practices are incredibly wasteful. Every year, fishing nets kill up to 300,000 whales, dolphins, and porpoises globally. Entanglement is the greatest threat to the survival of many species. Moreover, some fishing practices destroy habitats as well as inhabitants. Bottom trawling, for example, destroys entire ancient deep-sea coral forests and other delicate ecosystems. In some areas, it is the equivalent of plowing a field several times a year.

Unfair fisheries

As traditional fishing grounds in the north have collapsed, fishing efforts have increasingly turned to Africa and the Pacific. Pirates who ignore regulations and effectively steal fish are denying some of the poorest regions of the world much-needed food security and income, and those fleets fishing legally are giving only a small percentage of the profit to African or Pacific states.

Unsustainable aquaculture

Aquaculture (fish and shellfish farming) is often put forward as the future of the seafood industry, but it is not a solution to overfishing. Many modern aquaculture practices emphasize the unsustainable production of species for high-value export markets. Rapid expansion of intensive aquaculture has resulted in widespread degradation of the environment and the displacement of coastal fishing and farming communities.

Shrimp aquaculture industry is perhaps the most destructive, unsustainable, and unjust fisheries industry in the world. Mangrove clearances, fishery destruction, murder, and community land clearances have all been widely reported. The salmon farming industry also proves that farming is no solution; it takes approximately nine pounds of wild-caught fish to produce two pounds of farmed salmon.

Global warming

The ocean and its inhabitants will be irreversibly affected by the impacts of global warming and climate change. Scientists say that global warming, by increasing seawater temperatures, will raise sea levels and change ocean currents. The effects are already beginning to be felt. Whole species of marine animals and fish are at risk due to the temperature rise; they simply cannot survive in the changed conditions. For example, increased water temperatures are thought to be responsible for large areas of corals turning white (bleaching) and dying.

Pollution

Another significant impact of human activity on the marine environment is pollution. The most visible and familiar is oil pollution caused by tanker accidents. Yet despite the scale and visibility of such impacts, those of pollutants introduced from other sources dwarf the total quantities of pollutants entering the sea from oil spills. These other pollutants include domestic sewage, industrial discharges, urban and industrial runoff, accidents, spillage, explosions, sea dumping operations, mining, agricultural nutrients and pesticides, waste heat sources, and radioactive discharges.

Defending Our Oceans

Fundamental changes must be made in the way our oceans are managed. This means we must ensure that human activities are sustainable, in other words, that they meet human needs of current and future generations without causing harm to the environment. Accordingly, governments must set aside 40 percent of our oceans as marine reserves. Marine reserves can be defined as areas of the ocean in which the exploitation of all living resources is prevented, together with the prevention of exploitation of nonliving resources such as sand, gravel, and other minerals.

MONTEREY BAY AQUARIUM

www.montereybayaquarium.org

The mission of the Monterey Bay Aquarium is to inspire conservation of the oceans. It's a vision shared by all institutions accredited to the high standards of the Association of Zoos & Aquariums (www.aza.org). For us and other non-profit public aquariums, living exhibits are the most powerful and effective tools we have to win hearts and minds for a future with healthy oceans. With our colleagues, we're walking the talk—in our exhibits, operations, and our field conservation projects—as we inspire the public to action for our planet and its ocean life.

But we must do more—by giving people practical tools that they can use to make a difference. That's why we created Seafood Watch, the most recognized and respected program of its kind. Working with consumers, chefs, and major seafood buyers, we're harnessing the power of the marketplace to transform fisheries and fish farming in ways that support healthy oceans. And you can help.

Why Do Your Seafood Choices Matter?

Worldwide, the demand for seafood is increasing. Yet many populations of the large fish we enjoy eating are overfished and, in the United States, we import 80 percent of our seafood to meet the demand. Destructive fishing and fish farming practices only add to the problem. By purchasing fish caught or farmed using environmentally friendly practices, you're supporting healthy, abundant oceans.

You Can Make a Difference

Support ocean-friendly seafood fishing in three easy steps:

1. Purchase seafood from the Best Choices list on the facing page or, if unavailable, the Good Alternatives list; or look for the Marine Stewardship Council blue eco-label on store products and restaurant menus.
2. When you buy seafood, ask questions about where your seafood comes from.
3. Get and use the Seafood Watch pocket guides, mobile site, or iPhone app. And tell your friends! The more people who ask for ocean-friendly seafood, the better.

Support Ocean-Friendly Seafood

Seafood on the Best Choices list is abundant, well managed, and caught or farmed in environmentally friendly ways. Seafood items on the Good Alternatives list are options, but there are concerns about how they're caught or farmed, or with the health of their habitat due to other human impacts. Skip Avoid list items for now because they're caught or farmed in ways that harm other marine life or the environment.

Best Choices

Arctic char (farmed)
Barramundi (U.S. farmed)
Catfish (U.S. farmed)
Clams (farmed)
Cobia (U.S. farmed)
Cod: Pacific (Alaska longline)†
Crab: Dungeness, Stone
Halibut: Pacific†
Lobster: Spiny (U.S.)
Mussels (farmed)

Oysters (farmed)
Pollock (Alaska wild)†
Salmon (Alaska wild)†
Scallops: Bay (farmed)
Striped bass (farmed or wild*)
Tilapia (U.S. farmed)
Trout: Rainbow (farmed)
Tuna: Albacore (troll/pole, U.S.†
   or British Columbia)
Tuna: Skipjack (troll/pole)

Good Alternatives

Caviar, Sturgeon (U.S. farmed)
Clams (wild)
Cod: Pacific (U.S. trawled)
Crab: Blue,* King (U.S.), Snow
Crab: Imitation/Surimi
Flounder, Sole (Pacific)
Herring: Atlantic
Lobster: American/Maine
Mahimahi/Dolphinfish (U.S.)
Oysters (wild)*

Scallops: Sea (wild)
Shrimp (U.S., Canada)
Squid
Swai, Basa (farmed)
Swordfish (U.S.)*
Tilapia (Central America, farmed)
Tuna: Bigeye, Yellowfin (troll/pole)
Tuna: Canned Skipjack and
   Albacore*
Yellowtail (U.S. farmed)

Avoid

Caviar, Sturgeon* (imported wild)
Chilean sea bass/Toothfish*
Cobia (imported farmed)
Cod: Atlantic (imported Pacific)
Flounder, Halibut, Sole (Atlantic)
Groupers*
Lobster: Spiny (Caribbean)
Mahimahi/Dolphinfish
   (imported)
Marlin: Blue,* Striped*
Monkfish
Orange roughy*

Salmon (farmed, including
   Atlantic)*
Shark*
Shrimp (imported)
Snapper: Red
Swordfish (imported)*
Tilapia (Asia farmed)
Tuna: Albacore, Bigeye, Yellowfin
   (long-line)*
Tuna: Bluefin,* canned (except
   Albacore and Skipjack), Tongol
Yellowtail (imported, farmed)

---

* Limit consumption due to concerns about mercury or other contaminants. Visit www.edf.org/seafood.
† Some or all of this fishery is certified as sustainable to the Marine Stewardship Council standard.

www.noaa.gov/ocean.html

Protecting the Oceans and Providing Information So You Can Help

One of every six jobs in the United States is marine related, and more than one third of the U.S. gross national product (GNP) originates in coastal areas. The ocean is key to transportation and recreation, and its resources may hold the cures to many diseases. NOAA protects, preserves, manages, and enhances the resources found in 3.5 million square miles of coastal and deep ocean waters. NOAA's National Ocean Service provides products, services, and information that promote safe navigation, support coastal communities, sustain marine ecosystems, and mitigate coastal hazards.

Monitoring and Understanding

NOAA is the lead federal agency for implementing a national integrated ocean observing system that will be part of the greater Global Earth Observation System of Systems (GEOSS). The aim is to make twenty-first-century technology as interrelated as the planet it observes, to predict and protect, providing the science on which sound policy and decision making must be built. Sustained ocean monitoring helps people in ocean and lake-dependent industries such as shipping by providing them with information to make informed decisions. Long-term consistent monitoring improves our understanding of the ocean's role in many of Earth's systems.

NOAA maintains a network of buoys, tidal stations, and satellite measurements that provides a continuous picture of the state of the ocean and Great Lakes. Through the National Estuarine Research Reserves, NOAA tracks water quality, meteorology, and nutrient data. NOAA scientists are combining this information with other weather and climate data to begin addressing many important questions such as the dynamics behind climate change, the effects of human activities on ecosystems, and the impact of pollutants on the marine environment.

NOAA also maintains one of the world's largest archives of oceanographic data, used in long-term monitoring, ocean climatology, and ocean research, at the National Oceanographic Data Center.

NOAA's Office of Ocean Exploration and Research Program explores the unknown ocean by developing and using advanced technology for discoveries, including new undersea habitats, communities, species, and phenomena, and greater understanding of ecosystems. NOAA-led exploration is revealing clues to the origin of life on Earth, potential cures for human diseases, answers to help achieve sustainable use of resources, links to our maritime history, and information to help protect endangered species.

Understanding ocean ecosystem dynamics is critical for sustainable management of marine resources. NOAA's National Ocean Service, NOAA Research, and NOAA Fisheries work collectively to conduct leading-edge scientific research to provide resource managers with the information and tools needed to balance society's environmental, social, and economic goals.

Education

NOAA's mission is to serve the nation's need for oceanic and atmospheric information, but doing so also means helping ensure that the public understands how NOAA science affects their daily lives and future prosperity. Through its Office of Education as well as the National Marine Sanctuary Program, National Sea Grant Program, National Estuarine Research Reserves, and the NOAA Coral Program, NOAA is delivering educational tools and information supporting K–12 formal education, teacher professional development, and informal education to the American public.

NOAA Aquarius Underwater Laboratory is an underwater laboratory and home to scientists for missions up to ten days long. It allows scientists to work out on the reef up to nine hours a day. Increased research time on bottom is the key element that enhances scientific productivity beneath the sea. *www.uncw.edu/aquarius*

NOAA Coastal Services Center works with various branches of NOAA and other federal agencies to bring information, services, and technology to the nation's coastal resource managers. The center is a partner in more than one hundred ongoing projects geared to resolve site-specific coastal issues. *www.csc.noaa.gov*

NOAA Coral Health and Monitoring Program is an international network of coral reef researchers established to share knowledge and information on coral health and monitoring. CHAMP is now installing monitoring stations at all major U.S. coral reefs that will provide near real-time data. *www.coral.noaa.gov*

NOAA Marine Debris Program serves as a centralized marine debris monitoring capability within NOAA to coordinate, strengthen, and increase the visibility of marine debris issues and efforts within the agency, its partners, and the public. *www.marinedebris.noaa.gov*

NOAA National Geophysical Data Center Global Seafloor Topography provides stewardship, products, and services for geophysical data describing the solid earth, marine, and solar-terrestrial environments as well as Earth observations from space. *www.ngdc.noaa.gov/mgg/image/seafloor.html*

NOAA Office of Ocean and Coastal Resource Management provides national leadership, strategic direction, and guidance to state and territory coastal programs and estuarine research reserves. *www.ocrm.nos.noaa.gov*

NOAA Pacific Marine Environmental Laboratory (PMEL) carries out interdisciplinary scientific investigations in oceanography and atmospheric science. Current PMEL programs focus on open ocean observations in support of long-term monitoring and prediction of the ocean environment on time scales from hours to decades. *www.pmel.noaa.gov*

NOAA Undersea Research Center at UNC Wilmington supports undersea research off the southeastern United States from North Carolina to Texas. *www.uncwil.edu/nurc*

NOAA/NGS Sustainable Seas Expedition offers a comprehensive look at NOAA's 200-year history of ocean exploration through a series of chronological essays. Also included is a rich selection of historical quotations, arranged thematically, that capture the many advances, challenges, and misunderstandings through the years as both early and modern explorers struggled to study the mysterious ocean realm. *oceanexplorer.noaa.gov/explorations/explorations.html*

www.PewEnvironment.org/oceans

Using Sound Science to Advance Strong Environmental Policies

The Pew Environment Group (PEG), the conservation arm of the Pew Charitable Trusts, is dedicated to using sound science to advance strong environmental policies on climate change, wilderness protection, and ocean conservation. PEG manages a growing portfolio of domestic and international campaigns to end overfishing, protect and restore marine wildlife, safeguard ocean ecosystems, and ensure the sustainable development of marine aquaculture. PEG invests in scientific research to inform changes in policy and industry practices that will rebuild and strengthen our marine resources.

PEG's Campaign for Healthy Oceans has advocated for a national ocean policy that would protect, maintain, and restore the health of our marine ecosystems. Oceans sustain our coastal economies but, more important, oceans are essential to the health of the planet's air and water systems. Although a national policy should be carried out by the federal government, state governments need to be involved to ensure that all stakeholders are engaged in comprehensive, science-based, and precautionary management of marine resources.

Please visit our website, www.PewEnvironment.org/oceans, to learn more about PEG's ocean conservation efforts and how you can help protect our oceans. Whether you live near the coast or not, you can get involved in your community to ensure that the appropriate conservation goals are identified, meaningful benchmarks are established for measuring success, and government agencies are held accountable for achieving results in the water.

www.saveourseas.com

Save Our Seas

This is our moment of truth, and we cannot save our seas without you. Never before in human history has there been a more important time than the present to make a difference for our oceans. We have reached a turning point at which the future of our oceans hangs in the balance. No matter whether ocean water laps your borders or your country is surrounded by land, the ocean affects every single person on this planet. We call on every generation across the earth to act now and help us save our seas.

Respect our oceans.

Respect our oceans and those who live there. Remember that sharks have a history 200 million years older than the first dinosaurs. They are custodians of our seas, and we need healthy shark populations for us to enjoy healthy oceans. The ocean is their home, not ours.

Seafood on the menu?

Shark's fin soup is not on our menu—do not let it be on yours, and boycott all restaurants that serve it. Sharks are often caught as bycatch as well as targeted in longline fishing. Think about what fishing method was used to catch particular seafood and avoid seafood from fisheries that have high bycatch levels that destroy the marine environment. Avoid seafood that comes from bottom-trawl fisheries and choose seafood from sustainable sources.

Don't buy shark or ray products.

Avoid purchasing or supporting companies that buy, distribute, or sell shark or ray products. Do not buy any products, including medicine, that use gill raker or shark cartilage. Shark cartilage does not belong in your medicine cabinet; it belongs to the shark. Also, abstain from buying shark jaws, shark teeth, and any other parts from sharks or rays such as shark or ray skin purses, shoes, or knife handles. If shark or ray products are fashionable in your circles, make them unfashionable. Explain where they originate and how sharks are on the edge of extinction. It is up to us to keep shark and ray skins underwater on the animals that grew them and not on the high street.

Connect to the ocean.
Be inspired by the grandeur of the ocean. Connect to the ocean, study marine biology, or apply to become an intern with our researchers. Support ecotourism operators who follow good codes of practice when diving or interacting with sharks or manta rays. Donate to the Save Our Seas Foundation and help us learn more about sharks and rays to protect them better and create more marine protected areas.

Reduce your CO_2 emissions.
The world's oceans currently absorb over 25 million tons of CO_2 every day, and this has caused surface waters to become 30 percent more acidic since the widespread burning of fossil fuels began. An acid ocean not only will affect sharks and other marine life but, ultimately, will affect us. Reduce your carbon footprint.

Do not litter.
Sea turtles mistake plastic bags for jellyfish, one of their favorite foods. These bags fatally block the intestine, often causing the turtle to starve to death. One autopsy performed on a dead turtle revealed 1,000 pieces of plastic in its stomach.

Help stop light pollution on nesting beaches.
Whether you live or holiday on the beach, insist that the places where you stay minimize their light sources so that light from the sources does not reach the beach. Any artificial light source that is visible from a nesting beach can disorient sea turtles.

Sign petitions.
You can be directly involved with creating policies that protect sharks and rays and marine areas by signing petitions.

www.seaweb.org

Using Social Marketing Techniques to Promote Ocean Conservation

SeaWeb, founded in 1996 to raise awareness of the growing threats to the ocean and its living resources, is a communications-based nonprofit organization that uses social marketing techniques to advance ocean conservation. We envision a world in which all people act on the belief that a healthy ocean is vital to all life and essential to a sustainable future. By increasing public awareness, advancing science-based solutions, and mobilizing decision makers around ocean conservation, SeaWeb has brought together multiple, diverse, and powerful voices for a healthy ocean. Together, we are leading more voices for a healthy ocean.

The Concept of Sustainable Seafood

The word *sustainable* means different things to different people. Essentially, it is the capacity to endure and maintain. Sustainability is crucial in maintaining a long and healthy future for marine life and for our own society. More than 1 billion people depend on seafood as their primary source of animal protein, and several hundred million more depend on fish or shellfish as their main source of income. The sustainable-seafood movement was born from the realization that human demand for seafood was exerting an impact on the long-term viability of fish—one of the most widely traded and valuable wildlife commodities.

So what is sustainable seafood? Many organizations consider the following principles (adapted from the Marine Stewardship Council) to determine the answer to this:

- Fish and shellfish from a healthy population
- Fish and shellfish caught or farmed using methods that don't harm marine life
- Fish and shellfish from fisheries or farms that are responsibly managed

There also are social and economic issues relating to a sustainable supply of fish, as well as wider environmental concerns linked to climate change when defining sustainable seafood. Although all of this can be complex, you—the seafood consumer—can play a vital role in maintaining the sustainability of our ocean resources. By becoming informed, asking retailers and restaurants about the sustainability of their seafood, and making responsible choices, consumers can help ensure that there will be healthy seas and seafood now and in the future. For more information, visit www.seafoodchoices.org.

Seafood Sustainability for Our Kids

Two major factors affecting the ocean today, resource extraction and pollution, have direct impacts on seafood. In fact, seafood may be the most complicated food we eat. Many factors affect how safe and healthy a specific fish may be to feed to our families. Was the fish you're buying raised on a farm or caught in the wild? What part of the world did it come from? What did the fish eat? How long did it live?

Mercury, PCBs, and other contaminants find their way into lakes, rivers, and the ocean, in turn polluting the seafood humans rely on. Those toxins can be more serious for children than for adults because the children are growing and developing, and they consume more food and liquids based on body size than adults do.

In addition to health considerations, seafood we eat and serve to our families should be ocean-friendly, that is, sustainable. The reasons are obvious: If we want to have safe and healthy seafood for future generations, we must make sure the fish we eat today are caught or raised in a responsible manner. Considering all the factors that go into making a smart and healthy seafood choice, SeaWeb created the KidSafe Seafood Program to help parents make the best choices possible. When deciding on your next seafood meal for your family, visit www.kidsafeseafood.org to help you make healthy and sustainable choices.

Sustainability: Not Just About Seafood

Sustainability of ocean resources is about more than just the fish we eat; it's also about the places many fish live. Coral reefs exist in shallow tropical waters, providing 25 percent of all known marine life with places to find food, safe haven from predators, and natural areas for reproduction. There are roughly 5,000 species of corals, two thirds of which are considered deep-sea corals, found below depths of 200 meters. Corals also are important to the economy, providing nearly $30 billion per year in benefits from fishing, tourism, recreation, and coastline protection.

Unfortunately, like many of the species found in the ocean, corals are under threat. Shallow water reefs are suffering from climate change and ocean acidification in addition to extraction to meet global demand in curio objects and aquariums. Deep-sea corals face pressure from destructive fishing practices such as trawling and extraction for the home décor and jewelry trade.

Red and pink corals are prime examples. Found in the Mediterranean Sea and the Pacific Ocean, these "jewels of the sea" have been used for centuries in jewelry, fashion, and home décor designs. Demand for these species has caused catches to plummet by 60 percent to 80 percent since the 1980s. Unless there is a movement away from coral-derived creations to coral-inspired ones, the future of red and pink coral populations remains uncertain.

SeaWeb's Too Precious to Wear campaign addresses some of the threats posed to corals. The campaign works with top designers to raise awareness of coral as a living animal and encourages designers and businesses to use coral as inspiration only.

You can help decide the fate of corals as well. Be an informed consumer, and ensure that products you purchase don't contain real coral. For a list of designers and products that are coral-friendly, visit www.seaweb.org. Take the opportunity to reduce your carbon footprint as well, helping alleviate the pressure of climate change on corals.

WATERKEEPER®ALLIANCE

www.waterkeeper.org

Promoting Citizen Advocacy to Address Waterway Issues

Waterkeeper Alliance is a global environmental organization uniting more than 190 Waterkeeper groups around the world and focusing citizen advocacy on the issues that affect our waterways, from pollution to climate change.

Established in 1999 by Robert F. Kennedy Jr. and the other founding Waterkeeper members, the organization has grown rapidly over the past decade by championing the protection and restoration of the world's rivers, lakes, bays, and estuaries. With local Waterkeeper organizations on six continents, the Alliance today has the unique ability to confront environmental threats by engaging its grassroots network on a local, regional, or global level.

In virtually every part of the world, water resources are declining in quality and quantity. More than a billion people are living without access to safe drinking water; California faces the most serious water emergency in its history; Australia is in the midst of an epic, twelve-year drought—the first industrialized nation to deal with water scarcity on this scale. These are but a few examples of the daunting challenges we face.

Waterkeeper Alliance provides a way for communities to stand up for their right to clean water and for the wise and equitable use of water resources, both locally and globally. The vision of the Waterkeeper movement is for fishable, swimmable, and drinkable waterways worldwide. Our belief is that the best way to achieve this vision is through the Waterkeeper method of grassroots advocacy.

The Waterkeeper model began on New York's Hudson River in the 1960s. Commercial and recreational fishermen and fisherwomen, concerned about depleted fish stocks and industrial pollution, banded together to restore the health of the river. In 1983, they appointed a Riverkeeper to patrol the watershed and identify threats to clean water. The Riverkeeper became widely recognized as an effective environmental advocate and quickly became a model for watershed protection on rivers and beyond.

Today, Waterkeepers (Riverkeepers, Bayoukeepers, Baykeepers, etc.) patrol nearly 200 waterways, covering more than 100,000 miles of rivers, streams, and coastlines in the Americas, Europe, Australia, Asia, and Africa. Part scientist, teacher, and legal advocate, Waterkeepers combine firsthand knowledge of their waterways with an unwavering commitment to the rights of their communities and to the rule of law. Whether on the water, in a classroom, or in a courtroom, Waterkeepers speak for the waters they defend with the backing of their local community and the collective strength of Waterkeeper Alliance.

Waterkeeper Alliance ensures that the world's Waterkeepers are as connected to each other as they are to their local waters, organizing the fight for clean water into a coordinated global movement. United as one powerful force, Waterkeeper Alliance fights for the rights of communities everywhere as the voice for the world's waters.

Waterkeepers are full-time, privately funded, nongovernmental advocates for an identified river, lake, bay, or sound. They are recognized by their community, local government, and media as *the voice* for that particular body of water. They advocate compliance with environmental laws, respond to citizen complaints, identify problems that affect their identified bodies of water, and devise appropriate remedies to address these problems.

Waterkeepers employ a variety of strategies to curb pollution, including:

- Monitoring water quality.
- Investigating point and nonpoint pollution sources.
- Attending municipal board meetings.
- Submitting written and oral comments on discharge permit applications.
- Educating and motivating the public to act on behalf of its watershed.
- Participating in environmental scoping sessions.
- Devising solutions to water quality problems by using best practices and promoting best technologies.
- Pursuing litigation to enforce compliance with environmental laws.

Starting a Waterkeeper Organization

At the core of every Waterkeeper organization is a commitment to sophisticated and responsive grassroots advocacy and an unfaltering belief that everyone has the right to clean water.

Waterkeeper Alliance's board of directors and its Waterkeeper Support Committee meet regularly to approve prospective organizations. Interested groups must submit a formal proposal that reflects their commitment to Waterkeeper Alliance's model of aggressive water protection. Proposals should include an organizational vision, a strategic plan for sustaining a healthy nonprofit organization and achieving the mission of protecting and restoring the local waterway, and the means by which a full-time Waterkeeper will be employed.

If you would like to start a Waterkeeper organization, please email us at startawaterkeeper@waterkeeper.org, and one of our staff members will help guide you through the process. Thank you for protecting our waterways!

Environmental Organizations Working on Ocean Issues

Acoustic Ecology Institute focuses largely on the environmental effects of human sound. *www.acousticecology.org*

Alaska Marine Conservation Council advances conservation solutions that address the interdependence among healthy marine ecosystems, vibrant local economies, and rich coastal traditions. *www.akmarine.org*

Aldo Leopold Leadership Program provides academic researchers with the skills and connections they need to be effective leaders and communicators. *www.leopoldleadership.org*

Algalita Marine Research Foundation was founded by Captain Charles Moore, who discovered the North Pacific Garbage Patch; through investigative research on the impact of plastic marine pollution, it protects the marine environment and its watersheds. *www.algalita.org*

American Cetacean Society protects whales, dolphins, porpoises, and their habitats through public education, research grants, and conservation actions. *www.acsonline.org*

American Geophysical Union is a worldwide scientific community that advances, through unselfish cooperation in research, an understanding of Earth and space that is used for the benefit of humanity. *www.agu.org*

American Littoral Society promotes the study and conservation of marine life and habitat, protects the coast from harm, and empowers others to do the same. *www.littoralsociety.org*

American Rivers works in five key program areas—Rivers and Global Warming, River Restoration, River Protection, Clean Water, and Water Supply—to protect our remaining natural heritage, undo the damage of the past, and create a healthy future for our rivers and future generations. *www.americanrivers.org*

Animal Welfare Institute has sought to reduce the sum total of pain and fear inflicted on animals by people. In the organization's early years, its particular emphasis was on the desperate needs of animals used for experimentation. In the decades that followed, it expanded the scope of its work to address many other areas of animal suffering. *www.awionline.org*

Antarctic and Southern Ocean Coalition advocates on behalf of the Antarctic environment and ecosystems. Major campaigns include the Antarctic Krill Conservation Project, which works to protect the base of the Antarctic food web by regulating Antarctic tourism, protecting the Ross Sea, strengthening the Southern Ocean Whale Sanctuary, managing Southern Ocean fisheries sustainably, and implementing the Environment Protocol to the Antarctic Treaty. *www.asoc.org*

Aqua NIC is the gateway to the world's electronic resources for aquaculture information. *aquanic.org*

Aquatic Nuisance Task Force is an intergovernmental organization dedicated to preventing and controlling aquatic nuisance species and implementing the Non-indigenous Aquatic Nuisance Prevention and Control Act. *anstaskforce.gov*

The Association of Zoos & Aquariums is dedicated to conservation, education, science, and building personal connections with wildlife for the 180 million people who visit AZA-accredited zoos and aquariums each year. AZA's mandatory accreditation is the most stringent such process in the world, ensuring that AZA members meet rigorous professional standards for animal welfare, veterinary care, wildlife conservation, scientific research, education, expert staffing, and safety. *www.aza.org*

Atlantic States Marine Fisheries Commission serves as a deliberative body, coordinating the conservation and management of the states, shared near-shore fishery resources—marine, shell, and anadromous—for sustainable use. *www.asmfc.org*

Beacon Institute for Rivers and Estuaries is a center for scientific and technological innovation that advances research, education, and public policy regarding rivers and estuaries. *www.bire.org*

Biodiversity Hotspots leverages technology for biodiversity conservation. *www.biodiversityhotspots.org*

Biosphere Foundation has as its primary goal to inspire intelligent stewardship of our Earth's biosphere. Its projects aim to contribute to the existing body of knowledge about the biosphere and to inspire individuals to get involved through either hands-on fieldwork or virtual education and outreach programs. *www.biospherefoundation.org*

Birch Aquarium at the Scripps Institution of Oceanography provides ocean science education, interprets Scripps Institution of Oceanography research, and promotes ocean conservation. *aquarium.ucsd.edu*

Blue Ocean Institute is a conservation organization that uses science, art, and literature to inspire a closer bond with nature, especially the sea. It translates scientific information into language people can understand and use to make better choices on behalf of the sea. *www.blueocean.org*

BlueVoice features annotated video especially prepared for journalists and political leaders and provides ways for concerned citizens to communicate with their government representatives and to contribute to the preservation of the oceans. *www.bluevoice.org*

Bridge Sea Grant Ocean Sciences Education Center provides educators with a convenient source of accurate and useful information on global, national, and regional marine science topics, and gives researchers a contact point for educational outreach. *www.vims.edu/bridge*

California Academy of Sciences is a world leader in the scientific study of biological diversity. It supports twenty curators and eighty other scientists, students, and members of staff in their research activities. Their objectives in research are to explore and explain the evolution and maintenance of life. They seek knowledge about phylogenetic relationships, taxonomic and genomic diversity, and the mechanisms of evolutionary change. Their scientific research and collections provide empirical knowledge useful in sustaining life's future. *www.calacademy.org*

Caribbean Conservation Corporation & Sea Turtle Survival League ensures the survival of sea turtles within the wider Caribbean basin and Atlantic through research, education, training, advocacy, and protection of the natural habitats on which they depend. *www.cccturtle.org*

Caviar Emptor is a campaign to protect and restore threatened Caspian Sea sturgeon. *www.caviaremptor.org*

Cetacean Society International has the goal of "optimum utilization of the whale resources," as called for in the 1946 Treaty of the International Whaling Commission, through the protection of viable habitat and the cessation of all killing and captive display of whales, dolphins, and porpoises. *www.csiwhalesalive.org*

Clean Ocean Action works to improve the degraded water quality of the marine waters off the New Jersey and New York coasts. *www.cleanoceanaction.org*

Clean Water Action is an organization of 1.2 million members working to empower people to take action to protect America's waters, build healthy communities, and make democracy work for all of us. *www.cleanwateraction.org*

Clean Water Network is a coalition of more than 1,200 public interest organizations across the country, representing more than 5 million people, working together to strengthen and implement federal clean water and wetlands policy. It is the largest national coalition working to defend and strengthen the federal Clean Water Act. *www.cwn.org*

Coastal Resources Center mobilizes governments, businesses, and communities around the world to work together as stewards of coastal ecosystems. With its partners, it strives to define and achieve the health, equitable allocation of wealth, and sustainable intensities of human activity at the transition between the land and the sea. *www.crc.uri.edu*

Communication Partnership for Science and the Sea (COMPASS) works to advance marine conservation science and ensure that science is communicated to policy makers, the public, and the media. COMPASS provides ocean scientists with the communications tools and platforms to ensure that their science is shared in a credible and neutral manner. *www.compassonline.org*

Conservation International (CI), built upon a strong foundation of science, partnership, and field demonstration, empowers societies to care for nature responsibly and sustainably for the well-being of humanity. *www.conservation.org*

Conservation Law Foundation (CLF) works to solve the most significant environmental problems that threaten New England. CLF's advocates use law, economics, and science to create innovative strategies to conserve natural resources, protect public health, and promote vital communities in our region. *www.clf.org*

Consortium for Ocean Leadership represents ninety-four of the leading public and private ocean research and education institutions, aquaria, and industries with the mission to advance research, education, and sound ocean policy. The organization also manages ocean research and education programs in areas of scientific ocean drilling, ocean observation, ocean exploration, and ocean partnerships. *www.oceanleadership.org*

Coral Reef Alliance is the only international nonprofit organization that works exclusively to protect our planet's coral reefs. It provides tools, education, and inspiration to residents of coral reef destinations to support local projects that benefit both reefs and people. *www.coralreefalliance.org*

Coral Reef Science Studies is part of the scientific team of the Planetary Coral Reef Foundation (PCRF). The crew of PCRF's ship gathers data during intensive underwater studies as they continue to assess the health and vitality of coral reefs around the world. Observations are collected to add to the PCRF databank of impressions from reefs around the world. *www.pcrf.org/science/index.html*

Cousteau Society educates people to understand, to love, and to protect the water systems of the planet, both marine and freshwater, for the well-being of future generations. *www.cousteau.org*

Earth Communications Office is a nonprofit organization whose goal is to use the power of communications to help improve the global environment. *www.oneearth.org*

Earth Day Network was founded on the premise that all people, regardless of race, gender, income, or geography, have a moral right to a healthy, sustainable environment. Its mission is to broaden and diversify the environmental movement worldwide and to mobilize it as the most effective vehicle for promoting a healthy, sustainable environment. *www.earthday.net*

Earth Island Institute is a hub for grassroots campaigns dedicated to conserving, preserving, and restoring the ecosystems on which our civilization depends. *www.earthisland.org*

Earth Share provides an opportunity for caring employees and workplaces to support hundreds of environmental charities through workplace giving campaigns. A workplace giving campaign is an annual employer-sponsored program that enables employees to contribute a few dollars per paycheck as their charitable donation. *www.earthshare.org*

Envirolink is a nonprofit organization that has been providing access to thousands of online environmental resources since 1991. *www.envirolink.org*

Environmental Concern Inc. promotes public understanding and stewardship of wetlands with the goal of improving water quality and enhancing nature's habitat through wetland outreach and education; native species horticulture; and restoration, construction, and enhancement of wetlands. *www.wetland.org*

Environmental Protection Agency was established to protect human health and the environment through developing and enforcing regulations, giving grants, studying environmental issues, sponsoring partnerships, and teaching people about the environment. *www.epa.gov*

Essential Fish Habitat works to protect and conserve habitats important to NOAA trust resources. The division's primary mandates focus on ensuring that living marine resources have sufficient healthy habitat to sustain populations. Those mandates emphasize wetlands, coral reefs, diadromous fish habitat, and habitat of other marine and estuarine species. *www.nmfs.noaa.gov/habitat/ habitatprotection/efh*

Explorations E-Magazine educates the public, the alumni of Scripps Oceanographic Institute, the scientific community, and Scripps's friends and supporters about ongoing research and events. *explorations.ucsd.edu*

Fish List is an ocean-friendly consumer guide to making better seafood choices. *www.thefishlist.org*

FishWise is a nonprofit organization designed to improve the sustainability and financial performance of seafood retailers, distributors, and producers. Uniquely positioned between the seafood industry and marine conservation organizations, FishWise offers a range of services that create trust between seafood vendors and their customers, enabling businesses to sell more sustainable seafood more profitably. FishWise joins business imperatives with leading ocean conservation strategies. *www.fishwise.org*

Friends of the Earth exposes and fights pollution and exploitation of our ecosystems. Its Clean Vessels campaign is cleaning up the cruise industry, protecting marine sanctuaries, and reducing air pollution from oceangoing vessels. *www.foe.org*

Friends of the Sea Otter is an advocacy group dedicated to working actively with state and federal agencies to maintain the current protections for sea otters as well as to increase and broaden these preservation efforts. *www.seaotters.org*

Global Marine Litter Information—UNEP has developed and implemented a number of activities focused on the management of marine litter. *www.unep.org/regionalseas/marinelitter/ttp://www.marine-litter.gpa.unep.org*

Great Barrier Reef Marine Park Authority is the principal advisor to the Australian government on the control, care, and development of the Great Barrier Reef Marine Park. It is responsible for the management of the marine park and undertakes a variety of activities, including developing and implementing zoning and management plans, environmental impact assessment and permitting use, research, monitoring, and interpretation of data. It also provides information, educational services, and marine environmental management advice. *www.gbrmpa.gov.au*

Greenpeace International Defending Our Oceans campaign sets out to protect and preserve our oceans now and for the future by setting aside swaths of the global oceans from exploitation and controllable human pressure, allowing these areas the respite they so desperately need for recovery and renewal. *www.greenpeace.org/international*

Greenpeace USA advocates the creation of a network of no-take marine reserves, protecting 40 percent of the world's oceans, as the long-term solution to the overfishing of tuna, pollock, and other species and the recovery of our overexploited oceans. *www.greenpeace.org/usa*

Habitat Media is a nonprofit production group specializing in media for a mass audience that inspire their involvement in making positive change. Its landmark documentaries examine seemingly overwhelming problems, social and environmental, that are solved when "ordinary people" do their part. *www.habitatmedia.org/*

Humane Society International works on a variety of animal welfare issues in numerous countries. Its offices around the world cover topics such as the illegal wildlife trade, companion animal welfare, anti-fur campaigns, farm animal welfare, and disaster response. *www.hsi.org*

Institute for Ocean Conservation Science focuses research on advancing ecosystem-based fisheries management, a strategy that recognizes that the oceans' problems are interconnected and that species and habitats cannot be successfully managed in isolation, and on advancing knowledge about vulnerable and ecologically important marine animals that are understudied. *www.oceanconservationscience.org*

Intergovernmental Oceanographic Commission (IOC) works to promote international cooperation in researching and protecting the ocean. Today, the IOC is instrumental in monitoring the ocean through the Global Ocean Observing System (GOOS) and developing tsunami warning systems in vulnerable regions. *ioc.unesco.org/iocweb*

Intergovernmental Panel on Climate Change is the leading body for the assessment of climate change, established by the United Nations Environment Programme (UNEP) and the World Meteorological Organization (WMO) to provide the world with a clear scientific view on the current state of climate change and its potential environmental and socioeconomic consequences. *www.ipcc.ch*

International Coral Reef Action Network has been working to build resource stewardship within communities by providing opportunities to develop the skills and tools needed to ensure the sustainable use and the long-term vitality of coral reefs. *www.icran.org*

International Coral Reef Information Network is the only international nonprofit organization that works exclusively to protect our planet's coral reefs, providing tools, education, and inspiration to residents of coral reef destinations to support local projects that benefit both reefs and people. *www.coralreef.org*

International Marine Life Alliance works to end human influences that degrade and destroy the world's marine environment, at the same time improving the overall quality of life of people living in and communities dependent on coastal and marine resources. *www.marine.org*

International Rivers Network protects rivers and defends the rights of communities that depend on them. *www.irn.org*

International Whaling Commission has as its main duty to keep under review and revise as necessary the measures laid down in the Schedule to the International Convention for the Regulation of Whaling, which governs the conduct of whaling throughout the world. *www.iwcoffice.org*

IUCN—The World Conservation Union has as its mission to influence, encourage, and assist societies throughout the world to conserve the integrity and diversity of nature and to ensure that any use of natural resources is equitable and ecologically sustainable. IUCN develops and supports cutting-edge conservation science, particularly in species, ecosystems, and biodiversity, and the impact these have on human livelihoods. *www.iucn.org*

Jean-Michel Cousteau's Ocean Futures Society has as its mission to explore our global ocean, inspiring and educating people throughout the world to act responsibly for its protection, documenting the critical connection between humanity and nature, and celebrating the ocean's vital importance to the survival of all life on our planet. *www.oceanfutures.org*

Join the Voyage is a virtual online education and outreach program that uses extensive data, images, and film footage from its expeditions to guide people of all ages and from all cultures through the coral reef crisis. *www.jointhevoyage.org*

Marine Fish Conservation Network has as its primary objective to make conservation a top priority of marine fisheries management. To advance this objective, the network analyzes the ability of existing federal laws—chiefly, the Magnuson-Stevens Act (MSA)—to promote marine fish conservation adequately. *www.conservefish.org*

Marine Mammal Commission is an independent agency of the U.S. government, established under Title II of the act, to provide independent oversight of the marine mammal conservation policies and programs carried out by federal regulatory agencies. *www.mmc.gov*

Marine Stewardship Council runs an exciting and ambitious program, working with partners to transform the world's seafood markets and to promote sustainable fishing practices. Its credible standards for sustainable fishing and seafood traceability seek to increase the availability of certified sustainable seafood and its distinctive blue eco-label makes it easy for everyone to take part. It offers fisheries around the world a way to be recognized and rewarded for good management. By working in partnership with sustainable fisheries to create a market for sustainable seafood, the Council provides an incentive for other fisheries to change their practices. *www.msc.org*

Monterey Bay Aquarium has as its mission "to inspire conservation of the oceans." *www.mbayaq.org*

Monterey Bay Aquarium Research Institute (MBARI) is a world center for advanced research and education in ocean science and technology through the development of better instruments, systems, and methods for scientific research in the deep waters of the ocean. MBARI emphasizes the peer relationship between engineers and scientists as a basic principle of its operation. *www.mbari.org*

National Coalition for Marine Conservation works to prevent overfishing, reduce fish bycatch, and protect marine habitat for fish such as swordfish, marlin, sharks, tuna, herring, striped bass, and menhaden. *www.savethefish.org*

National Marine Mammal Laboratory conducts research on marine mammals important to the mission of the National Marine Fisheries Service (NMFS) and the National Oceanic and Atmospheric Administration (NOAA), with particular attention to issues related to marine mammals off the coasts of Alaska, Washington, Oregon, and California. *nmml.afsc.noaa.gov*

National Marine Sanctuary Foundation partners to create conservation-based research, education, and outreach programs for our nation's underwater treasures. *www.nmsfocean.org*

Natural Resources Defense Council uses law, science and the support of 1.3 million members and online activists to protect the planet's wildlife and wild places and to ensure a safe and healthy environment for all living things. *www.nrdc.org*

Nature Conservancy works in all fifty states and more than thirty countries, protecting habitats from grasslands to coral reefs, from Australia to Alaska to Zambia. Using a science-based approach aided by more than 700 staff scientists, it pursues nonconfrontational, pragmatic solutions to conservation challenges. *www.nature.org*

New England Aquarium redefines what it means to be an aquarium, combining education, entertainment, and action to address the most challenging problems facing the ocean. *www.neaq.org*

Notes from Sea Level is a unique blog by writer and filmmaker Jon Bowermaster that looks at the world from sea level, giving people a one-of-a-kind look at both the health of the world's ocean and the lives of the nearly 3 billion people around the globe who depend on it. *www.jonbowermaster.com*

Ocean Alliance collects a broad spectrum of data on whales and ocean life relating particularly to toxicology, behavior, bioacoustics, and genetics. From that data, it works with scientific partners to advise educators and policy makers on wise stewardship of the oceans to reduce pollution, prevent the collapse of marine mammal populations, maintain human access to fish and other sea life, and promote ocean and human health. *www.oceanalliance.org*

Ocean Conservancy believes it's time to change our national policies to protect entire ecosystems as the surest way to solve the most critical ocean conservation challenges we face. *www.oceanconservancy.org*

Ocean Conservation Society was organized to conduct scientific research and educational projects leading to the protection and conservation of our oceans. *www.oceanconservation.org*

The Ocean Foundation is a unique community foundation with a mission to support, strengthen, and promote those organizations dedicated to reversing the trend of destruction of ocean environments around the world. Its slogan is "Tell us what you want to do for the ocean, we will take care of the rest." *www.oceanfdn.org*

Ocean Futures Society. See Jean-Michel Cousteau's Ocean Futures Society.

Ocean Project advances ocean conservation by working in partnership with museums and others to educate visitors on the importance of protecting and conserving our ocean planet. *www.theoceanproject.org*

Ocean Research and Conservation Association (ORCA) is using the latest technologies to develop high-tech sensors and communications systems capable of detecting a wide range of water quality parameters, both chemical and biological, critical to keeping our waters clean and habitats healthy. These systems report back to ORCA's scientists and resource managers so better solutions can be implemented against threats to healthy marine ecosystems. *www.teamorca.org*

Ocean Revolution is a global movement of people and organizations working for the common cause of a healthy, wild, productive planet. Simple. *www .oceanrevolution.org*

Oceana has more than 300,000 members and e-activists in over 150 countries, the largest international organization focused 100 percent on ocean conservation. *www.oceana.org*

Oceanic Resource Foundation encourages the participation and support of individuals, corporations, and private foundations in the protection of Earth's marine environment. Contributions can be made to a variety of conservation and research organizations that support field researchers and graduate students studying coral reef systems and provide laboratory materials, scuba diving equipment, underwater survey reels and clipboards, and travel assistance. *www.orf.org*

Office of Ocean and Coastal Resource Management provides national leadership, strategic direction, and guidance to state and territory coastal programs and estuarine research reserves and leads the nation's efforts to manage and conserve ocean and coastal resources. *www.ocrm.nos.noaa.gov*

Partnership for Interdisciplinary Studies of Coastal Oceans is a long-term ecosystem research and monitoring program established with the goals of understanding dynamics of the coastal ocean ecosystem along the U.S. west coast, sharing that knowledge so ocean managers and policy makers can make science-based decisions regarding coastal and marine stewardship, and producing a new generation of scientists trained in interdisciplinary collaborative approaches. *www.piscoweb.org*

Pew Oceans Commission published a report in 2003 that was the first thorough review of ocean policy in thirty-four years, offering to guide the way in which the federal government can successfully manage America's marine environment. The report found that more than 60 percent of America's coastal rivers and bays are degraded by nutrient runoff, that crucial species such as groundfish and salmon are under assault from overfishing, and that invasive species are establishing themselves in the nation's coastal waters. The Pew Oceans Commission concluded its work, but its findings are still available online to aid researchers and policy makers. *www.pewoceans.org*

Planetary Coral Reef Foundation has just completed its fourteenth year of an expedition at sea dedicated to monitoring offshore coral reefs around the world. All of the forty-nine Coral Reef Studies, Studio of the Sea films, Singapore *Nautique* articles, and educational programs are featured online so you can join the voyage. *www.pcrf.org*

ReefKeeper International emphasizes coral reef monitoring. The overall objectives are to gather high-quality and widely distributed data on reef status, to determine long-term trends resulting from global climate change and anthropogenic stress, to assist effective management and conservation, and to determine the potential of reefs and reef organisms as early-warning indicators of global change. *www.reefkeeper.org*

Restore America's Estuaries is an alliance of eleven community-based conservation organizations working to protect and restore the vital habitats of our nation's estuaries. It's dedicated to working closely with communities and governmental organizations to preserve the extraordinary heritage of our nation's estuaries. *www.estuaries.org*

River Network is a nationwide movement to preserve and restore clean and healthy waters. Although rivers are its focal point, it works to protect the quality of all freshwaters and the health of all people and ecosystems dependent on them. *www.rivernetwork.org*

Save Our Seas implements and supports diverse programs centered on the protection of Earth's marine environment through CARE—Conservation, Awareness, Research, and Education. *www.saveourseas.com*

Save the Manatee Club funds manatee rescue, rehabilitation, and research efforts in the United States and the Caribbean. *www.savethemanatee.org*

Scripps Institution of Oceanography teaches and communicates scientific understanding of the oceans, atmosphere, Earth, and other planets for the benefit of society and the environment and is an international leader in originating basic research, developing scientists, and advancing the science needed in the search for a sustainable balance between the natural environment and human activity. *www.sio.ucsd.edu*

Sea Shepherd is an international nonprofit marine wildlife conservation organization. Its mission is to end the destruction of habitats and slaughter of wildlife in the world's oceans and to conserve and protect ecosystems and species. Sea Shepherd uses innovative direct-action tactics to investigate, document, and take action when necessary to expose and confront illegal activities on the high seas. By safeguarding the biodiversity of our delicately balanced ocean ecosystems, Sea Shepherd works to ensure their survival for future generations. *www.seashepherd.org*

Sea Turtle Restoration Project takes swift and decisive action to protect and restore marine species and their habitats and to inspire people in communities all over the world to join in as active and vocal marine species advocates. *www.seaturtles.org*

Seacology preserves the highly endangered biodiversity of islands throughout the world, searching for win–win situations by which the local environment is protected and islanders receive some tangible benefit for doing so. *www .seacology.org*

Seafood Choices Alliance helps the seafood industry—from fishermen, fisherwomen, and fish farmers to processors, distributors, retailers, restaurants, and food service providers—make the seafood marketplace environmentally, economically, and socially sustainable. *www.seafoodchoices.com*

SeaWeb is a communications-based nonprofit organization that uses social marketing techniques to advance ocean conservation. By raising public awareness, advancing science-based solutions, and mobilizing decision makers around ocean conservation, it is a leading voice for a healthy ocean. *www.seaweb.org*

SEE Turtles is a conservation tourism project that links people with turtle sites in ways that directly support protection efforts while increasing resources in communities to help residents thrive and value sea turtles in their environment. SEE Turtles is a project of the Ocean Foundation. *www.seeturtles.org*

Shark Research Institute was created to sponsor and conduct research on sharks and promote the conservation of sharks. A primary goal is creating value for sharks as sustainable natural resources for the dive tourism industry, particularly in developing countries. *www.sharks.org*

Smithsonian Institution provides Sant Ocean Hall and ocean education programs that will take you on a journey through the ocean, from ancient seas to living reefs. *www.si.edu*

Steinhart Aquarium is the most diverse aquarium in the world; its mission is to explore, explain, and protect the natural world. *www.calácademy.org/aquarium*

StopGlobalWarming uses the strength of numbers to urge the government to join the rest of the world in addressing global warming and to urge businesses to start a new industrial revolution of clean energy that reduces our dependence on oil. *www.stopglobalwarming.org*

Studio of the Sea is a floating movie and still-image production platform, based on the Planetary Coral Reef Foundation's sailing vessel. Its aim is to produce short films that expose the state of our oceanic planet, voyage through its island cultures, and portray elements of a life at sea. It places particular focus on the concurrent beauty and collapse of our coral reef ecosystems. *www.studioofthesea.org*

Surfrider Foundation is a nonprofit environmental organization dedicated to the protection and enjoyment of the world's oceans, waves, and beaches for all people through conservation, activism, research, and education. It specializes in beach clean-ups and restorations. *www.surfrider.org*

United Nations Environmental Programme—World Conservation Monitoring Centre provides leadership and encourages partnership in caring for the environment by inspiring, informing, and enabling nations and peoples to improve their quality of life without compromising that of future generations. *www.unep-wcmc.org*

Waterkeeper Alliance provides a way for communities to stand up for their right to clean water and for the wise and equitable use of water resources, both locally and globally. The vision of the Waterkeeper movement is for fishable, swimmable, and drinkable waterways worldwide. With nearly 200 Waterkeeper organizations on six continents, it aspires to protect every major watershed around the world. *www.waterkeeper.org*

Whale and Dolphin Conservation Society is the world's most active charity dedicated to the conservation and welfare of all whales, dolphins, and porpoises (also known as cetaceans). The money raised is spent on urgent conservation, research, and education projects that really do make a difference to their daily lives and long-term security. *www.wdcs.org*

Whale Remix Project works with governments, scientists, and local communities to end commercial and "scientific" whaling and is a leading advocate for whale sanctuaries, including the Southern Ocean Sanctuary in the waters around Antarctica, established to provide protection for 90 percent of the world's remaining whales. *www.stopwhaling.org*

Whaleman Foundation has as its primary mission to educate key decision makers while raising public awareness on the issues that affect cetaceans (dolphins, whales, and porpoises) and their critical habitats through its films, research, campaigns, and media outreach. *whaleman.org/index.htm*

Women's Aquatic Network (WAN) is led and organized by women, but its membership is open to women and men. Its mission is to bring together professionals with interests in marine, coastal, and aquatic policy as well as research, management, legislation, and other areas. WAN members are scientists, lawyers, policy makers, natural resources managers, entrepreneurs, environmental advocates, students, professors, and people from many other professions. *www.womensaquatic.net*

Woods Hole Oceanographic Institution is dedicated to research and education to advance understanding of the ocean and its interaction with the Earth system and to communicate this understanding for the benefit of society. *www.whoi.edu*

World Water Council promotes awareness, builds political commitment, and triggers action on critical water issues at all levels, including the highest decision-making level, to facilitate the efficient conservation, protection, development, planning, management, and use of water in all its dimensions on an environmentally sustainable basis for the benefit of all life on Earth. *www.worldwatercouncil.org*

World Wildlife Fund has as its mission to stop the degradation of the planet's natural environment and build a future in which humans live in harmony with nature by conserving the world's biological diversity, ensuring that the use of renewable natural resources is sustainable, and promoting the reduction of pollution and wasteful consumption. *www.panda.org*

For Further Reading

Alling, Abigail, Mark Nelson, and Sally Silverstone. *Life Under Glass: The Inside Story of Biosphere 2.* Johannesburg: Biosphere Press, 1993.

Ballesta, Laurent, and Pierre Descamp. *Planet Ocean: Voyage to the Heart of the Marine Realm.* Washington DC: National Geographic, 2007.

Bulloch, David K. *The Wasted Ocean: The Ominous Crisis of Marine Pollution and How to Stop It.* New York: Lyons and Burford Publishers, 1991.

Carey, Richard Adams. *The Philosopher Fish: Sturgeon, Caviar, and the Geography of Desire.* New York: Counterpoint, 2006.

Casey, Susan. *The Devil's Teeth: A True Story of Obsession and Survival Among America's Great White Sharks.* New York: Holt Paperbacks, 2006.

———. *The Wave: A Journey into the Dark Heart of the Ocean.* New York: Broadway, 2010.

Cicin-Sain, Biliana, and Robert Knecht. *The Future of U.S. Ocean Policy: Choices for the New Century.* Washington DC: Island Press, 2000.

Clover, Charles. *The End of the Line: How Overfishing Is Changing the World and What We Eat.* Berkeley: University of California Press, 2008.

Corson, Trevor. *The Secret Life of Lobsters: How Fishermen and Scientists Are Unraveling the Mysteries of Our Favorite Crustacean.* New York: Harper Perennial, 2005.

Cox, Lynne. *Grayson.* New York: Harvest Books, 2008.

———. *Swimming to Antarctica: Tales of a Long-Distance Swimmer.* New York: Harvest Books, 2005.

Cramer, Deborah. *Smithsonian Ocean: Our Water, Our World.* Washington DC: Smithsonian Books, 2008.

Davidson, Osha Gray. *Fire in the Turtle House: The Green Sea Turtle and the Fate of the Ocean.* New York: PublicAffairs, 2003.

Dean, Cornelia. *Against the Tide.* New York: Columbia University Press, 2001.

Dinwiddie, Robert, and Louise Thomas. *Ocean: The World's Last Wilderness Revealed.* New York: DK ADULT, 2006.

Earle, Sylvia A. *National Geographic Atlas of the Ocean: The Deep Frontier.* Washington DC: National Geographic, 2001.

———. *Sea Change: A Message of the Oceans.* Chicago: Ballantine Books, 1996.

———. *The World Is Blue: How Our Fate and the Ocean's Are One.* Washington DC: National Geographic, 2009.

Earle, Sylvia A., and Ellen J. Prager. *The Oceans.* New York: McGraw-Hill, 2001.

Ellis, Richard. *The Book of Sharks.* New York: Knopf, 1989.

———. *Book of Whales .* New York: Knopf, 1985.

———. *Deep Atlantic: Life, Death, and Exploration in the Abyss.* New York: Lyons Press, 1998.

———. *Dolphins and Porpoises.* New York: Knopf, 1989.

———. *The Empty Ocean.* Washington DC: Island Press, 2004.

———. *Encyclopedia of the Sea.* New York: Knopf, 2000.

———. *Men and Whales.* New York: Lyons Press, 1999.

———. *On Thin Ice: The Changing World of the Polar Bear.* New York: Knopf, 2009.

———. *The Search for the Giant Squid: The Biology and Mythology of the World's Most Elusive Sea Creature.* Boston: Penguin Books (Non-Classics), 1999.

———. *Tuna: A Love Story.* New York: Knopf, 2008.

Ellis, Richard, and John McCosker. *Great White Shark.* Palo Alto, CA: Stanford University Press, 1995.

Field, John G., Gotthilf Hempel, and Colin P. Summerhayes. *Oceans 2020: Science, Trends, and the Challenge of Sustainability.* Washington DC: Island Press, 2002.

Glover, Linda K., and Sylvia A. Earle, eds. *Defying Ocean's End: An Agenda for Action.* Washington DC: Island Press, 2004.

Grescoe, Taras. *Bottomfeeder: How to Eat Ethically in a World of Vanishing Seafood.* New York: Bloomsbury USA, 2009.

Helvarg, David. *Blue Frontier: Dispatches from America's Ocean Wilderness.* San Francisco: Sierra Club Books, 2006.

———. *50 Ways to Save the Ocean (Inner Ocean Action Guide).* Novato, CA: New World Library, 2006.

House, Freean, Jim Lichatowich, Richard Manning, Elizabeth Woody, and Seth Zuckerman. *Salmon Nation: People, Fish, and Our Common Home*. Portland, OR: Ecotrust, 2003.

Issenberg, Sasha. *The Sushi Economy: Globalization and the Making of a Modern Delicacy*. New York: Gotham, 2008.

Iudicello, Suzanne, Michael L. Weber, and Robert Wieland. *Fish, Markets, and Fishermen: The Economics of Overfishing*. Washington DC: Island Press, 1999.

Johnson, Paul. *Fish Forever: The Definitive Guide to Understanding, Selecting, and Preparing Healthy, Delicious, and Environmentally Sustainable Seafood*. New York: Wiley, 2007.

Knecht, G. Bruce. *Hooked: Pirates, Poaching, and the Perfect Fish*. Emmaus, PA: Rodale Books, 2007.

Kurlansky, Mark. *The Big Oyster: History on the Half Shell*. New York: Random House Trade Paperbacks, 2007.

———. *Cod: A Biography of the Fish That Changed the World*. New York: Penguin Books, 1998.

Lambert, Jill. *A Good Catch: Sustainable Seafood Recipes from Canada's Top Chefs*. Vancouver, BC: Greystone Books, 2009.

Land, Michelle D., and Susan Fox Rogers, eds. *A River's Pleasure: Essays in Honor of John Cronin*. New York: Pace University Press, 2009.

Maclean, Jay, and Daniel Pauly. *In a Perfect Ocean: The State of Fisheries and Ecosystems in the North Atlantic Ocean*. Washington DC: Island Press, 2003.

Matsen, Bradford. *Fishing Up North: Stories of Luck and Loss in Alaskan Waters*. Anchorage: Alaska Northwest Books, 1998.

———. *Jacques Cousteau: The Sea King*. New York: Pantheon, 2009.

Matsen, Bradford, and Tom Matsen. *Reaching Home: Pacific Salmon, Pacific People*. Anchorage: Alaska Northwest Books, 1995.

McPhee, John. *The Founding Fish*. 2002. Reprint. New York: Farrar, Straus and Giroux, 2003.

Moonen, Rick, and Roy Finamore. *Fish Without a Doubt: The Cook's Essential Companion*. Boston: Houghton Mifflin Harcourt, 2008.

Murphy, Dallas. *To Follow the Water: Exploring the Ocean to Discover Climate*. New York: Basic Books, 2008.

Navarro, Dawn, Wallace J. Nichols, and Robert E. Snodgrass. *Chelonia: Return of the Sea Turtle*. Los Osos, CA: Sea Challengers, 2000.

Nouvian, Claire. *The Deep: The Extraordinary Creatures of the Abyss*. Chicago: University of Chicago Press, 2007.

O'Barry, Richard, and Kenneth Coulbourn. *Behind the Dolphin Smile: A True Story That Will Touch the Hearts of Animal Lovers Everywhere.* Riverside, CA: Renaissance Books, 2000.

Roberts, Callum. *The Unnatural History of the Sea.* Washington DC: Shearwater, 2009.

Rothschild, David de. *The Live Earth Global Warming Survival Handbook: 77 Essential Skills to Stop Climate Change or Live Through It.* London: Virgin Books, 2007.

Safina, Carl. *Eye of the Albatross: Visions of Hope and Survival.* New York: Holt Paperbacks, 2003.

———. *Song for the Blue Ocean: Encounters Along the World's Coasts and Beneath the Seas.* New York: Owl Books, 1999.

———. *The View from Lazy Point.* New York: Henry Holt, 2010.

———. *Voyage of the Turtle: In Pursuit of the Earth's Last Dinosaur.* New York: Holt Paperbacks, 2007.

Savage, Roz. *Rowing the Atlantic: Lessons Learned on the Open Ocean.* New York: Simon & Schuster, 2009.

Sloan, Stephen. *Ocean Bankruptcy: World Fisheries on the Brink of Disaster.* New York: Lyons Press, 2003.

Veron, J. E. N. *A Reef in Time: The Great Barrier Reef from Beginning to End.* Cambridge, MA: Belknap Press of Harvard University Press, 2009.

Watson, Paul. *Seal Wars: Twenty-Five Years on the Front Lines with the Harp Seals.* Toronto: Firefly Books, 2003.

Whitty, Julia. *The Fragile Edge: Diving and Other Adventures in the South Pacific.* New York: Mariner Books, 2008.

Woodard, Colin. *Ocean's End: Travels Through Endangered Seas.* New York: Basic Books, 2000.

INDEX

Protecting Our Coral Reefs

In the opening week of *Oceans*, DisneyNature donated a portion of each ticket sale to The Nature Conservancy through Disney's Worldwide Conservation Fund.

These donations will help to establish new marine protected areas in the Bahamas. The protected areas will contain miles of vital coral reefs and provide natural habitat, nurseries, and feeding grounds for hundreds of marine species.

Creating the foundation for a healthy ocean environment, coral reefs provide food, shelter, and sanctuary to many of the reefs' incredible species. If the reefs die, so too will life in and around the Caribbean. It is estimated by some scientists that the Caribbean coral reefs could disappear in forty years without a network of well-managed protected marine areas.

The seven hundred islands that comprise the Bahamas contain 30 percent of the total reef area in the Atlantic Ocean, making it an important site for new marine protected areas. The coral reefs of the Bahamas are under threat by natural as well as human impact stresses, as are most other coral reefs. Through its "Adopt a Coral Reef" program, The Nature Conservancy is working hard to protect and maintain the coral reefs in the Bahamas and other areas throughout the Caribbean and the world at large. A leading global conservation organization, The Nature Conservancy manages and maintains more than one hundred marine conservation sites and projects in thirty-one countries and in all U.S. coastal states.

For more information about The Nature Conservancy's "Adopt a Coral Reef" program in the Bahamas, visit www.nature.org/disneyoceans.

I believe that a good story well told can truly make a difference in how one sees the world. This is why I started Participant Media: to tell compelling, entertaining stories that create awareness of the real issues that shape our lives.

At Participant, we seek to entertain our audiences first, and then invite them to participate in making a difference. With each film, we create social action and advocacy programs that highlight the issues that resonate in the film and provide ways to transform the impact of the media experience into individual and community action.

Twenty-five films later, from GOOD NIGHT, AND GOOD LUCK to AN INCONVENIENT TRUTH, and from FOOD, INC. to FURRY VENGEANCE, and through thousands of social action activities, Participant continues to create entertainment that inspires and compels social change. Now through our partnership with PublicAffairs, we are extending our mission so that more of you can join us in making our world a better place.

Jeff Skoll, Founder and Chairman
Participant Media

PublicAffairs is a publishing house founded in 1997. It is a tribute to the standards, values, and flair of three persons who have served as mentors to countless reporters, writers, editors, and book people of all kinds, including me.

I. F. STONE, proprietor of *I. F. Stone's Weekly*, combined a commitment to the First Amendment with entrepreneurial zeal and reporting skill and became one of the great independent journalists in American history. At the age of eighty, Izzy published *The Trial of Socrates*, which was a national bestseller. He wrote the book after he taught himself ancient Greek.

BENJAMIN C. BRADLEE was for nearly thirty years the charismatic editorial leader of *The Washington Post*. It was Ben who gave the *Post* the range and courage to pursue such historic issues as Watergate. He supported his reporters with a tenacity that made them fearless and it is no accident that so many became authors of influential, best-selling books.

ROBERT L. BERNSTEIN, the chief executive of Random House for more than a quarter century, guided one of the nation's premier publishing houses. Bob was personally responsible for many books of political dissent and argument that challenged tyranny around the globe. He is also the founder and longtime chair of Human Rights Watch, one of the most respected human rights organizations in the world.

. . .

For fifty years, the banner of Public Affairs Press was carried by its owner Morris B. Schnapper, who published Gandhi, Nasser, Toynbee, Truman, and about 1,500 other authors. In 1983, Schnapper was described by *The Washington Post* as "a redoubtable gadfly." His legacy will endure in the books to come.

Peter Osnos, *Founder and Editor-at-Large*